MORE PRAISE FOR *UNEASY PEACE*

"Admirably connects two stories about the criminal legal system that are usually told separately. One is that the country that Americans live in is safer than it has been for a long time. The other story is that for some citizens, especially African-American men, the country that they live in is not free."

—Paul Butler, *New York Times Book Review*

Uneasy Peace has enhanced my understanding of the decline in urban violent crime. Compelling too is Sharkey's discussion of ways to avert a possible new wave of national violence. This well-written and carefully researched book is a must-read for anyone residing in our nation's cities.

—William Julius Wilson, author of *More than Just Race: Being Black and Poor in the Inner City*

"Patrick Sharkey explains with accessible precision just how much the massive decline in homicide since the 1990s has mattered to the most vulnerable of city-dwellers, African American men. Sharkey also makes clear why this public health triumph is precarious. . . . Any student of cities will regard this book as essential reading."

—Tracey L. Meares, Walton Hale Hamilton Professor at Yale Law School

"Patrick Sharkey is the leading young scholar of urban crime and concentrated poverty. . . . *Uneasy Peace* is a must-read for mayors, city-builders, urbanists, and all those concerned with building and living in great urban places."

—Richard Florida, author of *The Rise of the Creative Class* and *The New Urban Crisis*

UNEASY
PEACE

ALSO BY PATRICK SHARKEY

Stuck in Place:
Urban Neighborhoods and the End of Progress Toward
Racial Equality

Spatial Foundations of Inequality
(coedited with George Galster)

UNEASY
PEACE

THE GREAT CRIME DECLINE, THE RENEWAL OF CITY LIFE, AND THE NEXT WAR ON VIOLENCE

PATRICK SHARKEY

W. W. NORTON & COMPANY

Independent Publishers Since 1923

New York | London

For information about permission to reproduce selections from this book,
write to Permissions, W. W. Norton & Company, Inc.,
500 Fifth Avenue, New York, NY 10110

For information about special discounts for bulk purchases, please contact
W. W. Norton Special Sales at specialsales@wwnorton.com or 800-233-4830

Manufacturing by Quad Graphics Fairfield
Book design by Chris Welch Design
Production manager: Julia Druskin

Library of Congress Cataloging-in-Publication Data

Names: Sharkey, Patrick, author.
Title: Uneasy peace : the great crime decline, the renewal of city life, and the next
war on violence / Patrick Sharkey.
Description: First Edition. | New York, N.Y. : W. W. Norton & Company, [2018] |
Includes bibliographical references and index.
Identifiers: LCCN 2017051652 | ISBN 9780393609608 (hardcover)
Subjects: LCSH: City and town life—United States. | Crime—United States—
History—20th century. | Crime—United States—History—21st century. | Crime
prevention—United States.
Classification: LCC HT123 .S535 2018 | DDC 307.730973—dc23
LC record available at https://lccn.loc.gov/2017051652

ISBN 978-0-393-35654-0 pbk

W. W. Norton & Company, Inc.
500 Fifth Avenue, New York, N.Y. 10110
www.wwnorton.com

W. W. Norton & Company Ltd.
15 Carlisle Street, London W1D 3BS

1 2 3 4 5 6 7 8 9 0

CONTENTS

PART III: THE CHALLENGE OF VIOLENCE AND URBAN INEQUALITY

ACKNOWLEDGMENTS

This book is a synthesis of observations, findings, and ideas that emerged through conversation, collaborative analysis, and written correspondence with a large group of mentors, colleagues, friends, family members, and students. I am grateful to all of them.

That group begins with Robert Sampson, who has been a continual source of inspiration, guidance, and insight since I began working with him in my second year of graduate school. We have discussed many of the ideas that made their way into this book, we wrote an article together that helped me clarify my own thinking about the relationship between violence and inequality, and his comments on the first draft had an enormous impact on the final version.[1] I thank Rob first and foremost.

The scholars who came together at the NYU School of Law in 2012–13 provided extensive feedback at an early stage of the project, and I'm grateful to all of them and to Ingrid Ellen and Vicki Been for inviting me to spend the year with such an extraordinary group of people. I carried out much of the empirical analysis that went into the book during my time as a William T. Grant Faculty

Scholar, under the mentorship of Larry Aber, Martha Farah, and Peter Bearman. I thank all three as well as other faculty scholars who discussed the ideas in the book with me, including David Deming, Stefanie DeLuca, Phil Goff, Elizabeth Oltmans Ananat, Sara Goldrick-Rab, and Candice Odgers. Several colleagues and friends provided particularly helpful thoughts on early drafts of chapters or the full manuscript, including Harry Blagg, Leah Platt Boustan, Stuart Butler, Eric Cadora, Charles Clotfelter, David Edwards, Ingrid Ellen, Elizabeth Glazer, Stuart Greer, Eric Klinenberg, Desmond King, Susan Lloyd, Jens Ludwig, and Mary Pattillo, as well as my parents, Eileen and Tom Sharkey. I would also like to thank Alison MacKeen of Sterling Lord Literistic and Alane Mason of W. W. Norton for their sharp insight and extensive effort in working with me to improve the manuscript.

Special thanks go to the doctoral students and undergraduates who assisted in gathering and analyzing data that became the foundation of the book. Gerard Torrats-Espinosa, a doctoral student at NYU, has been an integral part of much of the research. Most notably, he collaborated with me on the analysis of violent crime and economic mobility featured in Chapter 6.[2] We presented this work at a conference for small grant recipients at the Russell Sage Foundation and received valuable feedback from Raj Chetty, Nathaniel Hendren, Michael Hout, Christopher Jencks, and Sean Reardon, among others. Gerard also led the analysis of economic segregation in Chapter 6.

Michael Friedson collaborated on the study of neighborhood-level trends in violent crime featured in Chapter 2. He was lead author on an article based on the same data.[3] Michael also collaborated on the analysis of life expectancy featured in Chapter 4.[4] He provided feedback on multiple chapters of the book and gathered data on public transit that is referenced in the Preface. Kiara Douds, Delaram Takyar, and Gerard Torrats-Espinosa worked with me on the study of the relationship between nonprofit formation and violent crime described in Chapter 3.[5] Faria Mardhani assisted with obtaining and processing data on U.S. nonprofits. Ilha Youn helped gather data on crowd attendance in major league U.S. sports, which is referenced in the Preface and at other points. Annie Le helped gather national data on business improvement districts, described in Chapter 3. All these students provided excellent research assistance.

I would like to thank Susan Lloyd and John Gurda for their help in organizing my visit to Milwaukee and for their insights into the city. My conversations with Sharon Adams, Mayor Tom Barrett, Victor Barnett, Linda Bowen, District Attorney John Chisholm, Chief Edward Flynn, Mike Gousha, David Haynes, Carmen Pitre, Sister Patricia Rogers, Lauren Wechsler, and the group of organization leaders and community leaders were extremely helpful in illuminating the issues and the challenges facing Milwaukee. I thank everyone I met for taking out the time to introduce me to your city.

Harry Blagg was especially helpful in facilitating my trip to Perth, and his insights into the role of Aboriginal patrols provided the basis for my description in Chapter 9. I thank Maria McAtackney and Michael Wood for talking with me about Nyoongar Outreach Services, and Annie, Rachel, and the patrol staff for letting me observe the extraordinary work they are doing in Northbridge.

Last, thanks to Thomas and Kate for being such great kids, and to Alyssa, to whom this book is dedicated, for being such a wonderful person.

PREFACE

On October 12, 1977, television viewers across the nation were given a glimpse of life in the South Bronx. Game two of the 1977 World Series was being broadcast from Yankee Stadium, where the New York Yankees hosted the Los Angeles Dodgers. When Yankees second baseman Willie Randolph stepped to the plate to lead off the bottom of the first inning, the camera cut to an aerial view of the streets surrounding the stadium and focused the attention of the viewing audience on an enormous blaze that appeared to be consuming an entire block of the city.

Legend has it that Howard Cosell, the sportscaster with the iconic halting voice, described the scene to viewers in his matter-of-fact manner: "Ladies and gentlemen, the Bronx is burning." The truth is, he never uttered those words. Cosell's broadcast partner, Keith Jackson, was the one who first spoke when the camera showed the images of the scene less than a mile from the stadium: "That is a live picture, obviously a major fire in a large building in the South Bronx region of New York City."[1] The flames shot high in the air, illuminating a full block in a section of the city that otherwise appeared to be pitch-black, lifeless. Jackson, whose own voice had the natural urgency of a live on-the-scene reporter, was audibly stunned: "My goodness, that's a huge blaze."

The broadcast returned to the scene five times over the course of the game. Each time Jackson and Cosell marveled at the sight of the fire, providing updates on the effort to control it and assurances that no one had died. More than two hours into the game, in the bottom of the sixth inning, the last report showed that the blaze had finally been extinguished.

The fire that broke out during game two stunned the nation, but the sight of burning buildings was not unusual in the South Bronx. During a period in which New York City was shedding jobs and people, the value of real estate in the Bronx plummeted, and landowners were desperate to extract some value from their property. Dozens of neighborhoods across the Bronx lost more than half of their real estate to arson, and the community began to look as if it were the target of an aerial bombing campaign.[2]

The spectacle of a burning city may have evoked fascination and terror among viewers, but the nationally televised fire was just one relatively minor episode in a year of chaos, violence, and destruction in the South Bronx. In the 1970s this devastated section of New York City had morphed from a traditional poor, urban ghetto into a national symbol of urban blight, violence, disorder, and lawlessness.

The Bronx was the place where the serial killer David Berkowitz, who called himself "Son of Sam," roamed the streets for months, picking out victims at random and sending notes to newspaper columnists daring the police to find him. Berkowitz killed three of his victims in the Bronx during that summer of 1977, and several more in Queens, stoking the fears of New Yorkers as

the tabloids battled to document the most sensational details of
his murders and his life. It was a place where the lights could go
out in midsummer, as they did on July 13, 1977, when the city's
electrical grid failed and anarchy ensued. Shopping districts in
Brooklyn, Queens, and the Bronx were set afire and looted overnight, television stations went dead, and the city exploded. By the
time the power went back on, thousands of stores were destroyed,
and almost four thousand people had been arrested.[3]

The South Bronx came to be seen as a national disaster, the
most notorious section of a city that had reached the brink of
bankruptcy in 1976. Less than a week before the World Series
began, the *New York Times* ran a front-page photograph showing
President Jimmy Carter and several advisers touring a barren
stretch of Charlotte Street, just east of Yankee Stadium. Carter
and his aides looked as if they had stumbled upon a postapocalyp-
tic ghost town, a desolate landscape littered with piles of rubble,
beer bottles, scattered newspapers, and dirt.[4] A week later, when
the fire broke out in the first inning of game two, Howard Cosell
noted the irony: "That's the very area where President Carter trod
just a few days ago."

In 1977 the South Bronx became the most visible example of the
failed American city. The neighborhood would become the setting
for novels and films dramatizing the dystopia of postindustrial
urban life, and the dominant feature of the new urban landscape
was violence. Spike Lee captured the chaos of 1977 in his film
Summer of Sam. The Warriors, which told the story of a street
gang fighting to escape the Bronx and return to their home in
Coney Island, became a cult favorite. *Fort Apache, The Bronx* was
released in 1981, starring Paul Newman as a cop struggling amid
rioting and murder in the South Bronx. And in *The Bonfire of the
Vanities,* Tom Wolfe depicted public spaces like Franz Sigel Park,

just a couple of blocks south of Yankee Stadium, as places of lethal danger: "Nobody from the District Attorney's Office went out into the park on a sunny day in May to have lunch. . . . Not even a court officer, who had a uniform and legally carried a .38, ever did such a thing."[5]

Politicians used the South Bronx to weave their own tales of urban despair, dysfunction, and danger. Presidential candidate Ronald Reagan returned to Charlotte Street three years after President Carter's visit and blamed the incumbent for failing to create any visible change in the Bronx. Jesse Jackson, a Democratic hopeful in 1984, called attention to the plight of the urban poor by spending a night in the Forest Houses, a public housing development very close to the block that burned in front of a national audience of baseball fans.[6]

The horror of the South Bronx was sensationalized and exploited, used as a prop by filmmakers and novelists and politicians to capture the nightmare of urban America. But the reality was equally terrifying. The descent started with abandonment, destitution, joblessness, and hopelessness that were symbolized by the twelve thousand or so fires that were set in the South Bronx over the course of the 1970s. But over time the epidemic of arson turned into a plague of violence. Crime had been rising steadily in New York and across the country, but the market for crack cocaine ushered in an era of unprecedented violence.

The sociologist Randol Contreras, who grew up in the community in the late 1980s, recalls the drug dealers who ruled the streets. "I could not miss them," he writes. "They drove expensive cars, with shiny rims, with the sunroof open, or with the convertible top down, for all to see."[7] Dealers filled in the abandoned spaces created by years of arson, and open lots and vacant buildings became the sites for a booming business that was regulated by force. "Guns were drawn, people were shot, sidewalks were bloody, and children were hurt—dead bodies surfaced everywhere. Violence ruled the streets; there was no more public space."[8] At the start of the 1960s, fewer than 500 people were murdered annually in New York City, but by 1980 more than 1,800 homicides took place each year. A decade later the level of violence worsened: More than 2,000 people were murdered in each of the first few years of the 1990s.

In the years after a national audience watched the Bronx burn, Yankee Stadium was known as one of the country's most dangerous ballparks. To make their way to the stadium, fans had to venture into a subway system with graffiti so thick that signage within the tunnels was often impossible to see. Epidemics of smashed windows on subway cars broke out periodically, and service was unreliable as the cars broke down regularly. In 1982 the chairman of the Metropolitan Transit Authority revealed that he did not allow his own teenage children to ride the subway at night and that even he was nervous when he entered the subway. New Yorkers were nervous as well. Ridership, and revenue, plummeted to historic low points.[9]

The Yankees' owners, who had long sought to move the team away from the South Bronx, openly complained about the community surrounding the stadium. In 1994 Richard Kraft, the Yankees' vice-president of community relations, was quoted in *New York Magazine* referring to the kids who played basketball at Macombs Dam Park, across the street from the stadium, as "monkeys" who "crack the rim and bend the hoops."[10] He would later resign for his comment, but the animosity between the organization and the community remained. As the Yankees looked for an opportunity to escape the Bronx, warnings from the team alerted fans to the "perception of crime" in the area, essentially telling them to "come to Yankee Stadium at your peril."[11]

And fans heeded the advice. During a period in which thou-

sands of people were being murdered in New York City, attendance at Yankee Stadium was dismal. Part of the reason for the
small crowds was the performance of the team, but even when the
Yankees were competing for a playoff spot, about half of the seats
were empty for every home game. In some years, night games
drew ten thousand fewer fans than day games, as few New Yorkers were unwilling to make their way out to the Bronx after the
sun went down.[12]

From the subway system to the street corners to the public
parks to the hallowed ground of Yankee Stadium, the South Bronx
had become a place that was feared and avoided. Spaces that had
been created to support public life, to be enjoyed by all—those that
defined city life in America's greatest metropolis—were dominated
by the threat of violence.

————

In September 2014, a few months after I began writing this book,
I was asked to present a report to a room full of probation officers,
data analysts, and program administrators in the Bronx District
Attorney's Office. The meeting took place less than a block from
the municipal building that Tom Wolfe described in *The Bonfire
of the Vanities,* overlooking Franz Sigel Park.

As is often the case when academics present their research to
people working on the ground, the meeting was tense. I had been
asked to evaluate a unique program designed to engage violent
offenders as they returned from prison, and the results of the evaluation suggested the program may not have been as effective as
those in the room had hoped. I was the bearer of bad—or at least
mixed—news, and my inconclusive results didn't sit well with the
people who spent their time working with those who are leaving
prison. By the time the meeting ended, I needed to sit down.

On my way back to the subway, I decided to walk through

Franz Sigel Park. It was a place with benches and shade, and I was curious to see whether it resembled the description in Wolfe's classic novel, whether it still felt too dangerous to sit down on a park bench and eat lunch.

It was late afternoon on a hot, sticky day. The park has some remnants of 1970s New York, like the crumbling old concrete seating area that looks like it should have been torn down decades ago. But it also has beautiful stone walls that wrap around its edge, and rocky hills perfect for children to climb. Leafy trees separate the park from the street. A man and woman were talking quietly on a bench, kids played as their mother looked on, and a group of dogs ran off-leash as their owners chatted nearby. Some aging men who looked down on their luck sat talking in the shade, and a few others sat silently on their own. In a worn basketball court at the south end of the park, two young boys shot hoops lazily. I walked back up on the west side and sat for a few minutes on a wooden bench. Fellow New Yorkers strolled by slowly, taking advantage of the quiet and shade. Poverty was still visible inside the park and out, but there was not a hint of violence in the air.

Twenty-five years earlier Franz Sigel Park was a place most New Yorkers were not willing to enter. But on this day in September 2014, it felt like an urban sanctuary.

The calm of Franz Sigel Park reflected an atmosphere of peace throughout New York City. In the city where more than 2,000 people used to be murdered each year, 328 people were killed in 2014, the lowest tally since the first half of the twentieth century. And it wasn't just New York that had been transformed. Violent crime fell in almost every American city from the early 1990s to the early 2010s, and it plummeted in many major urban centers. In Atlanta, Dallas, Los Angeles, and Washington, the murder rate fell by 60 to 80 percent, similar to the crime drop in New

York City. Even in places that continued to have high levels of violence, like Oakland and Philadelphia, the homicide rate fell by at least 33 percent.

To write this book, I spent three years gathering data and investigating how the decline in violence had altered American cities and the lives of their residents. And with each analysis, I became more convinced that the drop in violent crime had led to a fundamental change in the nature of U.S. urban life. As violence fell, cities came back to life in ways that were both obvious and subtle. Families returned from the suburbs and moved into central cities, and the poorest urban neighborhoods began to attract new-comers. Schools became dramatically safer than they were twenty years ago, and test scores rose the most in the places that became safest. As academic performance improved and employment oppor-tunities returned to urban neighborhoods, children from families near the bottom of the income distribution became more likely to move upward, out of poverty. Most important, thousands of young people were no longer being gunned down and taken from their friends and families. The drop in homicides since the early 1990s led to an improvement in the life expectancy of black men that rivals any public health breakthrough of the last several decades.

As all this was happening, the feel of city life changed. Pub-lic spaces like Franz Sigel Park became peaceful and quiet, once again seen as welcoming to the residents of neighborhoods like the South Bronx. Subway cars, commuter lines, and buses in U.S. cities filled up, as residents and commuters became more willing to leave their cars behind and travel to and from work together. Public libraries began to brim with activity in the cities where crime fell, as parents no longer had to shield their children from the world outside the front door. Fans came back to Yankee Sta-dium in the Bronx, and just as many began to show up for night games as for day games.[13]

Cities, where public life is prioritized over private life, where property is used collectively and interaction is constant and unavoidable, came back to life as crime declined. The moment of peace I experienced on the park bench was shared across most of urban America. The year 2014 was the safest on record in New York, and one of the safest in U.S. history.

The decline in American violence is a stunning development that no one predicted and that many people still do not believe. The evidence I present in this book suggests it has been one of the most important social trends to hit cities over the past several decades. It is a victory for urban America.

But it is a tainted victory. And it is an uneasy peace.

As I sat in Franz Sigel Park, I didn't realize how fragile the moment was, but I probably should have. A few months earlier, in July 2014, forty-three-year-old Eric Garner, a black man, was killed while being arrested for selling loose cigarettes on the street in Staten Island. A bystander recorded the incident, and the video is chilling. It shows Garner arguing with officers for several minutes and refusing to be handcuffed.[14] An officer then wraps his forearm around Garner's throat, forcing him to the pavement, and attempts to hold him still with his arms locked around Garner's neck. Garner is shown gasping for air after being restrained, subdued, and handcuffed, and repeatedly pleading, "I can't breathe." And finally the video shows Eric Garner lying motionless on the sidewalk for several minutes as bystanders, emergency care workers, and police look on, before being rolled onto a stretcher and taken away in an ambulance.

Garner was declared dead an hour later at a local hospital. The official cause of death was listed as "compression of the neck and chest," but after watching the video of Garner's arrest, it is easy to see why many New Yorkers came to a simpler conclusion: He was choked to death.

What happened to Eric Garner has happened to others all across the country, and it has happened for a long time. Later in the same year, John Crawford was shot dead in an Ohio Walmart while carrying a BB gun from the store's shelves.[15] Four days later Michael Brown was shot and killed in Ferguson, Missouri.[16] While the nation watched Ferguson erupt in protest, Ezell Ford, a mentally ill black man, was shot dead when he was stopped by two officers in Los Angeles.[17] A few months later in Cleveland, twelve-year-old Tamir Rice was shot and killed while playing with a toy gun in a public park.[18] In April 2015 Walter Scott was shot in the back while running away from an officer, unarmed, after a traffic stop in Charleston, South Carolina.[19] And eight days later, in Baltimore, Freddie Gray was arrested for possessing an illegal knife and placed in the back of a police van, which made multiple unexplained stops on the way to central booking. By the time the van arrived, Freddie Gray was unconscious; he was dead a week later with spinal cord injuries.[20]

These deaths are not independent, isolated incidents. They are only the most visible examples of a national approach to confronting violent crime, and the larger problem of urban poverty, in the nation's poorest, most segregated neighborhoods. This approach began at the tail end of the 1960s, when the United States abandoned its efforts to confront urban poverty with a campaign focusing on justice and investment and settled on an alternative strategy that relied heavily on the police and the prison. Since then, police departments nationwide have been bolstered by growing federal and state funding and emboldened by a policy of aggressive, zero-tolerance policing that targeted low-income communities of color. The rise of intensive policing was accompanied by increasingly punitive criminal justice policies and more aggressive prosecution of offenders, leading to historically and internationally unprecedented levels of incarceration.

An honest assessment of the best evidence we have suggests that these changes in criminal justice and policing have contributed, at least partially, to the decline in violent crime.[21] But our national reliance on aggressive policing and mass incarceration has taken a heavy toll. As the criminal justice system has expanded its reach, the scale of imprisonment has torn families apart and destabilized entire communities.[22] At the same time, as videos of abusive or lethal police behavior have proliferated and gone viral, the policing tactics that have long been familiar in the country's most disadvantaged neighborhoods have become visible to the rest of the nation. The outrage that followed Eric Garner's death, the widespread protests against police brutality, the emergence of the Black Lives Matter movement, and the unrest that erupted in Ferguson, Baltimore, Dallas, Charlotte, Milwaukee, and elsewhere are clear signals that the methods our nation has used to confront urban violence are no longer acceptable to much of the American public.

As the movement for criminal justice and policing reform has gathered momentum, we have seen ominous reminders of what the old era of urban violence looked like. When the protests on the streets of Baltimore and St. Louis subsided and faded from media view, those same streets were hit by a wave of violence. After reaching a historic low in 2014, the national homicide rate rose by 11 percent in 2015, then rose again in 2016. The spike in homicides may represent little more than a short-term deviation from the long-term trend of falling violence. But there is fear in places like Baltimore and Chicago that the gradual decline in violent crime over the past two decades may have been wiped away after two years of unrest and killings. That same fear is now felt in Cleveland, Houston, Milwaukee, and St. Louis, where the sudden rise of violence may be an ominous sign of a new era.

The decline in violence that changed urban America is frag-

ile. It is threatened by the resentment of police officers who have
been asked, for the past twenty years, to take over dangerous city
streets by any means necessary—and who are now being vilified
in some quarters and told to change the way they do their jobs.
It is threatened by the outrage of the many Americans who are
now aware of the scale of mass incarceration, and the protesters who have now seen how police officers have long treated residents in the nation's poorest, most segregated neighborhoods. It is
threatened by the election of Donald Trump, whose law and order
rhetoric is a reminder of the language Richard Nixon used back
in 1968, just before the last century's sharpest rise in violence
occurred.

And lastly, it is threatened by a broader, more troubling trend
that has been developing for the past forty years: the rise of urban
inequality. As economic inequality has grown steadily since the
1970s, our cities have become increasingly segregated by income.
Poverty has become more concentrated in neighborhoods that are
detached from the rest of the city, the wealthy have moved into distinct areas of their own, and gated communities have proliferated.
The new American city is historically safe but shockingly unequal.

The developments that have taken place since I sat on the park
bench in September 2014 have presented mayors, state and federal legislators, police departments, community leaders, and advocates with a set of challenges that I consider crucial to the future
of American cities. First, how can we preserve and extend that
moment of peace, so that it is felt in every city and every neighborhood across the country? Second, how can we do so with a new
approach, one that reduces violence but also confronts the larger
problem of urban inequality?

PART I

THE NEW
AMERICAN CITY

1

THE END OF THE ERA OF VIOLENCE

The early 1960s are not remembered as a peaceful time in American history. President John F. Kennedy was assassinated in 1963, the same year that brutal images of police dogs attacking civil rights protesters in Alabama were broadcast to the nation. Casualties in Vietnam were just beginning to rise. One year later, in 1964, riots broke out in Harlem and Philadelphia, a preview of the unrest that would spread to hundreds of American cities in the years to come. But in the fifty years that followed, the homicide rate in the United States would never fall as low as it was in those early years of the 1960s. In both 1962 and 1963, there were only 4.6 homicides for every 100,000 people in the United States, according to data from the FBI.[1]

This period of domestic peace did not last. The national homicide rate rose steadily and quickly in the latter half of the 1960s, more than doubling between 1963 and 1974. From the mid-1970s through the early 1990s, the homicide rate fluctuated between roughly 8 and 10 murders per 100,000 residents, reaching a peak that was at least as high as any previous point in the twentieth century.[2] And it wasn't just the level of extreme violent crime that had changed; the character of violence had changed as well. Young people recruited into the crack trade were shooting and killing each other at rates that were unfathomable to other Americans.[3] The rate of juvenile homicides almost doubled from 1985 to 1993.[4] As the perpetrators of homicides became younger, the use of firearms became more prevalent, and the rise in lethal violent crime came to be seen as a problem most closely linked with one particular demographic group: young black men.

It was in this context that John DiIulio, a political scientist writing from Princeton, rose to prominence as the country's most influential expert on crime. DiIulio talked with criminals and law enforcement officials and tried to make sense of the wave of violent crime that had hit America's central cities. He diagnosed the problem of violence as a moral crisis and pointed to a new form of impulsive, remorseless youth criminal as responsible. DiIulio described this new breed of "superpredator" in language designed to shock politicians and terrify the public, calling them "fatherless, Godless, and jobless" and "radically impulsive, brutally remorseless youngsters, including ever more pre-teenage boys, who murder, assault, rape, rob, burglarize, deal deadly drugs, join gun-toting gangs and create serious communal disorders."[5]

Forecasting into the future based on demographic data on the American population, DiIulio predicted that a rising wave of young people would lead to an intensification of violence.[6] His warnings were not pulled out of thin air. In visits to juvenile prisons and in his perusal of crime statistics, DiIulio had seen a new type of criminal: very young boys, some barely into adolescence, who were angry, well armed, and lethal. He had heard the voices of prosecutors, parents, and even older prisoners who were shocked by the "stone-cold predators" roaming urban neighborhoods.[7] And he had scrutinized data on the age composition of the

U.S. population, which showed a demographic bulge in the cohort of four-to-ten-year-olds who would soon hit America's streets.[8]

DiIulio's voice was the loudest, and his language was the most incendiary, but he was not alone in his predictions.[9] James Alan Fox, a criminologist at Northeastern University who had written widely on trends in violent crime, focused on the same demographic shifts as DiIulio and predicted a steady rise of violent crime in the years to come. He offered an urgent warning: "unless we act now, when our children are still young and impressionable, we may indeed have a bloodbath of teen violence by the year 2005."[10]

In the midst of these dire predictions and warnings, as politicians from across the political spectrum battled to present themselves as tougher on crime than any opponent, a surprising thing happened. The homicide rate began to fall. It dropped just a small amount from 1993 to 1994, a blip in what appeared to be a rising wave of violence. Then in 1995 it dropped again, this time sharply, all the way back to the level of the late 1980s, a period before the rapid escalation of juvenile homicide. It fell again in 1996 and continued to drop in each successive year for the remainder of the 1990s. By the end of the decade, there were about 6 murders for every 100,000 Americans, a level that had not been seen since the late 1960s.

The stunning decline in violent crime made lots of experts look foolish and revealed just how difficult it is to predict human violence. The trend also revealed how challenging it is to explain the past. As the rate of violent crime leveled off in the late 1990s, a new set of criminologists entered the fray, took stock of how much things had changed, and started to publish research on what might have caused this miraculous decline in violent crime. Franklin Zimring wrote the seminal book on the 1990s crime drop, titling it *The Great American Crime Decline*.[11] Steven Levitt publicized a provocative and controversial theory of abortion and the crime drop made famous in the best-selling pop-science book, *Freakonomics* (more on this in Chapter 3).[12] But just as these debates heated up, crime began to inch down further. By the end of the first decade of the twenty-first century, the homicide rate had dipped below the rate of 5 homicides for every 100,000 residents, lower than half of what it had been at its peak.

By 2014, the homicide rate dropped to 4.4 murders for every 100,000 Americans.[13] This figure has historic significance. Because of shoddy data prior to 1960, it is impossible to know with certainty the exact rate of crime and violence in the first five decades of the twentieth century or at any earlier point in the history of the country. But the most persuasive research from historical mortality records concludes that the homicide rate was likely substantially higher in the first half of the twentieth century than it was in the second half. In fact, the prevalence of murder has been falling, albeit with spikes and troughs, throughout the country's history.[14] If the historical trends in murder derived from mortality records are roughly accurate, and all indications suggest they are, then we are led to a startling conclusion: 2014 was not only the safest year of the past five decades, it was one of the safest years in U.S. history.

If 2014 was the safest year in the nation's modern history, many Americans didn't seem to know it. A national poll conducted in May 2014 asked respondents whether they believed what the government figures were telling them about crime. "The government has reported a steady decline in the rate of violent crime over the last twenty years," the question began. "Do you think the government is correct and the rate of violent crime has decreased or do you think the rate of violent crime has remained the same or even increased over the past twenty years?" The wording appears designed to prime respondents to question the "official" figures on crime and violence, but even so, the responses are revealing. About a quarter of respondents said that they trusted the official figures and agreed that the rate of violent crime had fallen. A similar percentage thought that crime had remained the same, and others weren't sure. But the largest group—one-third of respondents—distrusted the government's statistics enough to claim that crime had *risen* over the previous twenty years.[15]

This finding means that I have written a book about a social trend that many Americans don't believe took place. And they have good reason to be skeptical. Most Americans have no personal experience with violence; only one out of every five American adults reports ever being physically harmed or even threatened with harm in the course of a crime.[16] Without direct experience of victimization, perceptions of violence are formed by a complex combination of media coverage, popular culture, and an informal, imperfect sense of the world surrounding us.

The news media play the largest role in distorting our "sense" of how much violence is out there.[17] National media coverage of crime and violence corresponds, at least loosely, with the actual level of violence in the country, but most Americans don't watch the national news.[18] Even in the Internet age, more Americans get their news from the local evening news than from any other source, and local TV newscasts are notorious for a bias toward blood.[19] The amount of coverage devoted to crime and violence in an area's local news bears almost no relationship to the actual level of violence in that area.[20]

Media bias is exacerbated by a tendency, among many different actors, to distort perceptions about the degree of violence in society. Politicians on the left are reluctant to acknowledge that conditions for the poorest Americans have improved, and politicians on the right are loath to admit that the behavior of the poorest Americans has changed in a positive way. Activists who work against violence and researchers who study violence have a strong incentive to present the problem that drives their work in the most urgent terms possible. Unwittingly, they provide fodder for journalists to stoke the fears of the public, and they provide cover for politicians eager to blame the country's problems on the menacing threat of inner-city criminals. To borrow the words of Steven Pinker, who wrote the definitive book on the decline in violence over the course of human history, "No one has ever recruited activists to a cause by announcing that things are getting better, and bearers of good news are often advised to keep their mouths shut lest they lull people into complacency."[21]

Most of the official figures on crime and violence come from statistics published by the FBI, which gathers and aggregates data reported by police departments around the country. The Unified Crime Reports (UCR) that police departments submit to the federal government have been in place since 1930, when the system was established to provide a reliable national measure of the level of crime and violence.[22] Over time the UCR system has played a larger role in criminal justice and law enforcement. UCR data are used to document how dangerous Philadelphia is compared to New York, how well the current mayor of Charlotte is fighting crime compared to his predecessor, and how violent the United States is relative to the nations of western Europe.

Police chiefs have an enormous incentive to show that crime has fallen under their watch, and they sometimes take creative, deceptive steps to ensure that the numbers look good.[23] One of the most comprehensive investigations of crime statistics was carried out by reporters from *Chicago Magazine,* who uncovered at least 10 cases in 2013 where someone in Chicago was "beaten, burned, suffocated, or shot to death" but was not counted as a homicide victim.[24] They found four more victims who were killed on Chicago's expressways, but those deaths were not counted in the city's statistics because the expressways are patrolled by state police. They found four cases where an injury took place in 2012 but the victim died in 2013. These deaths were switched over to the 2012 totals and ignored in 2013.

In the same year that *Chicago Magazine* published this investigation, the city's inspector general released a report concluding that the city's police department had undercounted the number of aggravated assaults and batteries by 6 percent and 3 percent respectively.[25] The department had undercounted the number of victims of violent crime by as much as 25 percent.[26]

Beyond Chicago, investigations of police crime statistics have raised troubling questions about the numbers reported in Atlanta, Baltimore, Dallas, Detroit, Los Angeles, Milwaukee, New Orleans, New York, Philadelphia, Phoenix, and Washington, D.C.[27] The investigations that have been carried out in many of the nation's big cities lead to a basic question about U.S. crime and violence: How reliable are the trends in violent crime that I report throughout this book? Or put more bluntly, how do we know for sure that the decline in American violence is real?

To begin to answer these questions, it is helpful to return to the investigative report from *Chicago Magazine* and consider its conclusions in more depth. The article was based on an extensive, case-by-case analysis of every suspicious death in Chicago occurring over the course of 2013. If every suspicious case that the reporters found was reclassified as a homicide, the total number of homicides in 2013 would have risen from the reported figure of 414 to a new total of 432. This is not a trivial change, but after adding in every single questionable death to the 2013 tally, there were still approximately 500 fewer homicides in 2013 than there were when violence was at its peak. No matter how inaccurate the department was in its reporting of criminal incidents, a very conservative accounting suggests that at least 100,000 fewer serious crimes were committed in Chicago in 2013 compared to twenty years earlier.

If the decline in violence is even partially attributable to misreporting of official statistics, one has to assume that there is more error in the measurement of crime now than there was in the past. This assumption is almost certainly wrong. Ever since cities began to collect systematic data on crime, police departments have been accused of fudging the numbers. An investigation by the *Chicago Tribune* in 1926 found that 40 percent of serious crimes in the city never made it into the police department reports.[28] In 1958 the Chicago Crime Commission accused the police department of taking steps to minimize the city's crime problem in official reports. An FBI review conducted in 1982 found that Chicago police were making crimes disappear by reclassifying incidents of crime as "unfounded." The number of unfounded crimes in Chicago was fourteen times higher than in comparable cities.

Today every incident of crime in Chicago is posted on the city's Data Portal, a groundbreaking public website that was launched in an effort to make city data visible and transparent to all its residents.[29] Maps of all crimes are readily available online and updated regularly. Even if the pressure to reduce crime is greater than it ever has been, this new transparency means that it is probably more difficult than ever to fudge crime data or to cover up crime.

Covering up homicides is particularly hard. Despite the worrisome cases documented in Chicago and elsewhere, research in criminology has led to the conclusion that homicide is a uniquely reliable measure of violent crime.[30] One reason is that bodies are very hard to hide. Homicide is a crime that is monitored not only by police departments but also by state offices of vital statistics, which rely on the reports of coroners and medical examiners to tabulate the cause of every single death. Those state offices send their reports up to the National Center on Health Statistics (NCHS).[31] Although the absolute number of homicides reported by the FBI and the NCHS may never align exactly, *trends* in the murder rate derived from police departments and aggregated by the FBI track almost perfectly with trends derived from medical reports gathered by state health departments and the NCHS.[32]

The residents of a given city may not be able to know exactly how many homicides there were in any particular year, but they can know, with some certainty, whether there are more or fewer homicides than there were a decade ago. The authors of the *Chicago Magazine* article were right that probably more than 413 homicides took place in Chicago in 2013. But it is also almost certain that many more than 943 homicides took place in 1992. Based on everything we know about the measurement of homicides, the changes that have taken place over a long period of time, in Chicago and elsewhere, will look basically the same no matter how crime is reported, no matter what source of data is used, and no matter who's in charge.

Perhaps more convincing, for the true skeptics, is the fact that Americans themselves have told us that violence is declining. The National Crime Victimization Survey (NCVS), designed to capture the level of criminal victimization as experienced by a national sample of U.S. residents, has been administered annually since the early 1970s.[33] It provides a useful complement to the official statistics compiled by the FBI because the NCVS is unaffected by changes in the way crime is monitored or reported by the police.

NCVS data not only confirm the patterns documented by the FBI but also suggest that the decline in violent crime may be underreported in official statistics provided by police departments. In 1993 about 80 out of every 1,000 Americans reported being the victim of a violent crime in the six months prior to the survey. By 2015, the latest year available, only 19 out of every 1,000 reported being a violent crime victim. The FBI's official crime statistics tell us that violence has been cut roughly in half. Americans' own reports suggest that violent victimization has dropped by more than 75 percent.

All the best sources of data on American violence—the national survey of victimization, the figures from vital statistics, and reports from police departments—tell the same story. The level of violence in the United States has fallen dramatically from its latest peak in the early 1990s. No matter which data source one trusts, it is impossible to argue that the nation is not safer than it was twenty years ago.

But just how safe are we at this moment? A single answer to this question is difficult, because the response depends entirely on the point of comparison. Relative to all nations of the world, the United States has a very low rate of violent crime and homicide. According to estimates from the UN Office of Drugs and Crime, there are more than 30 homicides for every 100,000 residents of Honduras, Venezuela, Zambia, and Jamaica, a rate that is six times higher than the U.S. rate.[34] In some regions of the world, extreme violence is a common aspect of daily life for most of the population. This is not the case in most U.S. communities.

This observation does not mean that the United States has become a particularly peaceful nation. Relative to most of the *developed* world, this country has an extremely high rate of homicides and a fairly high rate of violent crime. The U.S. homicide rate is more than twice that of Algeria, Canada, Japan, Germany, Switzerland, the United Kingdom, and many other countries, where there are fewer than 2 homicides per 100,000 residents. And since

2014, the U.S. homicide rate has begun to rise once again and is now above 5 murders per 100,000 people. The unrest that spread through urban America in the summer of 2016 may be a signal that the long period of declining violence has come to an end.

But before we ring alarm bells about an impending wave of violent crime, it is worth taking a moment to consider how much the nation has changed. The era of our urban history when cities were dominated by violence, politics were driven by the fear of violence, and urban policy was taken over by the problem of violence has ended. Although it now seems likely that the rate of violence will begin to inch back up, we are still living through one of the safest periods in U.S. history. And the places that have changed the most are cities.

2

THE NEW AMERICAN CITY

The modern history of urban America began back before the Bronx was burning on national television. It began in the mid-1960s, when crime started to rise and the nation's emerging conflicts, tensions, and problems all seemed to be concentrated in its cities. Urban neighborhoods became battlegrounds where African Americans who sought to live wherever they chose, to have equal status under the law, and to be represented in government faced fierce, violent resistance. New challenges like air and water pollution became impossible to ignore in the 1960s and came to be seen as urban problems. And in the latter half of the decade, neighborhoods in hundreds of U.S. cities exploded in anger as the rising tensions of the civil rights era spilled out onto the streets.[1]

For many, the promise of urban America seemed to fade away in the 1960s. Middle- and upper-income families, mostly (but not entirely) white, began to leave for the suburbs, and their departure created enormous fiscal stress on city governments. The rising costs of policing and social services placed cities in a tenuous financial state, and as the population shifted from the cities and into the suburbs, political influence shifted outward as well. Central cities started to lose their clout in state legislatures, and the federal government began to slash funding for city governments, leaving them on their own to handle mounting challenges with a declining tax base.

A new form of urban poverty emerged. Segregation intensified, poverty became concentrated in neighborhoods where joblessness was widespread, and surviving on welfare benefits became common. Institutions like churches and schools deteriorated. Deep poverty and institutional decay created a niche where illicit drug markets proliferated. The rate of violent crime rose quickly from the 1960s through the 1980s and remained high through the early 1990s. But the image of America's cities also began to change. The idea of the city became linked with the problem of violence in America. it got worse for them, lol

The sociologist Elijah Anderson wrote *Code of the Street,* his classic ethnography of street life in Philadelphia's ghetto, after spending years in the early 1990s observing public life and talking with residents.[2] He described desperate poverty, widespread joblessness, and lingering racial tension. But the dominant feature of public life in Philadelphia's poorest neighborhoods was neither homelessness nor drug abuse nor prostitution; it was violence.

During this period, Philadelphia's social world was organized and regulated by violence. Public parks were "staging areas," where young men adopted body language intended to make clear that they could handle any challenge that came their way. Older residents retreated from public spaces or entered them prepared to defend themselves. A longtime resident relayed the informal rules required to navigate the streets of his neighborhood: "Keep your eyes and ears open at all times. Walk two steps forward and look back. Watch your back. Prepare yourself verbally and physically. Even if you carry a cane, carry something."[3]

Children living within this social world were forced to adapt to its code, adopting informal rules of behavior that allowed them to avoid constant victimization yet maintain status on the street. A smaller segment of young people gave in to the "code of the street" entirely, spending their lives in a continuous campaign for status, which was earned through force. "When the boys admire another's property, they may simply try to take it; this includes that person's sneakers, jacket, hat, and other personal items," Anderson wrote. The quest for status, and respect, was a zero-sum game—respect gained by one young man was respect lost by another, making him vulnerable to more frequent attacks. "Many are uncertain about how long they are going to live and believe they could die violently at any time. They accept this fate; they live on the edge."[4]

Parents had to find ways to shield their children from the dangers of the neighborhood, while also preparing them to defend themselves if necessary. A young woman named Yvette told Anderson that she spent most of her childhood indoors, barricaded from the neighborhood inside a fortress created by her mother. "She's got iron doors in the front and the back. Steel windows. Bars on the windows. Our house looks like a little prison." Yvette spent her time inside, at home or at school: "My mom and my dad kept me in the house. I did not have any friends on my block." Parents often taught their children to survive by fighting back when necessary, even if they were reluctant to do so. Sometimes children had to do more than simply defend themselves. "It used to be the gangs, and you fought 'em, and it was over. But now if you fight somebody, they may come back and kill you. It's a whole lot different now."[5]

Anderson's vivid description of life in Philadelphia's ghetto was the most celebrated account of violence in the 1990s, but it bears close resemblance to what was being documented in many different cities across the country. In two seminal books on urban poverty, *The Truly Disadvantaged* and *When Work Disappears*, William Julius Wilson analyzed Chicago neighborhoods from which the middle class had departed, leaving behind communities where poverty was concentrated, where jobs had vanished, where schools had begun to crumble, and where violence flourished.[6] Loïc Wacquant, a French sociologist who came to Chicago to study with Wilson, described the city's poor, predominantly black neighborhoods as something close to a zone of terror. "Physical violence is a palpable reality that overturns all the parameters of ordinary existence. . . . Violence in its most brutal forms—including assault and battery, shootings, rape, and homicide—is so intense and prevalent inside the hyperghetto that it has forced a complete reorganization of the fabric of daily life."[7]

This reorganization of daily life reflected a new form of vulnerability for Chicago's residents. During a heat wave in 1995, the sociologist Eric Klinenberg documented that residents in communities that had been taken over by open-air drug markets and gang activity were unwilling to leave their apartments and venture into public space to find cooler air on their stoops or in the parks: "Throughout the city, but especially in the areas with high rates of violent crimes, people chose to suffer through the intense heat rather than cool themselves in the same areas in which their predecessors had congregated in severe heat waves of previous decades."[8] Hundreds of people died, most living in streets where stores had closed their doors and signs of government presence in this emergency were nowhere to be found.

Chicago's violence spilled over into the middle-class communities that bordered the ghetto. Mary Pattillo lived in and observed a middle-class neighborhood of Chicago and showed how proximity to the violence and gang activity of the ghetto altered the meaning of middle-class status for black families: "Unlike most whites, middle-class black families must contend with the crime, dilapidated housing, and social disorder in the deteriorating poor neighborhoods that continue to grow in their direction."[9] Families who had moved up in the income distribution and obtained stable middle-class jobs found themselves struggling to shield their children from the threats of violence, drugs, and gangs that dominated nearby public spaces.

This was Chicago during the era of violence. Baltimore was similar. In his memoir of his childhood in Baltimore, the author Ta-Nehisi Coates recounts that his most vivid memories were of nights spent sprinting through the streets to avoid crews of boys from Murphy Homes, a housing development near his home, undergoing repeated tests of fortitude in the halls and locker rooms of his school, and using an array of strategies to stay safe outside his home. "When crack hit Baltimore, civilization fell," wrote Coates. The threat of lethal violence on Baltimore's streets was new, different from the threats Coates's father had faced decades earlier: "Dad told me how it used to be. . . . The bad end of a beef was loose teeth and stitches, rarely shock trauma and 'Blessed Assurance' ringing the roof of the storefront funeral home."[10] Violence had become inescapable, and as Coates wrote years later, "when you live around violence there is no opting out."[11]

In urban neighborhoods where violence was always possible, street gangs proliferated. Teenagers in cities all over the country joined gangs at a young age, motivated in part by the need for protection. The sociologist Victor Rios recalls the day during his teenage years when he went with his closest friends to visit a group of girls in a neighborhood outside his own gang's territory in East Oakland, California.[12] A group of rival gang members found out that he was present and approached him and his friends. A brawl ensued. In the midst of the chaos, someone pulled a gun and began shooting. Rios fled and made it out safely, but his best friend was shot in the head and killed.

The horror of this episode played out continuously in the cities of California during the 1990s. Martin Sanchez-Jankowski, who spent years hanging out with gang members in Los Angeles and elsewhere, found that much of the violent activity of gang members was preemptive, driven by fear. In environments outside the control of the formal legal system, young men anticipated violence wherever they went and often struck first in an attempt to survive. An L.A. gang member explained his decision to attack a rival group as an effort to avoid being victimized: "We checked each other out and then my homies and I decided to attack the putas [whores] because if we would've got outside we would have been in some tightness [trouble]."[13] Another young man recounted his decision to instigate a fight with rival gangs, explaining, "We both saw each other and didn't do anything for a while. Then we just attacked them spics . . . 'cause you figure that you might as well attack them because they're going to jump us and, shit, you might as well do it when the situation is best for us."[14]

The environment that had emerged on the streets was one where victimization was always possible, where violence was seen as inevitable. In Los Angeles, homicide detectives had a name for that era in the city's history: "The Big Years."[15]

Neighborhoods across all five boroughs of New York were consumed by the rise of violence. The anthropologist Philippe Bourgois moved to the heart of Manhattan's Spanish Harlem to understand the lives of Puerto Rican men who sold crack at a time when the neighborhood had been taken over by the drug trade and the violence that went with it. In his first thirteen months in Spanish Harlem, Bourgois witnessed the fatal shooting of a young mother who sold drugs, an onslaught of gunfire from a machine gun into a nearby building, two separate firebombings, a shootout between police and a felon, and "a half dozen screaming, clothes-ripping fights."[16] Although those who were outside the network of illegal activity were rarely the victims of such incidents, he found that "street culture's violence pervades daily life in El Barrio and shapes mainstream society's perception of the ghetto."[17]

Across the East River in Bushwick, Brooklyn, young black men felt vulnerable the moment they stepped outside their homes and into public space. "If there's ten people there, they're just gonna come and spray the whole block and whoever gets caught gets caught. They're not even aiming at you, they're just . . . that's the crowd, he's in there somewhere, let's knock everybody. It's crazy."[18] The criminologist Richard Curtis interviewed young men who described the sound of gunfire as a constant source of background noise. "Nights here are like the Fourth of July, but all year round. There are always guns being fired."

These depictions of urban life come from some of the most influential studies written in the past fifty years. They describe neighborhoods that had emptied out over time, where economic opportunities had disappeared, where schools had become just as dangerous as the streets, and where institutions like churches had lost members and resources to sustain themselves. They describe communities where public spaces had been taken over by gangs and drug dealers, and where no one was safe.

These seminal studies of urban poverty have one other feature in common: They were all written before the decline in American violence. In fact, much of what we know about urban poverty is based on a set of classic studies carried out between the early 1960s and the mid-1990s, when violence was extremely high or was rising quickly. These are the books that are taught in seminars on urban poverty all over the country; these are the images that policy makers have in mind when they talk about the problem of "inner-city" neighborhoods. And these academic studies were reinforced by images of the ghetto in popular culture, as films like *Boyz n the Hood* and *Colors* dramatized the violence of everyday life in cities like Los Angeles, and television shows like *Cops* brought the brutality of life in the ghetto directly to viewers.

Our collective understanding of the look and feel of urban poverty was developed during the era of violent crime. But considering how far violence has fallen, it is time to consider whether the nature of urban poverty has changed, and to ask a basic question: Is everything we've been taught about the urban ghetto wrong?

The O Street Market lies at the intersection of O and Seventh streets in the Shaw neighborhood of northwest Washington, D.C., a section of the city that has long been seen as the "cultural and economic hub" for D.C.'s African American community.[19] When Martin Luther King, Jr., was assassinated in April 1968, Shaw was one of the many neighborhoods that exploded. Stores were looted, buildings were firebombed, and troops were called in to occupy the neighborhood and the city. In the years that followed, middle-class families began to leave. By the late 1980s, Shaw had become a symbol of the decay and violence that had taken over much of urban America. Washington's population fell from over 750,000 in 1970 to roughly 600,000 by 1990, and it continued to decline in the early 1990s.[20]

There were many low points in the 1980s and 1990s in Washington, a city that watched its mayor smoke crack in an FBI sting operation that was recorded and played back to the nation. But perhaps the most shocking incident occurred at the O Street Market, a center of public life within the neighborhood, on March 31, 1994.[21] At around seven that Thursday evening, a gunfight erupted between two groups of youths inside the crowded market. Violence was common at the time, but battles over turf and drug markets typically were waged on side streets away from crowds. On that evening in March, the violence of D.C. finally took over the most public of spaces. Fifteen-year-old Duwan A'Vant, who had just become a father, was killed in the gunfire. His best friends, all in their teens, were feuding with a rival group of teenagers from a few blocks over. Their rivalry left eight people shot, including two elderly women, two FBI security guards, and a toddler.

The shootings at the market are still remembered as one of the most disturbing events in an era of extreme violence. Between 1988 and 1992, the nation's capital had the highest homicide rate in the country.[22] If Washington, D.C., had been an independent country, it would have ranked among the top two or three most violent nations in the world.[23] The gunfight that erupted at the city's largest market was a signal that the violence that had engulfed the city finally had spread to all public spaces, that no one who was out in the open was safe. Lorren Leadmon, a detective who worked the case, expressed the collective feeling of shock and vulnerability: "It was so brazen, and it struck people from all over the city because people came from all over to that market. Next to running up into a church, it was about the worst thing you could do."[24]

The aftermath of the O Street Market shootings was predictable. As the public steered clear of the market, businesses left, and the space emptied out. The historic building was vandalized, and the roof collapsed. The once-vital market became yet another visible marker of urban blight, an example of what happens when violence takes over a community.

The changes that have taken place in the two decades since the shootings have been less predictable. As in the nation as a whole, the number of murders in D.C. fell in the latter half of the 1990s, but the decline in homicides was steeper in the nation's capital than almost anywhere else. At the peak of the era of violence, in 1991, there were 482 homicides in D.C., but by the end of the 1990s there were half that many. The annual count of homicides continued to fall in the 2000s, and since 2009 there have been between 100 and 150 homicides each year.[25]

The transformation of the Shaw neighborhood, and the infamous O Street Market, has been equally dramatic. The neighborhood became more closely linked to the rest of the city when the Shaw–Howard University metro station was opened in 1991. A municipal building was constructed at the corner of U and Fourteenth streets, gradually bringing a stream of city workers and residents to a place that had previously been occupied by drug dealers.[26] Several housing cooperatives were established to provide affordable homes for longtime neighborhood residents. And after more than a decade in which it stood dormant, the building that housed the market was purchased and restored.

A new playground has been built down the street from the site of the bloodshed two decades ago. Storefronts that were abandoned have been redeveloped and have begun to cater to a new clientele, as the neighborhood's population has slowly become more diverse. An article from a local paper documented the neighborhood's constantly shifting establishments: "One block up from the market, the neighborhood laundromat closed last week. It will be replaced by a gourmet coffee roastery. A long-empty corner storefront is expected to become a Mexican restaurant under the direction of a celebrity chef. Diagonally across, a beer garden, Dacha, draws a large, happy crowd."[27]

In this new environment, the primary concerns expressed by longtime Shaw residents have to do not with violence but with the community's shifting culture and demographics.[28] A neighborhood that was predominantly black now has a large presence of whites and Hispanics. Brand-new housing developments have sprouted up around the market, with units renting for several thousand dollars a month or selling for millions. Newcomers are ascending to leadership positions in the local political structure and are calling for bike lanes and dog parks. The neighborhood remains economically diverse because of subsidized housing, but otherwise it is far out of reach for middle-class families.

Occasional shootings still take place in Shaw, providing a reminder of what life used to be like there. But these days the major challenge is how to integrate a diverse community of residents into a neighborhood with a tremendous amount of history, culture, and economic value. These are important issues at a time when neighborhoods across the country are dealing with the challenges of affordable housing and gentrification. But it is also important to acknowledge just how much things have changed since the early 1990s. Longtime residents are justifiably concerned about the high-priced restaurants popping up in the neighborhood and about where they will do their laundry. But two decades ago the same residents of Shaw were worried about being shot while shopping for groceries.

The story of Shaw is familiar in dozens of cities, from San Antonio to Phoenix to Los Angeles to Minneapolis. The story is visible in two maps, shown in Figure 2.1. On the top, the largest cities across the country are shaded by the 1993 murder rate.[29] The lightly shaded cities were the safest places in the country that year, cities where there were fewer than 10 homicides for every 100,000 residents. The cities shaded in the darkest tones are places where more than 40 out of every 100,000 residents were killed each year, a level of violence unheard of in most of the world.

The same cities are shown in the bottom map, shaded by the murder rate in 2014. The map still shows splotches of dark-shaded cities, places that continue to have high levels of violence. But few of these places are left. Many of the cities that were intensely violent in the 1990s, like Washington, D.C., now have relatively low rates of violent crime. Many of the dark circles on the map have turned lighter.

The transformation that has taken place in these cities is com-

Homicide Rates in the Largest U.S. Cities, 1993

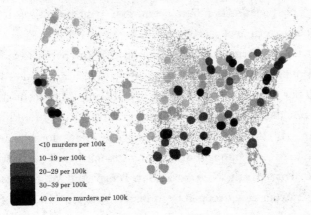

Homicide Rates in the Largest U.S. Cities, 2014

Fig. 2.1 Homicide rates in the largest U.S. cities, 1993 (top) and 2014 (bottom)

plex and nuanced. It is not only about the drop in violence and the reawakening of public life in neighborhoods like Shaw. It is also about gentrification, rising rents, and the new faces that have appeared walking along U Street in the nation's capital. It is about the expansive reach of the prison system, and the tenuous relationship between residents and the police. But more than anything else, it is about a transition from a time of horrific, relentless, brutal violence to a time of relative peace.

And it is a story that has played out in cities all over the country. In 1993 about 40 percent of big cities had a homicide rate above 20 per 100,000 residents, but in 2014 only 13 percent still had a homicide rate this high. A small group of cities, like Flint, Michigan; Hartford, Connecticut; Newark, New Jersey; and Baton Rouge, Louisiana, didn't change much by 2014. But in cities like Fort Worth, New York, San Diego, and Washington, D.C., the murder rate dropped by at least 75 percent. In Atlanta, Boston, San Francisco, Seattle, Tampa, and many other cities it fell by at least half. In just about every big city, murder became less common.

As the homicide rate fell, neighborhoods that used to be war zones began to transform. Although a lack of available data makes it extremely difficult to study very localized trends in violence over a long period, Michael Friedson, a postdoctoral researcher, and I were able to obtain data on neighborhood violent crime, going back a decade or longer, in six different cities: Chicago, Cleveland, Denver, Philadelphia, Seattle, and St. Petersburg.[30] To be clear, these six are not representative of all U.S. cities; nonetheless, our study was the first to utilize data from multiple cities to document how the crime decline has played out in local neighborhoods, and the patterns found in these six cities are revealing.

Friedson and I found that the most substantial drops in violence occurred in the most violent neighborhoods of each city. In Denver, for example, the violent crime rate dropped by 95 crimes per 10,000 residents in the city's most violent neighborhoods, but by just 11 crimes for every 10,000 residents elsewhere in the city. The decline in violence in the most dangerous neighborhoods of

St. Petersburg dropped by five times as much as it did in the rest of the city.

The case of Cleveland is particularly illuminating. Cleveland remains one of the most violent cities in the country, and it has experienced an increase in murder over the past few years. Relative to the early 1990s, however, the level of violence in Cleveland has fallen sharply. Friedson and I compared neighborhood rates of violent crime in 1990 and 2010 and found that the city's most violent communities had experienced the greatest changes over time. For every 10,000 residents of the most violent neighborhoods, there were 176 fewer violent crimes in 2010 than there were in 1990, a drop of 43 percent. In the rest of the city, the level of violent crime didn't change much—in fact, it rose slightly over this twenty-year period.

These changes do not mean that Cleveland's poorest residents are now safe; nor do they mean that the risk of violence is now spread evenly across the population. But they do mean that the drop in crime has had its greatest influence on everyday life in the neighborhoods where violence was the biggest problem. Before crime started to decline, the level of violence in the neighborhoods of the city's poor residents was about 70 percent higher than in the neighborhoods of its nonpoor residents. In 2010 a gap still existed, but it had shrunk considerably; the average level of violence in the neighborhoods of Cleveland's poor population was only about 24 percent higher than in the neighborhoods of its nonpoor population.

All six cities we studied showed similar patterns. As the degree of violence has fallen, the gap between the neighborhoods of the poor and nonpoor has narrowed, and the experience of urban poverty has become less distinct. There is still tremendous inequality in the distribution of violence across urban neighborhoods, but the degree of violence in communities where poverty is concen-

trated and in those where it is not has converged. In some cities, the transition is far from complete—in Chicago, for instance,
black and Latino residents continue to live in much more violent
communities than the city's white population. But in other cities,
like Denver, the average level of violence in the neighborhoods of
black and Latino residents has begun to look very similar to that
in whites' neighborhoods.[31] Poor residents of Philadelphia, Cleveland, and Seattle are still exposed to higher levels of community
violence than are those who do not live in poverty, but the neighborhoods of the poor no longer look dramatically different from the
neighborhoods of everyone else.

The connection between violence and poverty has not come close
to being severed in American cities, but in many places, that connection has frayed over time. After two decades of falling violence,
the look and feel of urban poverty have changed.

Roughly fifteen years after Elijah Anderson chronicled the daily
challenges faced by young people in Philadelphia's ghetto, the
sociologist Alice Goffman carried out her own research in another
segregated Philadelphia neighborhood, immersing herself in the
lives of a group of young black men.[32] In the years between Anderson's book and Goffman's fieldwork, street life in Philadelphia had
changed.

The young men whom Anderson studied spent their days avoiding
rivals and negotiating public space in the hopes of avoiding being
victimized. Although the police were present in *Code of the Street,*
which was written at a time when the national rate of incarceration
was rising quickly, the various representatives of the criminal justice system—including parole officers, detectives, judges, prosecutors,
and corrections officials—were not a constant presence in the lives
of young black men.

In Goffman's Philadelphia, the hierarchy of threat had shifted.

Violence remained a central concern, as the young men whom she describes were entangled in local rivalries and were always at risk of lethal violence. But the threat posed by other groups of young men was sporadic, whereas the threat of a cop or a parole officer was constant. When they looked over their shoulders as they walked down the street, the young men in Goffman's book were more worried about an officer trailing them than a member of a rival crew.

This shift in focus, from the threat of violent peers to the threat of abusive police, can be found in an array of recent studies of urban poverty. In 2015 Ta-Nehisi Coates published *Between the World and Me,* written in the form of a letter to his son. As in his earlier memoir of his own childhood in Baltimore, Coates focused his more recent book on the vulnerability of the black body in the United States. But Coates does not warn his son about the danger of rival crews of young boys from the housing projects nearby. Instead, he begins with a story about being pulled over in Prince George's County, Maryland, by members of the same police force that would later kill Coates's friend from college. It is the risk from law enforcement, and from the expansive criminal justice system, that preoccupies Coates as he writes to his son.

The long shadow of the criminal justice system may be the most visible change in America's poor, segregated neighborhoods, but other changes too have altered the character of the urban ghetto. Rising immigration has changed the face of cities, creating "global neighborhoods" in cities that used to be black and white.[33] After decades in which central city neighborhoods were places to be feared and avoided, scholars like Lance Freeman and Derek Hyra have documented the tension that has surfaced as newcomers more likely to be highly educated, better off, and white have made their way into neighborhoods that used to be segregated, poor, and violent.[34] Neighborhoods once occupied only by African Americans now have more diverse populations, and the overall level of racial segregation has slowly begun to fall.[35]

As new faces have entered urban neighborhoods and violence has fallen, other social problems have worsened. Deep poverty has become more prevalent in the decades since welfare reform, and in many cities housing has become increasingly expensive and unstable.[36] Even as new community organizations have proliferated in many parts of urban America, the challenges of surviving, raising children in a decent home, sending them to a nurturing school, and avoiding hunger have become more formidable at a time of state retrenchment and rising inequality.

The urban population has shifted, the safety net has shrunk, and the reach of the criminal justice system has extended, yet the visible, audible, tangible presence of urban violence, which used to dominate city neighborhoods across the country, has faded.

———

New York City may be the poster child for the Great American Crime Decline, but one doesn't have to travel far from New York to tell a very different story about American city life. Drive west ten miles from Lower Manhattan, through the Holland Tunnel, over the Pulaski Skyway, and you will find yourself in Newark, New Jersey. Twenty-five years ago that drive would have brought you into a city that didn't feel all that different from the one you left. The buildings are taller in Manhattan and the streets are more crowded, but the signs of urban decay that were once visible throughout Manhattan were similar to what you would have found in Newark.

The risk of violence also was similar. Back in the early 1990s, there were around 30 homicides for every 100,000 New York City residents, and 35 homicides for every 100,000 residents of Newark. In the years since, New York City has experienced a transformation that has been scrutinized and documented in excruciating detail. Newark, just ten miles to the west, hasn't changed much at all. By 2014, the homicide rate in New York City had fallen to 4 per 100,000, while the rate in Newark was 34 per 100,000.

In an era of relative urban peace, cities like Atlanta, Baltimore, Cleveland, Detroit, Flint, Kansas City, New Orleans, Newark, Oakland, and St. Louis remain unacceptably violent. And others, including Chicago, Milwaukee, and Houston, have experienced a sudden rise in violence since 2014. This group of cities tells us, very clearly, that the stunning transformation of American city life is incomplete and fragile. To paint a complete picture of what urban America looks like after the era of violence, one has to tell the story of these cities left behind.

In April 2016 I visited Milwaukee, a city where residents are concerned that things could go back to the way they used to be twenty years earlier. Up until a few years ago, the decline in violence that took place in Milwaukee looked very similar to what happened in most big cities across the country. Since the early 1990s, the level of lethal violence had fallen by 40 to 50 percent. Instead of 160 annual homicides, there were between 80 and 100 each year from 2010 to 2014. But then in 2015, the city seemed to explode. One hundred and forty-five people were killed in 2015, the highest number since 1993, and the violence continued into 2016.

I was invited to Milwaukee by Susan Lloyd, the executive director of the Zilber Family Foundation, an organization that is working with residents to rebuild the city's communities. She asked me to come for two days of meetings, to talk about my research on neighborhood inequality, and to try to help them understand why the city's neighborhoods had suddenly erupted in gunfire. When I arrived in Milwaukee, it was as if I was visiting a world where the crime decline never happened.

...

John Gurda is a historian with an encyclopedic knowledge of Milwaukee, which has made him something of a local celebrity. He has written multiple books about the city's neighborhoods, he writes a monthly column for the *Journal Sentinel,* sits on the boards of community groups and foundations, and serves as the city's informal ambassador.[37] On my first morning in Milwaukee, I was lucky enough to have John as my guide for a three-hour driving tour of the city. The city was sunny and warm on the morning of April 25, 2016. Before John arrived, I commented on the beautiful weather to the clerk at the hotel's coffee shop. He laughed and said it wouldn't last. He was right.

But that morning the sun shone brightly, providing the ideal setting to be introduced to the city. John, accompanied by Susan Lloyd, picked me up, and we quickly made our way past downtown and into the city's neighborhoods. John's voice provided a streaming narrative during our slow drive. As we passed each intersection, he identified the building, the school, the organization, the event, or the person most essential to understanding that particular block. We drove past nondescript intersections and learned about riots that arose there in 1967 during intense battles against discrimination and housing segregation. We stopped on quiet streets and learned about the tireless work that was going on to keep them from falling apart.

It was at one of these quiet corners, the intersection of West North Avenue and North Seventeenth Street, that a young man named Raymond Harris had been shot and killed two years earlier.[38] At the corner where he was killed, there now lies a community garden next to a renovated two-story house that is owned and operated by the organization Walnut Way. It is a place where young people from the community can go to access resources to help them deal with trauma, to share their emotions and receive support, and to come together in a safe space.

As we wound our way through the neighborhoods on the north side, from Harambee to Metcalfe Park to Lindsay Heights, John and Susan pointed out neighborhood institutions similar to Walnut Way, organizations run by people with an extraordinary commitment to their communities and to their city. But there were also stretches of city blocks where the running commentary slowed down, where crumbling, boarded-up homes on either side of the street dominated the landscape. I asked what was going on in these neighborhoods, and there wasn't much to say. The reach of organizations like Walnut Way and the Zilber Family Foundation could extend only so far. Some blocks in Milwaukee are on their own, and they are struggling.

Later that day I visited the Dominican Center, a faith-based organization run by Sister Patricia Rogers, a passionate, engaging, and talented woman who was doing everything she could in her own neighborhood of Amani. Near the Dominican Center, I noticed a prominent house on a corner with windows that were boarded up but painted to resemble windowpanes and shutters. The house was clearly vacant, but the grounds were well kept. I asked about the house and found out that the paint job was the work of Sister Patricia, who had the plywood on the windows painted so that the abandoned house looked nicer. The paint job made it clear to everyone who passed that the plot of land was cared for, that someone was watching over it.

That afternoon in Sister Patricia's conference room, I met with fifteen leaders of organizations that look out over their own communities in Milwaukee. I asked all of them the same questions: What happened last year? What changed in your community? Why did the city seem to explode with violence? No one had a definitive answer. Some pointed to April 30, 2014, the day Dontre Hamilton, a black man, was shot fourteen times by white officer Christopher Manney.[39] Hamilton, a man with paranoid schizophrenia, had been sleeping in a public park when he was woken by the officer and patted down. The interaction escalated, Hamilton grabbed the officer's nightstick and hit him with it, and Manney began shooting. Officer Manney was fired by decision of police chief Edward Flynn, but he was not prosecuted in court.

Some of the leaders in the room thought the killing of Dontre Hamilton had been the final straw for Milwaukee's young people. They gave up on their city. A representative from the Children's Hospital said that there had been no quiet periods in her emergency room over the past year. Usually there are lulls and slow periods, but in 2015 the stream of young people coming through hospital doors with gunshot wounds was constant. The director of an economic development organization said that he had always had a close connection with the young people in his neighborhood—but this past year those same kids started vandalizing the van used to help transport residents around the city.

After the group of organization leaders left the room, I stayed behind for a separate meeting with a dozen or so residents who were active within their neighborhoods. Most had been in Milwaukee for their entire lives. Some said the previous year was worse than it had ever been. They talked about how the kids in their neighborhoods couldn't get a job and ended up hanging out on the streets. They talked about how the police were destroying their communities, and locking up as many black people as they could. They worried about being poisoned with lead in their water, just like in Flint.[40] And they shook their heads when they described the attitudes of some children who were shooting each other over an insult or an argument about a girl. They blamed the mayor, they blamed the local labor market, they blamed the police, and they blamed parents throughout their own communities. They blamed themselves for not doing enough.

One father whose sons had left the city said even they couldn't understand what was going on back home in "Kill-waukee."

Another resident told her kids they should plan to leave as soon as they finished high school. I asked the others whether they would leave Milwaukee if they had the chance. "I've been here too long to leave," one woman responded. "But I tell my kids to get as far away as they can."

When the discussion with residents ended, I sat in the passenger seat of Susan Lloyd's car and we headed east on West Locust Street toward a dinner being held at the Sojourner Family Peace Center, a beautiful campus designed to provide support and services for families affected by any form of domestic violence. A few blocks east of the Dominican Center, we came to a stop at an intersection, and I noticed a crowd of young people gathering on a side street. Dozens of teenagers were converging in the middle of the one-way street, blocking a line of cars that were trying to pass. Two teenage girls were at the center of the pack, pointing and yelling at each other. Young men stood in between them, and others stood behind looking on.

We waited at the intersection and watched the crowd of young people become more tightly bunched in the middle of the street. The intensity of the crowd was growing; a fight seemed about to break out. The light turned, and we were in the midst of traffic, so we drove on before anything happened. But as I looked back, I noticed four or five young boys, no older than nine or ten, navigating up and down the street on their bikes, winding their way through the teenagers, onto the sidewalks, and around the cars that were stuck on the one-way street, with nowhere to go. The boys looked like they were about the same age as my own ten-year-old son, who had never seen a real, serious fight in person. These kids looked like they might have been about to watch something violent go down on a Monday afternoon, in the middle of the street, on their own block.

That night at dinner, when I described the crowd of young peo-

ple on the side street, the community leaders and police department officials at my table were not surprised. No record of an
incident had been logged by the police department, and it is possible that the confrontation did not escalate any further. But the
thought of those young boys on their bikes stuck with me.

Just as the clerk at the coffee shop had predicted, by the time I
left Milwaukee the sky was gray and the wind was blowing hard.
The weather matched my mood. After watching the chaotic scene
on the side street in Amani, seeing pockets of boarded-up homes,
and hearing the exasperated voices of community residents, I left
wondering whether things in Milwaukee were about to get worse.[41]

The ominous feeling in Milwaukee reflects a rapidly growing,
nationwide fear of an impending rise in violence. This fear is not
unfounded. The national spike in homicides in 2015 and 2016 has
left residents and community leaders in some cities thinking back
to the worst years of the 1980s and 1990s. And it has evoked
alarm across the country, as criminologists have documented the
sudden reversal of the long-term trend of falling violence, and as
sensational journalists have stoked Americans' fears by warning
of an impending crime wave.[42]

The national obsession over the idea that violent crime is on the
rise has some value. The fear of rising crime can bring urgency
to the constant battle to confront violence. I saw this urgency in
Milwaukee, where a single year of rising violence had leaders of
the city mobilized to do whatever possible to respond. Although
only a small number of cities have experienced a meaningful, sustained increase in the homicide rate, it is nonetheless important
to acknowledge that the long period of declining violence may have
come to an end. Something real, and troubling, is happening in a
growing number of U.S. cities.

But there is also a danger that comes with the obsessive focus
on spikes in violent crime that occur over a few short months, or

even over one or two years. There is a risk that a city like Milwaukee will be seen as hopeless, a place inevitably bound to be dangerous. There is a risk that the kids of those community leaders will give up on their city, and leave; and that visitors charmed by Milwaukee's beautiful tree-lined streets will have second thoughts as they consider where to raise a family. And there is the risk of ignoring the crucial distinction between short-term fluctuations and long-term trends, and misunderstanding what our country is like at this moment, and how it has changed over time.

If we consider what America's cities looked like twenty years ago, we find that many of the cities that continue to have high levels of violence have experienced meaningful changes over time. Detroit's *rate* of homicides has declined only by roughly 20 percent since the early 1990s, but that figure is somewhat misleading because hundreds of thousands of people have left the city, which has become notorious for urban blight, depopulation, and crime. Even in the city that has suffered the most from deindustrialization, the raw number of homicides has dropped to a historic low. Roughly 600 homicides used to occur in Detroit each year; over the past few years, the total has hovered around 300, lower than at any point since 1967. In Cleveland, Oakland, and Philadelphia, the homicide rate has declined by 25 to 40 percent. And in Atlanta, a city that is still violent, the homicide rate has dropped by more than half since the early 1990s.

After two decades of declining violence, murder is no longer a national crisis. Violent crime remains an urgent problem in many cities, but one that can now be defined in relation to specific places at specific times. In 2015 cities like Baltimore, St. Louis, and Milwaukee drew the attention of the nation when the number of murders rose after periods of unrest. In 2016 cities like Chicago and Las Vegas experienced a sharp rise in violence that provoked policy makers and heads of foundations to mobilize in response.[43]

As the country's focus shifts to cities that are experiencing spikes in violence, it is important to keep in mind the other cities that are out of the national headlines. Places like Fort Worth, Long Beach, Miami, San Antonio, and Santa Ana, California, used to have high levels of violence but are now historically safe. Denver, Fresno, and San Francisco, once relatively violent, are now among the safer cities in the country. And Anchorage, Colorado Springs, San Jose, and Tucson have always had extremely low levels of violence.

The United States has made it through a period during which its cities were places to be feared and avoided, and the problem of violence seemed hopeless and overwhelming. The problem has not disappeared, but the maps showing homicide rates in the largest cities capture a new reality: For the first time in decades, most big cities are no longer dangerous places. Why?

3

THE TRANSFORMATION OF
URBAN SPACE

As they pass La Brea Avenue, visitors walking east on Los Angeles's Hollywood Boulevard are usually looking down at the sidewalk, searching for a star bearing the name of Elvis Presley or perhaps Spanky McFarland of the Little Rascals (whose star is nearby). If they look up, however, they might notice something different about the famous street. Among the throngs of tourists, revelers, homeless people, and performers are uniformed men and women with dark blue T-shirts and pants, looking out over the sidewalks and intersections. The visitors might observe that those uniformed men and women carry guns and radio receivers, but no badge is visible on their shirts. They might notice the backs of the dark shirts, which read BID PATROL.

The armed officers walking east and west on Hollywood Boulevard are not from the Los Angeles Police Department. They are paid security for the Hollywood Entertainment District, one of the first business improvement districts (BIDs) formed back in 1996 in a state that now has more than any other.[1] A few years before the Hollywood Entertainment District was formed, there had been more than a thousand homicides each year in Los Angeles, one of the most violent cities in the country. Hollywood Boulevard always had its attractions, but at that time the area was known as yet another run-down, seedy, and sometimes dangerous L.A. street. The BID, which extends eighteen blocks from La Brea Avenue eastward to US 101, was a desperate attempt to reclaim and revitalize an iconic stretch of land that contains some of the country's most famous landmarks.

Business improvement districts are private entities created by property owners who agree to pay a tax in order to fund an enhanced set of services in a designated section of a town or city. For the Hollywood Entertainment District's founders, as for most BID founders, security and sanitation were the primary goals. Almost half of the BID's budget, which is now close to $4 million per year, goes to fund the armed security officers, mostly off-duty or retired cops, who can be seen patrolling the boulevard seven days a week. BID security officers make more than seven hundred citizens arrests each year and often work directly with the LAPD to respond to incidents of crime. The BID has provided funding for eight closed-circuit cameras overlooking key intersections on the boulevard, and the footage from those cameras is made available for the use of the LAPD. The line separating the Hollywood Entertainment District's privately funded patrol officers from the LAPD's publicly funded officers is sometimes blurry.

In 2011 the economists Phil Cook and John MacDonald designed a study to assess whether the introduction of BIDs like the one in Hollywood actually served their intended purpose; that is, whether they were effective in reducing crime.[2] The researchers took advantage of the fact that BIDs had been established in Los Angeles in different locations at different times, making it possible to see whether there is a noticeable decline (or increase) in crime from the period just before the introduction of the BID to the period just after. By comparing changes in crime to changes in areas outside the BID, but in the same police district, they were able to test whether the BID itself could be seen as an effective crime control strategy.

Cook and MacDonald analyzed the effect of the first BIDs formed in Los Angeles in the 1990s and continued the analysis to consider all thirty BIDs formed before 2005. They found that establishing a BID led to a reduction of roughly 28 crimes in the following year, a drop of 11 percent from the average annual total of crimes in each area where BIDs were formed. The impact stayed about the same from the first few years when BIDs emerged to the end of the period of study, when large swaths of the city were part of a BID. The researchers found no evidence that crime was simply displaced, shifted outward beyond the boundaries of the BID. In fact, neighboring communities may also have experienced some of the benefits to public safety, as certain types of crime, like assaults, dropped slightly in nearby streets as well.

Perhaps the most persuasive finding was that the greatest drops in crime occurred in the BIDs that devoted the greatest resources to public safety and security. By agreeing to tax themselves, the establishments within the BID were, in effect, using their private resources to provide a public good. Each incident of crime not committed meant that a visitor to Hollywood Boulevard was not injured or traumatized, individual property was not lost, a police officer's time was not spent writing up a report and showing up in court, the offender was not ushered through the criminal justice system, a judge had one fewer case to hear throughout a busy day, and one jail or prison cell was not occupied. All these consequences have costs, to the victim of the crime and to the public taxpayers of the city. Based on the best estimates of the "social costs" of crime, Cook and MacDonald calculated that every

$10,000 spent by a BID on security led to a reduction in robberies and arrests worth roughly $200,000 in value to the people of Los Angeles and California.

The private expenditures from groups like the Hollywood Entertainment District have generated enormous benefits to the public. And in the process, they have transformed one of America's most famous streets. Since the 1990s, Hollywood Boulevard has changed from a shady, crime-ridden area, where tourists paused to take a picture and then departed quickly, to a glitzy, clean, sanitized, and safe attraction catering to thousands of visitors each day. The website for the Hollywood Entertainment District BID boasts that "this District has served as a fundamental underpinning to the overall Hollywood revitalization success story."[3] There is likely some truth to the claim. The BID has spent millions of dollars cleaning up the streets and sidewalks, utilizing off-duty police to crack down on suspicious or criminal behavior, and trying to make the area as pleasant, safe, welcoming, and profitable as it can.

Interpreting the changes that have taken place on Hollywood Boulevard is not straightforward. The transformation of this iconic section of Los Angeles can be seen as an uplifting tale of urban revitalization or as a dark tale of sanitization in the name of profit. The tactics of armed private security officers are likely seen as reassuring to some but as repressive to others. The efforts to reduce the level of panhandling on the boulevard are undoubtedly welcomed by many and seen as cruel and unnecessary by others.

But the story of change on Hollywood Boulevard, no matter how it is perceived or evaluated, captures a broader change that has occurred across America's urban neighborhoods. It is about not only well-known places like Hollywood Boulevard but also poor neighborhoods, where community groups are the driving force behind efforts to transform public spaces to keep residents safe. It is a story about not just BIDs but also a set of people and organizations—public law enforcement, private security, private citizens, and nonprofit groups—that responded to the rise of violent crime by taking ownership, and oversight, over public and private spaces. Some pages of this story document brutal accounts of police violence and oppression, while others document inspiring accounts of communities' resilience. It is the tale of a new set of urban guardians.

More than thirty years ago the criminologists Lawrence Cohen and Marcus Felson developed what they called "routine activities theory" to solve a puzzle of rising crime in the 1960s.[4] During a decade in which poverty declined, unemployment dropped, and racial and ethnic inequality became less severe, they wondered how it could be possible that crime worsened. Cohen and Felson argued that to understand large-scale trends in crime, criminologists had to move beyond their focus on the characteristics or the motivations of potential offenders, beyond the simplistic notion that the presence of more poor people translates into more crime, and even beyond a pure focus on individual criminals. Instead of thinking about how many potential offenders there are in the world, they argued, criminologists should broaden their view to consider when, where, and why a crime is likely to occur.[5]

The basic insight of Cohen and Felson's theory is that the likelihood of a crime occurring depends on three elements: a motivated offender, a vulnerable victim, and the absence of a capable guardian. The two criminologists pointed to the way that Americans' everyday routines had shifted in the 1960s, leading a growing share of the population, particularly women, outside the home for work, school, or travel. The shift in routines led to more vulnerable victims walking public streets and more homes left unguarded. Home burglaries became more common. A larger share of murders was carried out by strangers, as opposed to relatives or romantic partners.

Routine activities theory has been criticized and refined over time, but it remains crucially important because it allows for a shift in the way that we think about why crime rises and falls. Many of the most prominent arguments about the decline in violence since the 1990s begin with the assumption that the behavior of potential criminal offenders has changed over time. Some argued that the drop in exposure to lead—a toxin that is known to have damaging effects on every aspect of children's development—changed the behavior of an entire generation of youth. Others argued that changes in abortion law have meant that many thousands of unwanted children, who are assumed to be more likely to grow up to be criminals, were never born. And still others suggested that improvements in the national economy, the proliferation of medications to treat attention deficit/hyperactivity disorder, or the drop in the relative number of young males in the population helped bring about a reduction in crime.[6]

The common link to most of these theories is the assumption that the level of violence must have fallen because of a decline in the number of individuals who are prone to violence. Cohen and Felson's ideas push us to think differently, to consider the possibility that the decline in violence was driven not simply by a drop in the number of potential offenders but also by a change in the nature of public and private spaces. It is not just that fewer people are roaming the streets looking for a victim, in other words, but also that more people, organizations, officers, and even cameras are looking out over those same streets to make sure no one is victimized.

After decades in which urban communities were mostly left on their own to deal with the problem of rising crime, the most fundamental change that has taken place since the 1990s is that a wide range of different people and institutions began to take over urban spaces. The most visible and most controversial of these urban guardians, then and now, are the police.

In the aftermath of the World Trade Center attacks in 2001, the Department of Homeland Security developed a system to monitor the imminent threat of a terror attack. The Homeland Security Advisory System was color-coded, with red indicating a "severe" threat level, orange indicating "high," and yellow indicating "elevated." Two additional levels of threat, blue ("guarded") and green ("low"), were never used in the nine years during which the system was operational.[7]

The threat advisory system was designed as a way to mobilize authorities in high-risk cities or areas with vulnerable targets. In the years immediately after the attacks, there were several periods, some lasting just a few days and some stretching over several weeks, in which the threat level was raised to "orange," indicating a "high risk of terrorist attacks."[8] In Washington, D.C., one of the highest-risk cities, these were periods in which the police department mobilized officers and sent them out across the city, creating a visible presence in public spaces by lengthening shifts and increasing the numbers on patrol. Although the primary purpose of these strategies was to prevent another terrorist attack, the terror advisory system generated another change on the streets of D.C.—it led, very simply, to more officers out in public.

The economists Jonathan Klick and Alexander Tabarrok realized that the erratic shifts in the terror threat system generated a unique natural experiment.[9] Criminologists have struggled for decades to figure out whether placing more police officers in public spaces actually prevents crime from happening. This basic question is difficult to answer because decisions about how many officers to put out on the street typically are driven by the level of criminal activity in different communities. If the number of officers on the street is dependent on the severity of the crime problem, it becomes extremely difficult to determine whether those additional officers actually affect the level of crime. In the years after 9/11, however, the terror alert system generated sudden changes in the number of officers assigned to patrol the neighborhoods of Washington, D.C., and these changes had nothing to do with the level of crime.

Klick and Tabarrok argued that the terror alert system could be used to provide evidence on one of the most basic questions in criminal justice research: Does the presence of police prevent crime? The researchers' analysis led to a very clear answer. On days when the terror alert system was set to "orange" or high alert, there were about seven fewer crimes in Washington, a decline of almost 7 percent from the normal average of roughly 110 crimes per day. The decline in criminal activity was greatest in the area surrounding the National Mall, where much of the increase in police presence was focused. The conclusion from this analysis, one of the strongest studies yet of how the sheer presence of police affects criminal activity, is that if police patrols are increased by half, one should expect crime to drop by roughly 15 percent.[10]

Though persuasive, this conclusion is not airtight. It is possible that residents and visitors to the nation's capital were wary of venturing into public spaces like the National Mall during periods when the government warned of "high risk of terrorist attacks," or that the entire city was vigilant during this period.[11] What makes the results more convincing is that the findings are consistent with a growing set of studies that have all reached the same basic conclusion: When more police are on the streets, fewer crimes occur.[12]

William Evans and Emily Owens, for example, found that police departments that received federal grants to help hire additional police officers experienced declines in crime in the period immediately following the grant.[13] Rafael Di Tella and Ernesto Schargrodsky studied the aftermath of a religiously motivated terrorist attack in Buenos Aires that led to an intense police presence near all Jewish and Muslim buildings in the city. They found that crime dropped, but only in the immediate vicinity of these buildings.[14] Mirko Draca and several colleagues carried out a similar study in the aftermath of the 2005 bombings in London and found that crime declined over a period of six weeks when extra police were deployed to Central London.[15] Using a different form of natural experiment, Steven Levitt found that police forces tend to be bolstered in election years, when politicians worry about spikes in crime, the support of police unions, and accusations of being soft on crime from potential opponents. These changes in the size of the local police force reflect political calculations and have nothing to do with local crime rates, yet they also bring about a reduction in violent crime.[16]

The accumulation of evidence has led to a relatively new consensus about police and crime. After a long period in which most criminologists believed that police were powerless to control crime, the new consensus is that more police on the street translates into less crime. And over the course of the 1990s, more and more police officers were hired to patrol the streets of America's cities. Bolstered with funding from the federal government, more than sixty thousand new officers were hired over the course of the decade, increasing the per capita rate of police officers by around 14 percent.[17] After surveying the evidence on how much crime falls with each additional officer, Steven Levitt estimated that the growth of police forces throughout the 1990s can account for somewhere between 10 and 20 percent of the crime drop that occurred during that decade.[18]

The enhanced presence of law enforcement on the streets of America's cities did not occur in a vacuum. Investments in law enforcement were part of a much broader effort designed to expand the reach of the criminal justice system and to respond to the problem of violent crime through tight surveillance and brute force. This effort took many forms. The number of private security guards more than doubled from the early 1980s through the mid-2000s.[19] Closed-circuit television surveillance systems were installed not only in homes and businesses but also on street corners, in public transit systems, and in schools.[20] A survey of 131 cities in California, conducted in 2007, found that 37 had public surveillance systems in place.[21] The American Civil Liberties Union estimates that there are now 22,000 cameras in use in Chicago's streets, buses, subways, and schools alone.[22]

As city streets became more closely watched, urban spaces began to change. The open-air drug markets that were responsible for some of the most visible violence in the 1980s were forcefully shut down. The distribution of crack cocaine, which emerged around 1985 and accounted for a sharp spike in gun violence committed by young black men, began to move indoors and away from the street corners that had been taken over by dealers willing to kill in order to protect their turf.[23] Street corners all across the country were no longer the sites of lethal gun battles to capture or retain prime real estate for the drug trade.

At the same time, a growing share of Americans were being placed into jails and prisons across the country, as stiffer sentencing laws and more aggressive prosecution resulted in the incapacitation of a large share of potential offenders. In the early 1970s, about 200,000 Americans were locked up in state and federal prisons. By the end of the 2000s, the prison population had exploded to over two million.[24] The progression toward mass incarceration is neither efficient, just, nor humane as a mechanism to control violence. But as violence rose steadily from the 1960s through the late 1990s, it was a brute-force approach to controlling violence that was endorsed by most Americans, including a large segment of African Americans, and supported by politicians from both major political parties.[25]

Although there is no consensus on how much of the crime drop can be attributed to the rise of incarceration, even the staunchest critics of mass incarceration acknowledge that the expansion of the imprisoned population contributed to the decline in violence.[26] A recent committee of experts on imprisonment reviewed the best available evidence and came up with three conclusions.[27] First, the impact of imprisonment on crime is largely the result of incapacitation, the removal of potential offenders from the streets. Second, as a greater share of the population is locked up, imprisonment is likely to be less and less effective in reducing crime further. And lastly, the rise of imprisonment in the United States contributed to the decline in violence. It is unclear how much of the crime drop can be explained by imprisonment, but there is no longer much debate that mass incarceration played a role in reducing violence.

The portrait of change in city streets that I have painted so far is a dark one. From the mid-1980s to the late 1990s, a wave of urban warriors clad in dark blue uniforms swept across urban neighborhoods, using brute-force tactics to take over city streets. They worked to shut down open-air markets for crack cocaine, a drug that had generated a surge of lethal violence. And the work of law enforcement was complemented by that of prosecutors who exploited increasingly harsh sentencing laws to take a rising share of offenders off the streets and put them behind bars. As public security forces grew larger and bolder, private security forces also proliferated, utilizing new technologies designed to monitor public and private spaces closely. Business improvement districts hired their own security forces, cameras were installed on the exteriors of parks and buildings, and private businesses invested in guards to look over their properties.

None of this is pleasant to think about. It evokes images of a police state, where private and public security forces work together, utilizing advanced technologies, to surveil urban spaces and to lock away anyone who may be seen as a threat.

But these were not the only changes that took place on city streets in the 1990s. At the same time that growing numbers of Americans were being arrested and locked away in prisons and jails, a new contingent of community organizations quietly began to emerge in neighborhoods across the country to combat the problem of violent crime. The story of these local organizations is crucially important, but is often left out of discussions of the crime decline. The response to violent crime in America's cities did not come only from external forces that occupied the most disadvantaged urban neighborhoods. It also came from within.

A twenty-minute drive south from Hollywood Boulevard takes you into a section of the city now known as South Los Angeles. If the name is unfamiliar, it is because the City of Los Angeles officially renamed the area in 2003. The old name, South Central Los Angeles, had become notorious as the setting for deadly gang wars between the Bloods and the Crips and for the 1992 Rodney King riots. The city decided that a new name might wipe away the image of bloodshed, brutality, blight, and poverty that had come to be associated with South Central.

A group of city residents took a different approach to creating change in South Central L.A. Back in 1985, Juanita Tate learned that the city was planning to put a trash incinerator in her neighborhood, at the corner of Long Beach Avenue and East 41st.[28] She took action, organizing her neighbors in a successful effort to block the plan. And this was just a starting point. Over the subsequent years, the group of neighbors who had success-fully protected their neighborhood from an environmental hazard decided to form a nonprofit. They had already taken responsibility for their neighborhood, but now they made it their organization's official mission. Concerned Citizens of South Central Los Angeles (CCSCLA) set formal boundaries that defined their community: "the I-10 Santa Monica Freeway to the north, the I-110 Harbor Freeway to the west, Slauson Avenue to the south and Alameda Street to the east."[29]

Then they got to work. Realizing that they could not oversee every street within the community, the leaders of CCSCLA orga-nized fifty-seven block clubs that would take responsibility for the streets that they look out upon every day. They took action to make sure that alleys were no longer used for dumping or drug dealing, they worked with the city to train formerly incarcerated residents to clean up sidewalks and maintain the streets, and they built more than one hundred units of housing in their community. Juanita Tate and her neighbors did not single-handedly transform South Central Los Angeles, a community with deep, entrenched poverty that was decimated by the emergence of crack cocaine. But at a time when the community had been abandoned by the city, and left to crumble and fall apart, this group of neighbors took responsibility for a section of their city and gradually, steadily, began to make it safer.

CCSCLA was part of a wave of community mobilization that spread across U.S. cities in the early 1990s, after decades in which community organizations struggled for public support. When the group of neighbors began to organize in 1985, roughly 2,200 non-profits existed in Los Angeles. A decade later 4,800 nonprofits had been formed across the city. Some were organized to promote the arts, others for medical research or other causes. But a large num-ber of nonprofits, in Los Angeles and beyond, were formed to deal with the crisis of concentrated poverty and violence that reached its apex in the late 1980s and early 1990s.

Of course, not every nonprofit has people like Juanita Tate at its helm, and not every nonprofit has a mission of overseeing an entire community, keeping streets clean and keeping residents safe. Not every community organization that arose in Los Angeles suddenly found a way to end the problem of violence. Yet something changed in L.A. neighborhoods and in other poor, violent communities across the country in the early 1990s. Groups of neighbors began to organize, on a large scale, to reclaim the streets around them. Foundations began to reinvest in neighborhoods, years after the government abandoned them. The community nonprofit became a crucially important organizational form that arose, in cities throughout the country, to look out over public and private spaces.

The idea that community groups contributed to the crime decline is comforting, but how do we know that the rise of nonprofits actually had a causal impact? Unlike the studies showing the impact of policing and incarceration, virtually no research has been done on the effect of nonprofits on crime.[30] Along with doctoral students Delaram Takyar and Gerard Torrats-Espinosa, I set out to change this by analyzing data on every nonprofit organization formed in the nation's largest cities from 1990 to 2012.

Identifying the impact of nonprofits on crime is not straightforward, because places with more antiviolence organizations are, of course, places with higher levels of crime.[31] This doesn't mean that community organizations cause more crime, but rather that cities where the problem of violence is more severe are also places where new organizations are likely to sprout up to combat the problem. To determine whether nonprofits have an impact on crime, one needs to do more than analyze the association between rates of nonprofits and rates of crime. We began by focusing on a very short time frame, analyzing whether year-to-year shifts in the number of new community organizations formed in a city bring about changes in the level of crime in the following year. We adjusted for everything else about the city that might be changing from one year to the next, like the characteristics of the population and the rate of poverty, and we found that as the number of community nonprofits rises, every kind of violent crime falls.

To push the analysis further, we looked for situations in which antiviolence nonprofits were formed not because of a recent rise in violence but rather because new sources of funding became available to community groups and leaders.[32] In these situations, we can more confidently assess whether the newly formed organizations had a causal impact on the level of violence. Our results were similarly strong and led to the same conclusions. In a given city with 100,000 people, we found that every new organization formed to confront violence and build stronger neighborhoods led to about a 1 percent drop in violent crime and murder. On the basis of these results, which provide the strongest evidence to date of the causal impact of local nonprofits, we concluded that the explosion of community organizations that took place in the 1990s likely played a substantial role in explaining the decline in violence.

Some of these new organizations were business improvement districts, formed to increase public safety within a city's shopping districts. Others were community centers set up to provide safe spaces for local youth after school, community groups that set out to transform abandoned lots into cooperative gardens, and neighborhood organizations like Juanita Tate's Concerned Citizens of South Central Los Angeles, which set out to make sure their blocks were cared for and watched over.

In the Rio Grande Valley, an intensely poor area on the southern tip of Texas, Valley Interfaith was formed when a collection of community and school institutions came together to organize for change. The Harvard political scientist Robert Putnam studied the organization, describing how it developed leaders from a community of immigrants who saw their young people remain in poverty or swept up into gangs, and fought for repairs to dilapidated schools, resources for job training, paved streets, drainage systems, and streetlights.[33] In the process, it helped establish networks of residents who worked together to solve common challenges. Lupita Torres, a retired farmworker who became a leader within the organization, explained the shift: "We got to know each other. There used to be squabbles and jealousy, little groups that gossiped about each other. Now there's more friendship, and we know how to gather people to deal with problems."[34]

When the Washington Heights section of northern Manhattan was overtaken by gang violence and paralyzed by fear, community leaders began to mobilize to bring people together and to fight back.[35] Robert Snyder, a journalist who lived through the transformation of Washington Heights, documented the efforts of residents and community groups to retake streets and parks and reclaim their community. Snyder described the work of Alianza Dominicana, which organized meetings of community groups and came together with other organizations, including the "Community League of West 159th Street, the Dominican Women's Development Center, and the Asociación Comunal de Dominicanos Progresistas," to march for public attention to the problems within their community and for resources to help.[36] Mothers Against Violence took over a playground in a park that had been dominated by drug addicts. A group called Friends of Fort Tryon Park raised funds, gathered volunteers, and organized events to retake the neighborhood park for community residents and visitors. The New York Restoration Project was formed to care for smaller parks throughout the city, including the array of smaller parks within Washington Heights. According to Snyder, the collective efforts of these organizations transformed the public spaces in this section of northern Manhattan: "In Washington Heights, as elsewhere, residents stepped out of their homes, reclaimed parks and sidewalks, and overcame the fear that had driven so many people indoors during the years of high crime."

The stories from the Rio Grande Valley and Washington Heights are similar to anecdotes from Dudley Square in Boston, Little Village in Chicago, South Central Los Angeles, and East Lake, Atlanta.[37] To those who worked for years and decades to change their communities, the decline in violence was no accident of history, no side effect of changes in abortion law or the amount of lead in gasoline; rather, it was hard work by residents, organized into community groups and block clubs, that transformed urban neighborhoods. My own research results suggest that they are right. The new guardians looking out over city streets are not just public and private security guards but also residents, mobilized in new organizations specifically formed to build community life and control violence. And their presence is a crucial part of the story about how urban communities have changed over the past twenty years.

Why did violent crime fall? Since the early 2000s, when it became clear that the drop in violence was more than a short-term trend, this question has puzzled sociologists, criminologists, and economists. Scholars have searched for a change in society that might explain such a radical, unexpected shift in the behavior of Americans. In the language of empirical researchers, they sought to identify an "exogenous" shock that caused the decline in violence—a change that had nothing to do with crime or criminal justice yet created widespread drops in criminal behavior. Journalists have latched on to these theories, often rewarding the most counterintuitive ideas with the greatest publicity.

The most celebrated theory came from economists John Donohue and Steven Levitt, who proposed that the liberalization of abortion law led to smaller birth cohorts and thus a decline in the number of children born to mothers who were not equipped to provide the types of resources, attention, and nurturing that children require for successful and healthy development. As a result, they argued, thousands of potential offenders were never born. The abortion hypothesis became the best-known theory of the crime drop.[38]

But problems emerged with this hypothesis. Researchers studying abortion pointed out that the changes in law had little impact on fertility rates or the number of children born to "high-risk" caregivers.[39] Other evidence emerged showing that the cohorts that should have been most affected by changes in abortion law continued to show high rates of violent offending into the early 1990s, well after the time when we should have seen a drop in violent offenses according to the theory.[40] And research on changes in abortion laws in other times and places found mixed evidence on the impact of abortion on violent crime.[41] By this point, many criminologists dismiss Donohue and Levitt's theory about abortion and crime altogether, concluding that it was simply wrong.[42] My reading of the evidence persuades me that changes in abortion law may have had a causal impact on levels of crime, but the impact was likely small in magnitude. Violent crime did not fall because more American women had abortions.

Another prominent theory proposed that the drop in exposure to lead, a toxin known to have damaging effects on every aspect of children's development, changed the behavior of an entire generation of youth and led to the crime decline. Strong evidence indicates that exposure to lead impedes the development of cognitive skills and increases impulsive behavior, and that the steep drops in lead exposure have made American children less vulnerable to developmental delays. Recent research presents compelling evidence that exposure to high levels of lead may in fact have a causal impact on the likelihood that a child will be suspended from school or incarcerated.[43] However, advocates of this theory tend to vastly overstate the strength of the relationship between declines in lead exposure and crime rates. Although legislation reducing the amount of lead in gasoline and paint is a true public health breakthrough, the evidence available does not lead me to the conclusion that the drop in lead exposure played a major role in generating the crime decline.

Others who have proposed that the crime drop was caused by an exogenous force point to shifts in the age distribution of the population, improvements in the economy, the growth of immigration, declines in alcohol use, the increased availability of air conditioning, increased time spent indoors playing video games or on social media, and even the spread of medication for attention deficit/hyperactivity disorder as potential explanations. Some of these theories are purely speculative, and others have preliminary, tentative, or conflicting evidence behind them. I would not rule out any of these factors in the discussion of what might have contributed to the drop in crime until we have better evidence with which to evaluate them. But I think it very unlikely that any single factor altered the behavior of Americans in such a stark manner that it can explain why violent crime has fallen so sharply, and so substantially, since the 1990s. I find it difficult to believe that the crime decline was caused by any exogenous shock to society, by a social change that had nothing to do with crime or violence. Instead, I have come to believe that violent crime fell because many different segments of American society mobilized to confront it, and that the crime decline was largely caused by "endogenous" forces—changes that were a response to the crisis of violence itself.

In his impressive book on the historical decline in human violence, the psychologist Steven Pinker argues that the rise in violent
crime in the United States from the 1960s through the 1990s was
a historical anomaly.[44] Over the last several centuries, all forms
of interpersonal violence have become less common. A "civilizing"
process has taken hold across the world, and the exercise of violence
has become less acceptable to humans in all societies. The period
of rising violence in the United States represents a departure from
this long-term trend. Despite the imagery of "flower power" and
nonviolent protest associated with the 1960s, Pinker argues, commonly shared norms prohibiting the use of violence as a means of
securing a given outcome began to break down in that tumultuous
decade. Some began to see violence as an acceptable way to advance
one's interests or social agenda. This disruption in the long-term
civilizing process, according to Pinker, resulted in the 1960s–90s
rise of violent crime. And the crime decline that followed should be
understood as a correction, a reversion to the longer-term world-
wide rejection of violence that has occurred over centuries.

Pinker's argument helps to make sense of why violence fell
the most in places with the most severe, most visible crime
problems—like New York, Washington, D.C., and Los Angeles.
It helps to explain why violence began to fall in the years when
crime ascended to the top of the political agenda and when Americans, for the first time on record, considered it the most pressing
problem facing the United States.[45] And it helps to explain why
crime fell most sharply in the neighborhoods and cities where the
problem had reached catastrophic levels and where every segment
of society had mobilized to respond.[46]

If the crime drop was the result of a society-wide response to
violent crime, a universal rejection of the bloodshed that came to
dominate America's impression of central cities in the 1990s, then
what form did this rejection take? It came, first, in the form of mass

incarceration. Increasingly severe sentencing laws and aggressive policing and prosecution took hundreds of thousands of individuals off of city streets and placed them in jails and prisons. As more and more Americans were placed behind bars, the lucrative, lethal market for crack cocaine gradually cooled off, partially because the demand for crack had run its course and partially because of the intensive battle fought against the gangs who controlled drug distribution on the streets of major U.S. cities.[47] Street corners in city blocks were no longer the sites of gun battles fought among rival groups of dealers who used force to earn their livelihood, and violent crime driven by the drug trade fell sharply.[48]

At the same time, the number of "guardians" of urban spaces grew rapidly. Federal funding paid for tens of thousands of new police officers whose job was to watch over the most dangerous neighborhoods. The tactics they used were sometimes oppressive and sometimes brutal but were also more effective, focusing resources on the precise locations where crime was most intense. The surveillance of city streets extended to private properties and urban schools. Officers appeared in schools across the country, along with cameras and metal detectors, firms hired security guards, homeowners purchased alarm systems, drivers used remarkably effective technologies to monitor the location of their cars, and cities installed closed-circuit cameras to watch over public space.[49]

As the surveillance of urban populations intensified and the criminal justice system expanded, another set of guardians emerged in the nation's urban neighborhoods, offering a more positive, hopeful addendum to the story of how urban spaces have transformed. In the early 1990s, thousands of local community organizations were established to provide social services and safe spaces for young people, to create stronger neighborhoods, and to confront violence.

The evidence I have presented confirms anecdotal accounts of journalists, activists, and researchers who have argued that violent crime fell because of years of hard work by people and organizations hit hardest by the 1980s–90s epidemic of violence. I believe they are right, but they have left out the other, more troubling half of the story. It was the hard work of community groups, combined with the enhanced presence of law enforcement, the criminal justice system, and private security forces that helped bring about the drop in violence across urban America. The most fundamental change that took place in U.S. cities was the transformation of public spaces. Streets that had been abandoned for decades were taken over by police officers, security guards, and community groups. Opportunities for criminal activity began to shrink, and violence began to fall.

These changes have come with costs, but they have also brought about great benefits. And it is the most disadvantaged groups of Americans who have benefited the most.

PART II

THE BENEFITS OF
THE CRIME DECLINE

4

THE PRESERVATION OF BLACK LIVES

Over the course of 2009, 459 people were murdered in the City of Chicago, and three out of every four victims were young black men.[1] One of these victims was a sixteen-year-old honors student named Derrion Albert, who was killed when he got swept into a brawl on his way home from Fenger High School, in the Roseland neighborhood of the South Side.[2] His murder was unspeakably tragic but not all that unusual in a city that often has more annual homicides than any other in the nation. What was unique about this murder was that it was caught on video. Because someone was recording the chaotic scene near Fenger High, the world outside Roseland was given a glimpse of the horror that occurs on a regular basis in some of America's most intensely disadvantaged communities.

The video shows a street packed with African American teenagers on their way out of the school. Most of them are wearing the school uniform of polo shirts and khakis, with backpacks on their shoulders. It is immediately apparent from the video that trouble is in the air. As voices rise and become panicked, a few young men begin to run, and the continuous scream of a car horn booms in the background. Small groups of young men face off in the streets, throwing blows and then jogging onward. The shouts get louder, and the fighting intensifies among a small group on the sidewalk. A man in a black T-shirt picks up a wooden board, at least eight feet long, and attempts to swing it down on another with his back turned. His blow does not land, but the newly discovered weapon changes the tone of the fight. A group of men pick up more boards, which look like railroad ties, and advance toward the others. Girls scream, and the crowd of high schoolers drifts quickly away, heading down the street.

One young man is surrounded by the group armed with the makeshift weapons, and he gets knocked brutally to the ground. Another faces off with an attacker and absorbs a partial blow but stays on his feet. And finally, amid the chaos, the video focuses on sixteen-year-old Derrion Albert, who is on the ground, attempting to get up. A man in a black T-shirt runs directly toward him, holding an enormous wooden board behind his head. He swings it as hard as he can, and it lands directly. After another lighter swing, he heads off down the street, jogging away from his victim.

As the street clears, several girls make their way to Albert. They are screaming as he lies still on the ground. They pick him up by the arms and drag him into an open doorway, as a small group of adults enter the picture, looking around at the chaos on the street. Amid the shrieking voices crying out for help, one voice is heard pleading with the lifeless body, "Derrion, get up! Derrion, get up please. Derrion. Derrion, please."

If you want a partial, voyeuristic sense of what violence looks like, what it sounds like, what it feels like, my description is not sufficient. Take a few minutes and Google "Derrion Albert murder." A warning: The full video is shocking, brutal, and incredibly sad to watch. If you're like me, watching the video will leave you with a strange, sick, deeply unsettling sensation that lingers within as you close your browser. Your heart will beat faster, and your breath will be quick. You will find yourself distracted, just as I am as I type these sentences. The disturbing images will remain in your mind for a few hours, like a weight on top of your head, making it difficult for you to concentrate as you try not to dwell on what you watched.

My goal is not to sensationalize the brutal violence that ended Derrion Albert's life, but to make the statistics on crime and violence more human. Violent crime is about bodies torn apart and disfigured, about mothers and friends crying out, and about bloodstained city streets. To understand the impact of violence, one has to see it. The video of Derrion Albert's murder is nothing more than a quick, blurry glimpse into the death of a teenager who was navigating the dangerous streets of Roseland. But even when watched through the safety of a computer monitor, it provides a sense of the unique nature of violence.

When an incident of violence occurs, the anger, terror, and fear are experienced by everyone who knows the victim, everyone who hears the police sirens, and everyone who walks the streets where the threat of violence lingers. Unlike any other public health problem, violence is felt beyond the victim and the perpetrator. It takes over entire communities. And violence differs from the other leading causes of death, like heart disease and cancer, in another way: It is a young person's disease. The overwhelming majority of victims and perpetrators of violence are young men like Derrion Albert, age fifteen to thirty.[3] But the shock of violence is felt by everyone who is associated with those young men, everyone linked to them through the networks that connect youth to each other, and everyone who walks the same streets. When a young person is killed, every parent must worry about her own child and the possibility of death enters the minds of youths throughout the community.

The unique nature of violence should change the way we think about incidents like the murder of Derrion Albert. If one is affected, at a physical and emotional level, by watching a video shot years earlier in a place that may be hundreds or thousands of miles away, then what must it feel like to walk the streets that Derrion Albert walked on a daily basis? What was life like, in the days and weeks that followed his death, for Derrion Albert's friends and classmates who watched the incident unfold and tried to save him in the aftermath? In the period following Derrion Albert's killing, how did the young men and women perform when they returned to Fenger High School, sat down in their classrooms, and attempted to focus on a history, math, or English test?

I will return to these questions in the next chapter. In this chapter, I focus on the most basic, most tragic dimension of the horrific scene that took place outside Fenger High School: the loss of a young man's life. Throughout this book, I write about violent crime as an issue related to urban policy, neighborhood dynamics, criminal justice, and policing. But fundamentally it is about young people who never get to see adulthood, about sons, brothers, cousins, boyfriends, husbands, fathers, and good friends who are taken from the world. It is about human life that is wasted.

The decline in violence, on the other hand, means that thousands of young people, like Derrion Albert, no longer have their lives cut short by violence. It is about human life that is preserved.

The life table is a tool used by demographers to calculate the average life span of a human born today. It is constructed by measuring the rate of mortality for different groups of the population at all ages, then putting all the information together in one table, with one row representing every year in a human's life. The table starts with 100,000 hypothetical people, then uses mortality data to predict how many of them will die in each year of their lives, until no one is left. If one takes the total number of years lived by everyone in this hypothetical population, and divides by the original 100,000 people, the result is called life expectancy at birth. This statistic provides the answer to a basic but meaningful question about the current state of a population's health: How long can a newborn entering the world today expect to live?

To understand how the decline in homicide has changed our answer to this core question about American society, I conducted a thought experiment. I imagined that the crime decline never happened and that the rate of homicides had remained the same since the early 1990s. And I asked: How long could different segments of the American population expect to live if the national murder rate never fell?

With Michael Friedson, a postdoctoral researcher, I gathered detailed mortality data going all the way back to the 1990s.[4] The data were available for only four groups of Americans—white and black men and women—so we focused on these segments of the population. We started in 1991, the year the homicide rate reached its latest peak, and continued through 2014, the year at which the homicide rate reached its trough. And we calculated the life expectancy for each group, without considering the decline in violence.

Across this entire time span, white women always lived the longest, on average, followed by black women, white men, and black men. Life expectancy has been improving steadily for everyone, but the gaps separating these four groups reveal the persistence of inequality in this most basic measure of health. The average white female born in 2014 can expect to live to 81; the average African American female can expect to live two years fewer, to 79; the average white male can expect to live to 77; and the average African American male can expect to live to 73. This is the disturbing reality of racial inequality in American public health.

But a longer-term perspective, and a closer examination of

the gaps between these four groups, tells a very different story. In 1991 black men could expect to die about eight years earlier than white men, on average. By 2014 the gap in life expectancy between white and black men was four years. Despite continuing racial inequality, these figures mean that black men have experienced the greatest improvements in life expectancy, and the gap between black men and every other group has declined considerably over time.[5]

What would these trends look like if the decline in violence had never happened? To carry out the thought experiment, Friedson and I calculated life expectancy for each of the four groups after adding all the additional homicides that would have occurred if the homicide rate had never dropped. For black and white women and for white men, there is virtually no difference between trends in life expectancy with and without the crime decline. Homicide is not an important cause of death for people in these groups, at any age. For black men, on the other hand, the trend in life expectancy would look significantly different. Our estimates indicate that an African American boy born at the end of the crime wave could expect to live, on average, about four-fifths of a year longer due purely to the drop in homicides that took place from 1991 to 2014.[6]

This impact may not seem like much, but it is incredibly uncommon for any medical advancement or public health intervention to raise life expectancy by this amount. For some perspective, consider a different thought experiment conducted by Dr. Jay Olshansky, a national leader in the study of population longevity. In a "special report" published in the *New England Journal of Medicine,* Olshansky and several coauthors used a set of exercises to project how life expectancy in the United States might change over the coming years and decades in response to one of the most important public health crises in America, the obesity epidemic.[7]

The prevalence of obesity in the United States rose by half in both the 1980s and 1990s. When Olshansky's article was published in 2005, two-thirds of American adults were classified as either overweight or obese, with the largest increases found in the tail of the distribution reflecting extreme obesity. Every group of American adults has experienced a similar rise in obesity, but the most substantial increases have occurred among racial and ethnic minority groups, particularly black Americans.

The authors of the article carried out an even more extreme thought experiment than the one we conducted on homicide. In our simulation, we simply assumed that the level of homicide returned to the rate from 1991. Olshansky and his coauthors, on the other hand, imagined what life expectancy would be if the national epidemic of obesity vanished altogether. According to their estimates, if every American adult suddenly shed all excess pounds, life expectancy of the population as a whole would rise by one-third to three-quarters of a year. If not one black man across the country was overweight, life expectancy for black men would rise by somewhere between .30 and 1.08 years. In other words, the impact of the decline in homicide on the life expectancy of black men is roughly equivalent to the impact of eliminating obesity altogether.[8]

The rise of obesity is the focus of some of the most prominent U.S. public health experts and the subject of conferences and countless journal articles. In 2017 the National Institutes of Health will spend over $900 million on obesity research. About $65 million, on the other hand, will go to research on homicide, youth violence, and violence prevention combined.[9]

And yet while much of the health community has focused on the epidemic of obesity, a public health triumph has played out in the nation's black communities. It is true, of course, that the decline in American homicide has not had a dramatic effect on the health of the entire population, because violence is a phenomenon that is not common for most of the population. But for the most disadvantaged segment of the American population, black men, violence is the most urgent health crisis, and the crime decline is the most important public health breakthrough of the past several decades. It is a breakthrough that is fundamentally different from advances in cancer research or drops in heart disease, which target people at the end of life. Violence targets young people before many of them have had a chance to start a career, a serious relationship, or a family.

Years of potential life lost (YPLL) is a statistic that measures how many years of life are missed when an individual dies at an early age. To calculate YPLL for a single homicide victim, one simply measures the difference between the number of years that individual could have expected to live, or life expectancy, and the number of years that he or she actually lived before being killed. This calculation is then summed over all homicide victims to get a measure of the total years of potential life lost due to the tragedy of homicide.

The disparities in years lost to violence are striking. For every 100,000 white women, just 77 years of life were lost to homicide in 2014. For every 100,000 white men, 177 years of potential life were lost, and for every 100,000 black women 218 years of potential life were lost. For every 100,000 black men, on the other hand, 1,239 years of potential life were lost due to homicide.

Even though these disparities are extreme, they would be much larger if not for the decline in violence. If the homicide rate hadn't changed from 1991, the years of potential life lost for every 100,000 black men would have almost doubled, rising from 1,239 to 2,396. The decline in homicides has meant that thousands of young black men have lived into adulthood, avoiding having their lives cut short and being lost to their families, friends, and communities. For every 100,000 black men, over 1,000 more years of time with friends and family have been preserved because of the drop in the murder rate.

———

In the four winters following Derrion Albert's death in September 2009, his mother and sister barely celebrated Christmas. It was a holiday that Derrion and his sister had loved and celebrated with their family traditions on Christmas Eve. But in the months following Derrion's death, his mother, Anjanette Albert, moved, and the decorations were still in boxes on Christmas Eve 2009. In the years that followed, she did not have the energy to find a tree, or any extra money to spend on gifts or stockings; or she was too busy with court proceedings for the five people charged in her son's death.[10]

Since her son was killed, Anjanette Albert's life was dominated by the void left by his murder. For almost four years, his gravestone was blank, without any marking noting who lay beneath it. His mother could not afford to pay for the engraving, and she told a reporter that the unmarked gravestone "had been eating me up inside." She struggled to pull her life back together, to survive financially, and to help support Derrion's sister, who sat silent in counseling sessions after his murder.

Toward the end of 2013, a local news station following up on the murder discovered that Derrion Albert's grave was unmarked. After the report, an anonymous donor provided funding to engrave his name, and others donated gifts and money for groceries and a Christmas tree. Four years after Derrion's death, his mother and sister were able to experience some semblance of joy during the holiday season.

For many families, however, that joy never returns. Most families of murder victims in Chicago see their loved ones buried anonymously, with no justice for the killer, no mention in the local newspaper, and no donations over the holidays. The stories of homicide victims are rarely told in full, and the stories of siblings, parents, and children left behind are ignored altogether. Yet losing a family member, whether it is a spouse, child, sibling, or parent, can often lead to a wide range of mental health problems, from depression to post-traumatic stress syndrome.[11] And the burden of family death is felt most acutely by African Americans, often at a young age. A national study found that African American adolescents are more than three times as likely as white adolescents to experience a death in their family. Even in families with similar levels of education and income, black adolescents are more than twice as likely as whites to go through the death of a family member.

Violence takes siblings away from their brothers and sisters, boyfriends and husbands from their romantic partners, children from their parents. It takes away life in an unnatural way, at a time when its victims are vibrant, energetic, and strong. And the loss lingers over time. Michael Javen Fortner, a political scientist, has written a history of black sentiment toward crime and punishment in New York, a book he was motivated to write because of his own experiences with violence in Brownsville, Brooklyn. "I was only a couple of years old when one of my brothers was stabbed to death," he wrote. "I do not remember him, but the pain and sorrow of that day stayed in my home like accumulated dust."[12]

When I wrote the first draft of this chapter, I ended it by celebrating the fact that the number of homicides in Chicago had fallen to a level not seen since the 1960s. I noted that the decline in homicide has meant that roughly ten thousand people are no longer taken from their families every year, about half of them black men. Even in Chicago, a city that has always had a high level of violence, hundreds of young men are still around to hang out with friends, spend holidays with family, enter the workforce, and start their own families.

But as the book came closer to publication, I decided to rewrite the end of the chapter. More than 750 homicides occurred in Chicago over the course of 2016, a figure that hadn't been reached since the early 2000s. The number of homicides was still almost 20 percent lower than at the peak of the era of violence, but by the end of the year, there were about 350 more homicide victims than in 2014. Across the country there were 1,300 more homicide victims in 2015 than in 2014, and the national homicide rate rose again in 2016. The time to celebrate the drop in Chicago's homicides has passed. After two years of rising violence, it is time to acknowledge that the problem has returned, and to call attention to the growing number of victims who have been lost over the past two years.

Homicide Watch is a network of websites that was developed, several years ago, to track every homicide victim in U.S. cities. The motto of the site is simple: "Mark every death. Remember every victim. Follow every case." In Chicago, the *Sun-Times* partnered with local journalism schools to begin its own version of Homicide Watch, with the goal of covering every homicide that occurred in the city. Their task has become more difficult over time, as the number of victims has risen sharply. But their efforts serve a tremendously important purpose: They attach a human face to the statistics on violence.

One homicide victim, twenty-one-year-old Shaquille Alexander, was shot in the head near his home in West Englewood. At the scene, a reporter described a crowd of people crying openly around the police tape that barricaded the young man's body. One woman was screaming "That's my baby" as she was consoled by others around her. Alexander's father stood among the crowd, as others cried around him, quiet and uninterested in talking to anyone. "My son's body.is lying in the street," he told the reporter. "I got a lot on my mind."

Arian Smith, a thirty-two-year-old father of three who was said to dote on his children, was shot and killed in his own kitchen in September 2016. Smith had passed the written and physical exams to join Chicago's Police Department. He was the primary caregiver to his three children, and "his life centered around them," according to his brother, who was quoted in an article. A video posted to a fundraising page showed Arian encouraging his three kids as they jumped on a hopscotch course, laughing as his youngest son ignored the lines and jumped straight ahead from the start to the finish. "He was someone . . . I looked up to," his brother said, ". . . because a lot of things he did, I wish I would be able to do."[13]

In 1995, at the age of seventeen, Raygene Jackson was convicted of murder and served twenty years. His own daughter was struck by a bullet that went through the gate of her mother's yard in 1997, and she died at the age of three. When he was released from prison on parole, at thirty-seven, Jackson reconnected with Faydra Rhinehart, the mother of his deceased daughter. Jackson and Rhinehart planned to buy a house and get married. The couple was determined to start life anew after two decades apart, and Jackson was working hard at making it outside prison, according to everyone who knew him well. As soon as he was released, he began taking care of the tasks he would need to reenter the labor force. He worked long days at a temp agency before he was shot and killed in West Garfield Park in the early morning hours of Sunday, July 17.

He led a troubled life, but the family he left behind remembered him with love and fondness. One of his best friends told a reporter, "He'll be remembered for his heart. He would never let anything bad happen to anybody." His godmother said, "He was a compassionate person. He was a lovely, caring person." And his fiancée expressed her sadness and her devotion to him. "When he was with me, he was the young sweet boy his mother raised," she said. "I've known him since I was a kid. I've loved him my whole life." The words that followed expressed the fatigue and anger of a woman who had sacrificed too much to the violence in Chicago: "When my lease is up, I'm getting out of Chicago. It's sad. This city is in ruins."[14]

5

LEARNING IN FEAR

At six p.m. on October 2, 2002, James Martin was shot and killed in the parking lot of Shoppers Food Warehouse in Wheaton, Maryland, just beyond the northern border of Washington, D.C.[1] The murder was thought to be an isolated incident. But the next morning, around 7:40, another man was shot while riding a lawnmower on the grounds of a nearby business. Just after eight the same morning, a taxi driver was shot while pumping gas at a Mobil station in Aspen Hill, Maryland, only a few miles away. Twenty minutes later a woman was shot while sitting on a bench outside a post office in Silver Spring. Finally, around ten that same Wednesday morning, another woman was shot while vacuuming her minivan at a Shell station in nearby Kensington.

All five shootings took place within a narrow stretch of Montgomery County, Maryland, a diverse, affluent, and generally safe suburban area north of the nation's capital. All five of the targets were killed. Beyond these similarities, nothing made sense about the spree of shootings. The victims were men and women, they ranged in age from twenty-five to fifty-five, and they were white, black, and Hispanic. There was no theory to explain the shootings, and no clue as to the shooter. The only information available was that the shooter was a skilled marksman—a sniper.

The series of random shootings put the region, and the country, on edge. Things worsened that night when a seventy-two-year-old man was shot while walking along Georgia Avenue on the north side of Washington, D.C., the first victim outside Maryland. The following day another woman was shot in a store parking lot, fifty miles south of D.C. in Fredericksburg, Virginia. The radius of threat had expanded southward.

After a quiet weekend passed, the terror reached a new level. On the morning of Monday, October 7, a thirteen-year-old boy was shot outside his middle school in Prince George's County, Maryland. The fear that gripped the D.C. area turned into outright panic. School districts canceled outdoor events, and some shut down altogether. Even in districts that remained open, many parents kept their kids at home.

The state of terror lasted two more weeks. Two days after the child was shot, a man was killed while filling his gas tank in Manassas, Virginia. Then another man at a gas station, a woman in a Home Depot parking lot, a man outside a Ponderosa Steakhouse, and another man standing on the top step of a commuter bus, on his way to work.

It was not until October 24, twenty-two days after the first random shooting in the grocery store parking lot, that the serial killers—John Allen Muhammad and a teenage accomplice, Lee Boyd Malvo—were arrested. In those three weeks, they had killed ten people and wounded three more. In the process, they paralyzed an entire region.

Alex Mitchell was a middle school student in Montgomery County, Maryland, when the "Beltway sniper" shootings took place.[2] Looking back, he described how he and his friends had altered their routines during the killing spree:

> It was normal to walk quickly (or to run) between rows of cars, barely dodging a scraped knee or bruised leg on the license plate covers of cars in parking lots, anything to keep out of plain view. I often found myself making strange and sporadic movements when jogging from basketball practice, school, or out to the mailbox from my garage, as if to throw the snipers off if they were aiming at me. Going to the grocery store was especially frightening; the idea of standing by one's trunk for several minutes while putting bags of groceries into the car almost seemed absurd. Was food really worth leaving oneself out in plain view for the snipers to have an easy shot? The casual walk out to the car from school had turned into packs of friends moving quickly together, walking one another from car to car until the last brave soul ran over to his or her car alone.

One particular night Mitchell found himself alone in his locker room after taking longer than his teammates to pack up and get ready to leave for the night. As captain of his team, he was responsible for carting the bag of basketballs back to his home in his car. But as he prepared to exit the gym, he was overcome with fear. He debated staying in place and waiting until someone got worried enough to come and get him. Instead, he decided to make a run for his car.

> Running down the long walkway to the parking lot, I began moving strangely, bopping my head this way and that, stepping side to side while running. The basketballs, which were in a sack and slung over my shoulder, were hitting my back very hard. I was glancing around frantically, noticing all of

the dark spots beyond and around the parking lot, prime locations to stand with a deadly assault weapon. Then there was
the sweeping baseball field next to the parking lot. My heart
began racing uncontrollably. . . . How had I been so stupid?
Why hadn't anyone waited to go out with me to the parking lot?
Just as I neared the beginning of the parking lot, my foot hit a
rock and I slipped momentarily. The sack fell off my shoulder,
spilling the basketballs all over the south corner of the lot. Not
feeling I had any other choice, I recklessly chased after the
basketballs, shoving them back into the sack. One ball bounced
over the curb and down into the dark field; this one I decided
was lost forever and did not even consider giving chase. Running to my car, I scraped the paint around the keyhole in the
process of jamming the key in its place, tossed the sack into
the backseat, and drove off with my head down by the wheel
and out of view.

What Mitchell describes is what happens to our bodies, and
our minds, when we are threatened with the possibility of death.
Instead of a leisurely walk from the gym to his car, Mitchell
describes a frantic dash, resulting in a lost basketball and scraped
paint on the car door. On a usual night, his mind might have wan-
dered back to a drill from practice or to his homework assignments
for the night. On this night, he identified and recorded every dark
spot in the vicinity of the parking lot.

Alex Mitchell was not a direct victim of the Beltway sniper, but
his life was overtaken by the fear of violence. His recollection of
those three weeks in 2002 illuminates a feature of violence that
makes it different from any other public health challenge. Violence doesn't just affect the physical body, it gets into the mind.
Although the most tragic toll of violence comes in the form of lives
lost, if we are to understand the full impact of violent crime then

the annual tally of homicide victims tells only a small part of the story. What makes violence so destructive is the way that it affects the friends and families of victims, the children who witness it, and the residents of city blocks where it strikes. Violence reverberates around entire communities, altering the daily lives of everyone within them. Social scientists tend to focus exclusively on how children interpret and respond to violence, but it is impossible to understand the full toll of violent crime without considering the physiological mechanisms by which a stressor in the environment comes to affect the behavior and functioning of the millions of young people who have never been shot and may never have been in a serious fight, but who live in fear.[3]

Here is a crude summary of what happens to the body when it is faced with the threat of violence.[4] To begin with, we receive information about the threat through our senses and transmit it to certain key areas of the brain, most notably the amygdala (an area associated with emotional processing) and the hippocampus (an area associated with learning and memory formation).[5] Our brain then triggers a set of automatic responses to the threat, or the possibility of a threat, nearby. In response, our body exits the state of rest and regeneration and enters a state of vigilance. Stored energy is mobilized for action. The sympathetic nervous system transmits messages of vigilance from the brain throughout the body. Nerve endings release a surge of epinephrine (adrenaline) and norepinephrine (noradrenaline), giving rise to a set of physiological changes, which may include an elevated heart rate, a rise in blood pressure, sweating, quick breathing, or goosebumps arising from fear. The HPA axis (the hypothalamus, pituitary gland, and adrenal glands) releases glucocorticoids, like the hormone cortisol, which act to maintain our heightened state of awareness and vigilance in the face of the continuing stressor.

These physiological changes are designed to enable us to focus on the immediate threat in the environment, escape, survive, and learn key details from the experience. When the threat has passed, a new sequence of processes slows the body down and shifts it from the state of vigilance back to a state of rest, growth, and energy storage.

The body's stress response system is meant to keep us alive when there is danger nearby, and in some situations it can make our brains function more efficiently. When humans are subject to moderate stressors or given stress hormones during the process of learning, for instance, they are often better able to recall later what they have learned.[6] But the stressor is helpful for learning only when it is directly related to the task at hand, and if the individual experiences it while learning.[7] If a child is trained for a spelling bee while being peppered with words by a ruthless tutor with demanding parents looking on, that child might have a better chance of recalling the spelling of the same words months later.[8]

Stress becomes much less useful when it is unrelated to the task at hand. After walking briskly through a dangerous block, a child who enters a classroom setting may remember every detail of the street but will have a much harder time focusing on a pop quiz in the first period. Individuals under stress typically are less able to retrieve and utilize information that they already know.[9] This pattern may be due to the direct effects of stress hormones on information retrieval, but some neuroscientists think that it may be the product of a competitive process in which the brain is deciding on which tasks are most important at any given moment. During a moment of acute stress, the brain focuses on the most pressing challenge or task facing it, leaving fewer resources to grapple with the less urgent task of remembering extraneous information learned previously.[10] When deciding whether to focus on the possibility of being jumped on the way to school or on the words one learned for a weekly vocabulary test, the brain picks the former.

This is the neuroscientists' model of our brain under stress. But while researchers in a lab can ask subjects to make a speech in public in order to induce a mild level of stress, the experience of witnessing a human being shot or stabbed cannot be replicated in a laboratory. To capture the impact of violence, it is necessary to move outside the lab and generate evidence from humans exposed to the real thing.

The Project on Human Development in Chicago Neighborhoods is the long, awkward title of one of the most ambitious studies ever carried out by social scientists.[11] In the early 1990s, a team of eminent researchers from several different disciplines, led by the sociologist Robert Sampson, came together to try to understand how children's lives unfolded in the context of overwhelming inequality, segregation, and violence that was present in Chicago's neighborhoods.

As part of the project, researchers carried out a survey of residents' perceptions of their neighborhoods. They mapped out a network of the ways community leaders and institutions were linked across the city. Before Google Street View existed, the research team from the "Chicago Project" drove an SUV block by block through the city and coded the amount of trash on each street, the presence of graffiti, and the number of boarded-up windows or abandoned lots. Most importantly, they began a longitudinal survey of children ranging in age from zero to eighteen, following their physical development, their family conditions, and their progress in school over the course of childhood—they called it the Longitudinal Cohort Study (LCS). The LCS began in late 1994 and has continued for three waves of data collection, following the children of Chicago for a substantial chunk of their formative years.[12]

I began working with data from the LCS back in graduate school, studying under Sampson's guidance. I spent years trying to understand how living within some of the most disadvantaged neighborhoods of Chicago affected kids' progress in school, their behavior, and the development of the cognitive skills that are measured in IQ tests.[13] I began this research using data from Chicago, then expanded to study the nation as a whole.

My first book, titled *Stuck in Place*, emerged out of this research and focused on the role that neighborhood disadvantage has played in the persistence of racial inequality in America.[14] To truly capture the degree of neighborhood inequality in the United States, I found, one has to think of Americans' exposure to neighborhoods from a multigenerational perspective, something that is passed on from parents to children. Most children who currently live in poor neighborhoods are from families that have been there for generations, particularly if those children are black. I showed that the consequences of growing up in disadvantaged neighborhoods accumulate over generations, as parents who grew up in poor neighborhoods carry with them the consequences of living in more violent communities, attending lower-quality schools, and having access to fewer opportunities in the labor force. The intergenerational transmission of neighborhood disadvantage goes a long way toward explaining why racial inequality in academic achievement, cognitive skills, and economic success has been so persistent.[15]

There was one problem, however. I produced virtually no evidence explaining why. In fact, the research literature focusing on how neighborhoods affect the life chances of children offers very little insight into the precise mechanisms that lead to worse outcomes for kids. The more progress I made with collaborators in understanding the impact of growing up in poor neighborhoods, the more I began to focus on a new set of difficult questions: What was happening in poor neighborhoods that affected the development of children so substantially? What was it about growing up in Chicago's poor neighborhoods, in particular, that was so harmful to children?

In March 2008, my first year out of graduate school, I found myself in a lecture hall at Columbia University listening to Dr. Frances Champagne, a brilliant neuroscientist who was teaching a two-day "short course" on the emerging field of epigenetics.[16] The course, which focused on how our experiences in our environments change the way our genes function, was utterly fascinating to a social scientist like myself who had spent little time studying genetics or the brain. But one particular line of research caught my attention. As she was describing the various methods that psychologists use to study stress in rats, Dr. Champagne mentioned a set of studies conducted in the lab of David Diamond, a cognitive neuroscientist at the University of South Florida.[17]

To understand how stress impairs the memory of rats, Dr. Diamond's team uses a novel approach: They place a cat outside the rat's cage. In a series of experiments spanning many years, Diamond and his colleagues have demonstrated how exposure to such "predator stress" impairs the rats' memory, making it difficult for them to learn the ins and outs of the mazes that Diamond and his students put them through. Exposure to a predator leads the rats to make more errors as they navigate through mazes—in human terms, it makes it appear as if they didn't study very hard or are not all that smart. The observations from Diamond's lab are not entirely surprising; after the rats spend a few moments fearing for their lives, it makes sense that they would be distracted when they set out on the mundane task of trying to find the hidden compartment that leads them out of the maze.

But that day, while I sat and tried to absorb the new insights from the field of epigenetics, a thought stuck in my head. Diamond's findings might be essential to understanding what goes on in the neighborhoods of Chicago. If children are exposed to extreme violence, if they spend their days trying to find ways to stay safe, if they fear that a "predator" might be nearby, then how might they react when they're asked to sit down to complete an assignment in school?

Diamond's experiments gave me an idea that has altered the trajectory of my research. It is not possible (or ethical or humane) to expose children to an actual incident of violence and see how they react. But real incidents of violence are going on every day, all across the country. To understand how children respond, it might be possible to see how children perform on standard cognitive tests if they are assessed right after an incident of violence has taken place. For the study of violence, Chicago is, unfortunately, an ideal lab.

The children interviewed for the Longitudinal Cohort Study had been given a set of cognitive assessments that measured their verbal, reading, and language skills, and these measures served as the outcomes for my study. After locating and geocoding every child's home address in the Chicago sample, I recorded the exact date on which they were assessed. I then gathered information from the Chicago Police Department on every homicide that had occurred in Chicago over the same time frame and matched the information on the timing and location of each homicide with the same information about the children who took the assessments.

The timing of each child's interview was completely random, which allowed for a kind of "natural" experiment that is roughly equivalent to the controlled experiments carried out in the lab by researchers like David Diamond. By pure chance, some children in the study were given a cognitive assessment (the analog to Diamond's water maze) just hours or days after a homicide occurred in their neighborhood. Other children in the same neighborhood were given the same assessment just before similar incidents, or several weeks or months later, at a time when no recent violence had taken place.[18] My question was simple: If rats perform worse when they're exposed to a nearby cat, what happens to children if they are assessed just days after a homicide down the street?

Once all the data sets were merged and I began the analysis, the answer emerged quickly. Just as rats perform worse when they're exposed to a nearby cat, children do substantially worse on standard tests of cognitive skills—the assessments commonly thought of as IQ tests—when there has been a homicide near their home. When they experience the shock of local violence, children appear to be less intelligent than they are.

This finding may not surprise many readers. When I present it to educators teaching in tough neighborhoods, they nod their heads and tell me that spending a week in their classroom could have saved me the trouble of all that data analysis. But what is shocking is just how much children's functioning drops in the aftermath of extreme violence. In my first study, I found that black children who were given the assessment in the days after a local homicide took place performed about four-tenths of a standard deviation worse on tests of verbal and language skills, on average, than black children in the same neighborhoods who were assessed at a different time. To put this impact in perspective, it was as if the children who were assessed right after a local homicide had missed the previous two years of schooling and regressed back to their level of cognitive performance from years earlier. The impact of local violence on children's functioning was more severe if the homicide occurred right before the child took the assessment, and it was more severe if it occurred in close proximity to the child's home. Most troubling, the impact of local violence was greatest for black children, the group most frequently exposed to violence.

The findings from the initial analysis were so disturbing that I thought they might be wrong. To make sure the results were real, I replicated the analysis with an entirely different survey of children in Chicago that was carried out independently by a different set of researchers but over roughly the same time period. This survey included a broader array of measures capturing different dimensions of cognitive skills. Using this second data set, I found the impact of recent, local violence to be even larger than in the initial analysis.

I discussed the results with Cybele Raver, a colleague at New York University who is one of the world's leading researchers on children's cognitive skills development. Dr. Raver studies executive function, the crucially important ability to delay gratification, control impulses, and maintain focus on the task at hand. We decided to use data that she had collected, years earlier, to test whether local violence might have had an impact on children's test performance simply because they were distracted, less able to focus. We took advantage of the fact that her research team had conducted assessments with the same children at multiple points in time. We compared the performance of children who took the assessments in the days after a local homicide to the performance of the same children at a time when no recent violence had taken place. The results showed the same drop in reading and language skills that I had found in the previous study, but Dr. Raver's tests of executive function gave a hint as to why the kids were performing worse. We found that when children were assessed in the aftermath of a local homicide, they were less able to control their impulses during the assessment and were less able to maintain their attention on the test.

Local violence does not make children less intelligent. Rather, it occupies their minds. The shock of a local homicide means that everyone who drives through the neighborhood is a potential threat, that a killer might be nearby, that more violence might be coming. It means sirens at night and police tape on the walk to school. For young men of color in particular, it means walking through one's own neighborhood as a potential target and a potential suspect. It means living within a crime scene.[19]

The consequences are tangible. In a subsequent study carried out in New York City, my colleagues and I explored whether students scored lower on the city's high-stakes standardized assessments of academic progress if they took the exams in the days after an episode of violence near where they lived. The previous studies

I had carried out focused on assessments of cognitive skills that were conducted within the children's homes, in a relaxed atmosphere, with no consequences for poor performance. The results from the tests in New York City, on the other hand, were used to evaluate teachers and schools and to determine whether students advanced to the next grade. Using the high-stakes assessments, we found that black students were three percentage points less likely to pass the city's English and language arts exam if there was an incident of violence on the child's block in the week before the test.[20] In a subsequent study, we found that the impact of violence accumulated, as each incident of major violence on a child's block led to a larger decline in performance.

The results shed light on a reality that policy makers in the field of education might not fully understand. Although standardized assessments are thought of as high-stakes tests, the stakes are much higher on the street, where children are worried about who will be the next to get shot in their neighborhoods. Children carry the burden of violence with them into the school and into the classroom. When they sit down to learn, they do so with a range of emotions running through their heads and elevated levels of stress hormones running through their bodies. Evolution has prepared them to maintain a state of vigilance as they navigate threatening streets where violence is possible. But children are on their own when they make it to school and prepare to focus on the lesson of the day, or the exam that will determine whether they advance to the next grade.

Seth Gershenson and Erdal Tekin are researchers at American University, located in the northwest section of D.C., very close to the epicenter of the Beltway sniper shootings. Going back to data from the period around the shootings, Gershenson and Tekin analyzed changes in the test scores of students in schools located within five miles of a sniper shooting, and compared them to changes in the scores of students from schools that looked similar but were farther removed from the shootings.[21] All students throughout Virginia were affected by the sniper shootings, but the researchers hypothesized that the students who went to school near an actual site where someone was shot would have experienced the most intense fear.

Compared to students who went to school farther away from the shooting sites, Gershenson and Tekin found that students attending schools within five miles of a shooting were somewhere between 5 and 9 percentage points less likely to pass their state English and language arts or math assessments. Every different way the researchers conducted the analysis produced the same results. More troubling, the impact of proximity to the sniper shootings was much more intense for students in more disadvantaged schools, with more low-income students and more students from racial and ethnic minority groups. Schools serving disadvantaged students tend to have weaker support services, many have larger student bodies, and students are more likely to take public transportation to and from school. For these students, the stress of the sniper shootings was particularly severe.

Years later, after Malvo had been imprisoned and Muhammad executed, the Prince William County (Virginia) police chief Charlie T. Deane was interviewed about the sniper shootings and asked if any lessons had been learned from them.[22] He didn't think so. "The sad thing is, the biggest lesson from this is that two fools with a rifle can put an entire region of the country in a state of absolute fear."

For those interested in understanding the full toll of violence, Deane's words are more poignant than he realized. The Beltway sniper shootings, which took place over three weeks in October 2002, did in fact reveal something unique about the phenomenon of violence: It has a long reach. An assault or attack involves an interaction between an assailant and a victim, but the impact of that interaction extends beyond the two involved. When a man is shot at random in Wheaton, Maryland, the possibility of death enters the minds of people in Washington, D.C. When gunfire is heard on a city street, the fear of a bullet enters the minds of every child and parent in the neighborhood. Violence is a corporal phenomenon, but its consequences are psychological.

When the threat of violence is present, public spaces shift from welcoming settings for collective life into areas of fear, suspicion, and stress. But when they become safe, those same spaces become calmer, quieter, more welcoming. Children within those spaces no longer have to worry about their well-being, about the threat of being shot or jumped. They can start to worry about the lesson plan for the day, their homework, and the test that is on the horizon. They can start to learn.

On December 14, 2012, Adam Lanza shot a bullet through a glass door, walked into Sandy Hook Elementary School in Newtown, Connecticut, and opened fire within the school, killing twenty elementary school students and six adults.[23] It was the second worst episode of school violence on record, trailing only the shootings that had occurred five years earlier at Virginia Tech. Sandy Hook was a tragedy that united the entire nation in a shared moment of grief. It created a national wave of concern over school violence, as children all over the country were taught what they should do if a shooter was inside their school building. The same shock and outrage over school violence returned in 2018 when seventeen students and staff members were killed by a former student at Marjory Stoneman Douglas High School in Parkland, Florida.

The horror, tragedy, and randomness of mass shootings on school campuses create a unique form of terror and anger that may be sufficient to generate a national movement for gun control. But these features of school violence also distort our perceptions about the scale of the problem. Mass shootings committed with automatic rifles make up a tiny percentage of all gun violence, and very few of these incidents take place at schools.[24] The intense focus on school shootings has distracted attention from a trend that many Americans might not believe: The nation's public schools have become much safer than they were in previous decades. Just as American adults now report less victimization than two decades earlier, student reports of violent victimization have plummeted over time. At the peak of America's violent era, about 89 out of every 1,000 students reported being the victim of a violent assault in school. By 2015, just 18 out of every 1,000 students reported being victimized.[25] Trends in victimization at school and away from school are almost identical, suggesting that the same decline in violence that occurred across America's neighborhoods also occurred inside the hallways of the nation's schools.

As victimization has fallen, students' behavior has changed. Whereas in 1991 26 percent of high school students reported that they carried a weapon to school in the previous thirty days, 17 percent did so in 2011.[26] Black students were the most likely to report carrying a weapon in the 1990s, but by the late 2000s, they were the group least likely to do so.

Perhaps more important than reports of actual victimization or use of weapons is the fact that students now feel safer in school. The proportion of all students who fear being attacked on their way to school or in school dropped from 12 percent to 4 percent from 1995 to 2011.[27] An even sharper change is reported among black and Hispanic students. Over 20 percent of black and Hispanic students feared being attacked in or on their way to school in the mid-1990s, compared to 8 percent of white students at the same time. In 2011 less than 5 percent of black and Hispanic students reported the same fear, compared to 3 percent of white students. The racial gap in perceived school safety is just about gone.

————

We now live in a moment when students feel more secure in their classrooms than they have in two decades. Racial gaps in school safety have narrowed, and the vast majority of children no longer feel the need to bring a weapon with them to school. Victimization on school grounds has fallen by roughly 80 percent since the early 1990s. If violence is as important to the learning process as I have argued, then these dramatic improvements in school safety should have generated visible changes in academic progress. The drop in school violence should have improved learning, and reduced racial and ethnic gaps in academic achievement. Has it?

Unfortunately, the available data allow only for hints as to the answer. The one data set designed to provide a reliable measure of change in academic performance of all American students is the National Assessment of Educational Progress (NAEP), sometimes referred to as "The Nation's Report Card."[28] The NAEP is composed of assessments given on a regular basis to a national sample of fourth-, eighth-, and twelfth-grade American students, allowing for the most reliable measure of change in academic performance over time. Students take the assessment only once, and teachers do not prepare them for it. The content is similar each year, as are the testing conditions. For all these reasons, the NAEP has become the gold standard for tracking academic achievement among American students over time.

What does the data from the NAEP reveal about the relationship between the crime decline and academic performance? First off, data from the NAEP (and other international assessments) make clear that the national drop in violent crime has not yet made America's students the smartest in the world; nor has it ended racial inequality in academic achievement. The conclusions from analysis of trends in the NAEP are more modest, yet are crucially important for those concerned with educational inequality: In the places where violence has declined the most, there have been very visible improvements in academic performance and declines in racial achievement gaps.

States where violent crime remained stable or increased have seen the smallest improvements in academic performance in both reading and math, and states where violent crime dropped the most have seen the largest improvements.[29] Although children from all racial and ethnic groups have benefited from the decline in violent crime, African American children have benefited the most. States where violent crime has fallen furthest are also the places where the gap in academic achievement between black and white students has narrowed the most. In states as diverse as California, Florida, and New Jersey, violent crime dropped substantially and the black-white gap in reading performance declined by 20 percent or more. Crime dropped only slightly in other states like Wisconsin, Tennessee, and Oklahoma, and black-white gaps in reading performance remained stable, or widened, over the same period.

This evidence is not sufficient to prove that the decline in violence caused the racial achievement gap to narrow. The best data available are only at the state level, so it is impossible to carry out the fine-grained analyses at the level of cities or neighborhoods that would be necessary to claim that the crime decline caused the improvements in performance or the narrowing of the racial achievement gap. But the evidence from the NAEP is reassuring.

If violence is as important to children's learning as I have claimed, then the changes that have taken place across the country should have produced some noticeable change in academic performance. The data from states where violence has declined show the type of improvement in reading and math scores that one would expect. If the burden of violence is disproportionately felt by black Americans, then one would expect to find the greatest reductions in racial inequality in the places where crime has dropped the most. This is exactly what I find in the data.

Other sources of data provide more evidence in support of the same conclusion. Gerard Torrats-Espinosa and I analyzed the relationship between declining violent crime and educational attainment in counties across the country. We found minimal evidence indicating that the drop in violence has affected college attendance, suggesting that the crime decline is less important for the select group of young people who are most likely to be thinking about a college degree. However, we found strong evidence that falling violent crime makes it less likely that young people will drop out of high school.[30]

This finding aligns with decades of research in education and psychology showing that a feeling of safety is a prerequisite for learning and engagement in school.[31] Students who report feeling unsafe in the school setting have difficulty concentrating, are more likely to stay home from school, and have worse academic performance.[32] When there is violence nearby, students are less able to focus on academic tasks, and their performance suffers.[33] And when students move away from intensely violent neighborhoods, they show strong improvements in core cognitive skills.[34] All of this research leads to a conclusion that no educator would dispute: When there is a threat of violence in the school or classroom, it is virtually impossible for young people to learn.

But when violence becomes less common, learning becomes pos-

sible once again. The crime decline has not come close to eliminating educational inequality in the United States, but it has made
students feel safer as they walk through their school hallways and
enter their classrooms. And it is the students who live in the most
disadvantaged environments, at greatest risk of leaving school at
an early age, who appear to benefit the most.

6

INEQUALITY AFTER THE CRIME DECLINE

entral Park is an urban landmark that stretches up and down the northern part of Manhattan. The expansive green fields, rocky hills, and winding paths are nestled between some of the most expensive real estate in the city, occupied by some of the wealthiest people in the world. But to many Americans, the park is not known for its distinctly urban beauty or for the obscene wealth that surrounds it. It is known for a single incident that took place on the evening of April 19, 1989. On that cold evening in the early spring, thirty or so black and Hispanic teenagers entered Central Park and carried out a series of brutal assaults on anyone who crossed their paths.[1] They attacked bicyclists and threw rocks at cars, they assaulted joggers, hitting one in the back of the head with a pipe, and they beat multiple people in the park so badly that they were left bloody and unconscious. The violence was random and senseless.

One of the victims was an investment banker named Trisha Meili, a white woman who was out for her nightly run. She would become known as the Central Park Jogger. What happened to

Meili that night is difficult to think about. When she came across the group of teenagers, most of them between the ages of fourteen and seventeen, she was attacked, knocked down, dragged, beaten, stabbed, gagged, tied up, raped, and left for dead in a shallow ravine.

Meili was found several hours later. She had hypothermia, severe brain damage, gashes all over her body, and a fractured skull. She lay in a coma for twelve days and was expected to die. Meili survived, but when she woke up from her coma, she could neither move nor speak. Miraculously, she slowly recovered and returned to work within a year of her attack.

The case of the Central Park Jogger was shocking even to New Yorkers who were used to the most sensational headlines in the city's tabloids, and it generated an outcry for justice and for vengeance.[2] Investigators zeroed in on five teenagers, four black and one Hispanic, who took part in the mayhem going on that night in Central Park. After hours of coercive interrogation, all five offered confessions, and they would all serve at least six years in prison. But more than a decade after the incident occurred, a serial rapist and convicted murderer named Matias Reyes admitted that he was the one who raped Meili and left her there to die. Reyes had acted alone in sexually assaulting her.

The case of the Central Park Jogger is perhaps the ugliest, most brutal episode from the era of violence in New York City. It is a tale about racial hatred, media sensationalism, and the miscarriage of justice, but it is also about a night of disgusting behavior and horrific crimes in the most public space in New York. For many who remember the episode, Central Park still evokes terrifying images of violence, lawlessness, and danger. For those who weren't around in the 1980s, on the other hand, it is almost impossible to imagine that the assault of Trisha Meili could have happened in Central Park.

Over the past two decades, the park has turned from a disorderly, perilous place into a beautiful, safe, open-air fortress that is idyllic, natural, and serene and yet closely watched and secured. Virtually every foot of the trails is now monitored closely by a new set of "guardians." The park has its own dedicated police force and is run as an independent precinct. Staff from the Central Park Conservancy, the organization that manages the park for the city, now carry cell phones and walkie-talkies, communicating with one another and working directly with the NYPD. Thirty surveillance cameras are located around the perimeter of the park, capturing images of who is entering and who is leaving. And a one a.m. curfew is now strictly enforced.[3]

Some readers may shudder when they hear about the new surveillance of Central Park. But in the 1980s, more than seven hundred people were robbed each year in the park, and now the number of annual robbery victims is in the teens. The number of rapes that occur each year can be counted on one hand, and there has not been a single homicide in the park for fifteen years. Use of Central Park has tripled since the 1980s. Surveys of park users once showed that two out of every three people in the park were men; now a majority of the park's users are women. Entire sections of Central Park used to be dark and dangerous, off limits to most people at night. Now four out of five respondents say there is no part of the park that they avoid for safety reasons.

The contrast between the Central Park of 1989 and the Central Park of today is reflected in the words of a white woman who was interviewed for a story about safety in the park. Described as a "petite Wall Street trader," she shares an almost identical profile with the Central Park Jogger. Completely at ease as she walked her two Dalmations at ten p.m., she explained to the reporter why she was unafraid to be alone in the park, even at night: "I can't remember the last time I came across something that made me uncomfortable."[4]

...

The story of change in Central Park is about the drop in crime and the rise of the new urban guardians, but it is also about how the decline in violence has made the city safe and comfortable for the wealthiest New Yorkers. It is a story about the way two trends—the decline in violence and the rise of inequality—have converged in the nation's biggest city.

To this point, I have focused on the former trend, but the rise of inequality has hit America's cities with an equal or greater force. The share of the nation's income and wealth going to the most affluent Americans began to rise in the 1970s, and it continued to grow even after violent crime began to fall in the 1990s.[5] The steady growth of economic inequality is most apparent in the nation's cities, where the wealthy and the poor have gradually moved away, literally, from everyone in the middle. Back in 1970 about 15 percent of Americans lived in neighborhoods that were either extremely affluent or extremely poor. That figure had risen to 34 percent by 2012.[6] Since the turn of the century, the number of Americans living in exclusive, gated communities has risen by more than 50 percent, while the number of families living in high-poverty ghettos and barrios has doubled.[7] And many of the places that have experienced the greatest declines in violence, like Dallas, Los Angeles, and New York City, are among the country's most unequal cities.

The decline in violence may have saved thousands of lives, and created calm classrooms and safe parks, but the question remains: Has it given children a better chance in life and allowed them to rise up out of poverty? Has it had any impact on inequality, or has the long-term fall of violent crime simply made cities more comfortable for the new urban elites?

Located on the northern border of Central Park is Harlem, the section of Manhattan that has served as the center of African

American cultural life for more than a century. Harlem was the setting for Marcus Garvey's call for a large-scale return of black Americans to Africa, and for the Harlem Renaissance, an artistic movement that produced some of the greatest American writers and artists. In the first half of the twentieth century, Harlem became the symbol of "the aspirations for what blacks could achieve," in the words of Lance Freeman, a professor of urban planning at Columbia University who has studied the transformation of the iconic neighborhood. "Harlem was not just another ghetto," he writes, it was the "spatial manifestation" of the idea that the "new Negro would blaze his own trails and knock down barriers before him."[8]

Although Harlem may not have been like any other black community, it was not immune to the forces that devastated many such neighborhoods in the decades following World War II. Discrimination in New York's housing and employment markets led to overcrowded, dilapidated slums where Harlem's poor became concentrated, and decades of destructive housing policies led to crumbling homes, declining property values, and urban blight. Joblessness rose as New York's economy shifted away from the manufacturing sector, and the middle class began to leave northern Manhattan as conditions deteriorated, crime and drug abuse spread, and the boundaries of the black ghetto became less rigid.[9]

Harlem lost a third of its population in the 1970s alone, and more than 40 percent of its residents lived below the poverty line.[10] Despite its grand history, the neighborhood began to look like any other ghetto in urban America.

But in the 1990s, signs of change began to appear on the streets north of Central Park. Community development corporations, with help from the city, acquired abandoned lots and began to redevelop homes and rebuild neighborhoods.[11] Violent crime began to fall, and the neighborhood's unique history, elegant rows of townhouses, and bustling commercial streets attracted new investment. Restaurants opened, old crumbling buildings were redeveloped, major retail chains opened shop, and home values started to rise. Harlem, which had long been almost entirely black, drew a new population of Latinos and other immigrants, along with a growing trickle of whites and highly educated African American newcomers. Neighborhoods with extreme poverty rates slowly became more diverse, and the problem of concentrated poverty, which was seen for several decades as the most pressing challenge facing American cities, became less severe.

The changes that have taken place in Harlem can also be seen in many of the cities where crime has fallen the most. Examining data from U.S. cities, Gerard Torrats-Espinosa and I analyzed how the drop in violence from 1990 to 2010 has affected economic segregation, or the degree to which the rich live apart from the poor, in city neighborhoods. We did not find that the decline in violence had brought about a new era of integrated neighborhoods where the upper- and lower-class live together in harmony. In fact, the overall segregation of high- and low-income Americans has continued since the 1990s, and the concentration of poverty has not subsided in the years since crime began to fall.

And yet we found that the gradual separation of the rich from the poor is moving slowest, and in some cases is reversing, in the cities where crime has fallen the most. This is most strikingly the case in neighborhoods like Harlem that once had extremely high rates of poverty. Taking advantage of natural experiments that produce sharp changes in violent crime, we found that the drop in violence had a meaningful impact on the degree to which the poorest urban residents are isolated from the rest of the city, in communities of concentrated poverty.[12]

The crime drop has not reduced the enormous gap between rich and poor city dwellers, in other words, but it has led to a shift in the distribution of the urban population. The poorest city neighborhoods have started to gain new residents as they have become safer, and poverty has become less concentrated. The decline in violent crime hasn't ended the rise of urban inequality, but it has changed its form.

In much of the country, this finding simply means that the fall of violent crime has opened up the poorest neighborhoods of cities to a broader segment of the population, creating communities with a greater mix of poor and middle-class individuals and families. But to anyone who has spent time in cities like New York, Chicago, San Francisco, or Washington, D.C., the signs of change that have emerged in Harlem are more complicated, and they come with a dreaded label: gentrification.

As violence declined, neighborhoods like University Village on the Near West Side of Chicago experienced exploding demand for housing and have become unattainable for middle-class families. In neighborhoods like Fort Greene and Clinton Hill in Brooklyn, new coffee shops and restaurants have emerged, catering to the newcomers instead of the long-term residents. In communities like Shaw in Washington, D.C., resentment has grown as norms of behavior have shifted, as new arrivals have inserted themselves and their perspectives into public spaces and local political debates.[13]

And these same issues are present in Harlem, where Lance Freeman carried out dozens of interviews with residents to understand how they interpreted the changes going on around them. Some people in Harlem worried about being displaced from their homes and pushed out of their community as demand for housing rises and rents start to soar.[14] Although these are very real concerns in many cities, research carried out in New York City (which has more extensive protections for renters than many other cities) provides little evidence that gentrification leads to any detectable increase in displacement. The more salient threat for many long-term residents is *cultural* displacement, the sense that the neighborhood will become unaffordable to anyone except wealthy, highly educated newcomers, and the character of the community will change.

Many of the long-term residents of Harlem expressed frustration and resentment at the changes they saw unfolding around them, complaining that they no longer felt at home and wondering out loud why the city never before paid such attention to their neighborhood. When asked about the new restaurants and cafés in Harlem, a man who had lived in a public housing project there for his entire life said that he avoided the new cafes, telling Freeman, "Obviously they don't want too many of us in there." Residents saw the trash being collected more regularly and the police becoming more visible, and they questioned why the city ignored them for so long. When asked why the city was trying to clean up the community, one resident told Freeman, "It's not for the people who are in the community. It's not for us at all. . . . Anything that they're doing in Harlem, it's not meant for the poor blacks."

These sentiments have been documented in a range of different studies of neighborhoods undergoing gentrification. They reveal the tensions and public policy challenges that arise when a new population moves into a community like Harlem: Rents begin to rise, norms begin to shift, and the feel of the community begins to change.

But despite the visibility of gentrification in places like Harlem, the changes that have taken place in urban neighborhoods across the country typically look very different from our common conceptions of gentrification. When poverty begins to fall in the most disadvantaged neighborhoods, they usually do not shift from black to white, from poor to rich. Instead, the neighborhoods where poverty

has fallen the most over the past few decades have experienced a
slight decline in the percentage of black residents, an increase in
Hispanic and foreign-born residents, and a rise in employment.[15]
In fact, one study found that predominantly black neighborhoods
in Chicago were the least likely to undergo the process of gentrification.[16] This research does not mean that gentrification is unim-
portant; it just means that it is not nearly as common as one might
think, and that our image of what gentrification means is heavily
influenced by a small number of neighborhoods in only a few cities.

And even in neighborhoods undergoing very visible racial
change, like Harlem, longtime residents sometimes express an
ambivalent, or begrudgingly positive, attitude toward the changes
going on around them. "Well I'm a realist," one man told Freeman.
"I think gentrification is good in certain respects in that it brings
things to a neighborhood that it really never had. Like an all-black
neighborhood never had as much police protection as their white
counterpart. So it brings that. Plus it brings investment."

Although few of Freeman's respondents owned their homes,
those who did stood to reap enormous wealth from rising property
values. And some of the people who had lived through Harlem's
worst years welcomed the decline in violence and the shifting perception of the community: "I think it's a general positive because
it's maintaining its racial diversity and like I said it's safer, above
anything it's safe." Another respondent agreed: "So if other people
wanna live there then there is something good about Harlem. And
we have some nice places in Harlem."

Most of the literature on gentrification ignores this perspective, but Freeman's research reveals the potential benefits that
can come when neighborhoods become more economically diverse
and safer, attracting new resources for schools, new businesses,
and new attention from public agencies. "Residents of the 'hood
are sometimes more receptive because gentrification brings their

neighborhoods into the mainstream of American commercial life with concomitant amenities and services that others might take for granted," writes Freeman. Gentrification "represents the possibility of achieving upward mobility without having to escape to the suburbs or predominantly white neighborhoods."

Freeman's conclusions reflect the deeper meaning of the changes that have been going on in city neighborhoods over the past two decades. Twenty-five years ago the problems of violence and concentrated poverty were seen as the most pressing issues facing big cities. An enormous body of research showed that when children grow up in communities where poverty is concentrated, their chances of obtaining a high-quality education, finding a decent job, and moving upward in the income distribution are small. Both policy makers and academics assumed that if children spent their lives in neighborhoods that were less poor and less isolated, their life chances would improve substantially.

The decline in violence has provided a chance to test this idea. Cities where violence has fallen the most have seen the greatest changes in the concentration of poverty, leading to neighborhoods with a greater mix of low-, middle-, and upper-income residents. As these communities change, new conflicts and tensions have emerged, and in some places problems like affordable housing have become more acute. But the underlying hope of urban researchers back in the 1990s was that if neighborhoods became safe and concentrated poverty declined, children would have a greater chance to rise out of poverty.

Were they right?

Raj Chetty is an economist at Harvard who has contributed more to our understanding of economic mobility in America than perhaps any other researcher in the world. Years ago he established an agreement with the IRS that allows him to analyze data from tax returns, over time, for all Americans who file with the federal government. By tracking most of the adult population's reported income over time, the data provide more complete answers to an essential question about U.S. economic opportunity: Are children raised in poor families likely to be stuck in poverty throughout their lives, or can they rise out of poverty as adults?

In a series of groundbreaking studies, Chetty and a team of researchers demonstrated that the life chances of children from poor families vary dramatically depending on where they are raised.[17] Children growing up in high-opportunity areas like Seattle and Minneapolis can expect to earn about 10 percent more than peers who are raised elsewhere, and children growing up in low-opportunity areas like San Antonio and Baton Rouge can expect to earn about 10 percent less than peers raised elsewhere.

Chetty and his team compared siblings who moved across urban areas, spending different portions of their lives in high-opportunity areas and low-opportunity areas. Although the siblings shared the same family background, their experience of childhood differed simply based on how many years they spent in different places. For each additional year spent in a high-opportunity urban area, the research showed that adult income rises in a linear fashion. The finding is straightforward, yet striking in its implications. It demonstrates that the chance to rise upward depends not only on our personal characteristics and our families, but also on the environments in which we live.

But on another question, the research team at Chetty's Equality of Opportunity Project has made much less progress. What is it about these places that matters so much to the life chances of children? Chetty's research has demonstrated that something about places affects the life chances of kids, but we don't know exactly what it is.

Along with Gerard Torrats-Espinosa, I set out to see whether violence might be part of the answer. Why violence? As we have seen, children carry the burden of violence with them throughout childhood, creating a constant level of stress that disrupts their cognitive development and their academic progress. Children living within intensely violent settings are forced to navigate strategically through threatening streets, shifting their schedules and their routines in order to minimize the risk of assault. Parents in these environments often find creative ways to manage their children's lives in order to avoid violence, but they do so in ways that minimize the child's capacity to engage in social life within their neighborhoods and schools. Instead of taking advantage of resources and opportunities in school, children in violent environments are more likely to be kept inside behind closed doors.

But it is not only individual children who experience the impact of violence. Violence undermines entire communities, making it less likely that quality teachers are willing to remain at a tough school or that business owners will invest in a neighborhood. When neighborhoods are unsafe, economic activity dries up, and opportunities in the labor force wither away. When young men and women look for their first job, they may have to travel far outside their neighborhood to find an opportunity. Holding down a job is more difficult, and establishing a track record in the labor force, developing references, and becoming enmeshed in networks that lead to stable employment become less likely. As a result, children who begin near the bottom of the income distribution are more likely to stay there.

When violence begins to fall, on the other hand, children's experiences start to change, economic activity reemerges in the community, and opportunities open up. Young people are more likely to stay in school when their classrooms are safe, businesses are more likely to return to their neighborhoods, and jobs reappear. Upward mobility becomes more likely.

The data that Chetty and his team collected confirm these ideas. Torrats-Espinosa and I analyzed national data on violent crime and economic mobility and found that upward mobility is much less likely in cities with high levels of violence. But Chetty's data also allowed us to carry out a different kind of analysis, one that is more relevant for understanding how the decline in violence has affected the life chances of children. Instead of comparing children who live in more or less violent places, we compared children from the same places who grew up during a time when the level of violence was falling. The question that we asked was simple: As the level of violence in a child's environment begins to decline, does the chance that the child will experience upward mobility improve?

We took advantage of different types of "shocks" that affected the timing of the crime drop within cities, and analyzed the fortunes of young people from the same cities who grew up in times when violence was relatively high or low. We found that children who reached their teenage years at a time when the level of violence had subsided were substantially more likely to move upward in the income distribution by early adulthood, advancing further than their parents and further than others in the same city who had lived through a more violent time.[18]

Our results suggest that children who lived in an area where violence had declined by roughly half—which was not uncommon during this period—could expect to earn about $2,000 more in income every year during early adulthood. The magnitude of this impact is roughly equivalent to the effect of spending one's childhood in Denver, an urban area with greater opportunities for mobility, instead of Las Vegas, a place where opportunities to move upward have been more scarce. It is enough to provide economic stability during the crucial period of early adulthood, when young men and women are trying to start their own families and establish a track record in the workforce. For many, it is enough of a boost to give individuals a long-term chance at upward mobility, and for some it is sufficient to end the intergenerational cycle of poverty.

What happens when cities become safe? I have argued that public spaces awaken when violence becomes less common. Residents become more willing to venture out to places like Yankee Stadium, in the heart of the Bronx, for a night game. The city's labor force is more likely to come together in a train, subway, or bus instead of retreating to their individual cars and making their way to work, one by one, on their own. Visitors return for trips to landmarks, parks become crowded, and street performers entertain onlookers. Families from the surrounding suburbs consider moving back into the central city.

These are the changes most visible to urban planners, to city mayors, and to visitors. But when cities become safe, a less visible series of changes takes place in the neighborhoods that are not shown on city bus tours or tourists' brochures. Instead of shielding their children from the world outside the apartment, parents feel more comfortable allowing their children to walk home from a park or a community center after school. Neighbors begin to talk to one another about themselves and their kids, shopping districts begin to show signs of life, local libraries start to fill up. Children move through the city without the constant worry that they may be on the wrong street, with the wrong person, at the wrong time. When they enter school, students no longer have to think about surviving and can begin to focus on learning. The most visible people in the neighborhood are no longer drug dealers, and young people can start to see themselves as potential college students, workers, young professionals, and parents. Small business owners start to wonder whether it might be worth it to set up shop, and parents stop looking for a new, safer place to live. And as they figure out what they want to do with their lives, young adults can find opportunities to work nearby.

All the evidence from the past few chapters suggests that the greatest benefits of the crime drop have been experienced by the most disadvantaged segments of the urban population. And yet despite all these changes, the decline in violence has not ended the rise of urban inequality. When violence began to fall in the mid-1990s, inequality grew more severe. The most affluent Americans have continued to enjoy rising income and wealth, while families in the bottom half of the distribution have seen their income stagnate.[19] The share of wealth held by the top 1 percent has grown steadily since the 1980s, and the separation of the rich from the poor has not subsided. Racial disparities in income and wealth have not narrowed over time, even as the nation's cities have become dramatically safer.

These trends serve as a reminder that the rise of inequality is driven by economic and social forces much broader than violence, and it would be naïve to think that the fall in violent crime could counteract this trend on its own. But even if the crime drop has not reversed the growth of urban inequality, it has had a profound impact on its form and its consequences. As American cities have become more unequal, the decline in violent crime has changed the way rich and poor people are distributed across urban neighborhoods. In the cities where crime has fallen the most, the poorest neighborhoods have become less isolated from the remainder of the city. Areas of concentrated poverty have become more diverse, attracting new populations into communities that used to be on their own, excluded from the life of the city.

In some places, old problems of abandoned streets and violent crime have turned into new problems of shifting cultural norms and rising rents. Although these problems are very visible, they are not all that common. These problems are severe in a small number of cities struggling with the challenge of gentrification, and in these hot markets it is up to city leaders and policy makers to utilize tools like inclusionary zoning, land trusts, and subsidized housing to make sure that residents are not pushed out or priced out as their neighborhoods become more safe and more desirable.[20] But the new demand for land and housing in poor neighborhoods is a development that would have been difficult to imagine in the early 1990s, when the concentration of poverty was the most pressing problem in urban America. It is a problem that arises when people are interested in moving into low-income neighborhoods, instead of feeling desperate to get out.

The drop in violence has not only created less isolated neighborhoods, it has also made the consequences of urban inequality less damaging and less persistent. Poverty is sticky in the United States, passed on from parents to their children to a much greater degree than in most of the developed world.[21] But when violent crime falls, children who grew up in poverty are more likely to rise upward in the income distribution as adults. The decline in violent crime may not have slowed the rise of inequality, but it has disrupted the transmission of poverty from one generation to the next.

The final way that the decline in violence has affected American inequality is the most obvious, and perhaps the most important: It has changed the daily experience of inequality. In an "age of extremes," individuals from the most disadvantaged segments of the population have had their daily lives altered the most as violence has become less common.[22] In the early 1990s, being poor in the United States meant living with an extremely high risk of victimization. If you were poor, you had a very good chance of being the victim of a robbery, an assault, or something worse. If it didn't happen in one year, there was a strong possibility that it would happen in the next. The threat of violence was a regular part of daily life.

If there is a single fact that reveals just how much urban life has changed over the past twenty years, it is this: The poorest Americans are now victimized at about the same rate as the richest Americans were back at the start of the 1990s. Think about that for a moment. A poor, unemployed city resident in 2015 had about the same chance of being robbed, beaten up, stabbed, or shot as a well-off, high-paid urbanite in 1993.

Rates of victimization are not just abstract metrics that can be analyzed like the gross national product or unemployment rate. They are measures of how many of our fellow citizens have been assaulted or beaten in the previous six months. They are measures of how we interact with our neighbors and anonymous strangers, how vulnerable are the poorest among us. The figures on victimization indicate that all of us have become safer over the past two decades, but the greatest changes have been experienced by the poorest Americans.

This is the paradox of urban inequality after the era of violence. As economic inequality has grown, our nation's cities continue to become more stratified by income and wealth. Rich and poor Americans live apart, in separate communities, and their children go to different schools. Black and Hispanic Americans continue to live in entirely different social worlds than white Americans, even if they have similar income.[23] Yet the decline in violence has slowed these trends, leading to neighborhoods with both high- and low-income residents and raising the chances that a child born into poverty will move upward as an adult. And one of the most destructive features of urban poverty—the daily threat of victimization—has become much less common, for everyone.

PART III

THE CHALLENGE
OF VIOLENCE AND
URBAN INEQUALITY

7

ABANDONMENT, PUNISHMENT, AND THE NEW COMPROMISE

Officers from the New York Police Department stopped, questioned, and sometimes frisked civilians on the street more than 685,000 times over the course of 2011. One of those civilians, a young man named Alvin, was stopped by two officers as he walked down the street near his home in Harlem, on June 3, 2011. Alvin had already been stopped once that day, and as the police approached him for a second time, he decided to discreetly record the interaction.[1] Like the video of Derrion Albert's murder, the audio of Alvin's encounter with the approaching police officers provides an introduction to a world that has been hidden from most Americans who live outside the nation's most disadvantaged neighborhoods. It is a world where young men of color are subjected to the constant threat of being targeted by the police, and where they navigate the streets around their homes under a cloud of suspicion.[2]

Alvin was stopped during the year when the use of "stop, question, and frisk," a police tactic actively defended by former mayor Michael Bloomberg and former police commissioner Ray Kelly, reached its peak. The number of "reasonable suspicion" stops has plummeted under the reforms implemented by Mayor Bill de Blasio and by William Bratton, who served for two years as police commissioner beginning in 2014.[3] But in 2011 the police were stopping young men of color at a shocking rate. Young black and Latino males made up about 5 percent of the city's population, but they were targeted in 42 percent of all police stops. Mayor Bloomberg described the use of stop, question, and frisk as a crucial part of the city's efforts to prevent crime and confiscate weapons, but only about 5 percent of these interactions led to arrests, and only about one-tenth of 1 percent turned up a gun.[4]

In their reports on each incident, officers were required to list a reason why the individual was stopped. During this period, the most common reason given in the official reports was "furtive movement."[5] In Merriam-Webster's dictionary, the first definition of *furtive* is "done in a quiet and secret way to avoid being noticed"—a perfect adjective to describe a young man looking over his shoulder, trying not to be noticed by the police.

But one can get a better sense of what this meant on the streets of Harlem by listening to Alvin's recording. As the officers exit their car and approach the young man, Alvin tells them that he has just been stopped a few blocks away, to which the officer responds: "You know why? You look very suspicious."

As Alvin tries to respond to their questioning, the interaction escalates.

Officer: "Why do you have a fuckin' empty bookbag?"
Alvin: "'Cause I had my hoodie in there."

Alvin's response generates more anger in the officers, and their voices get louder.

Officer: "You have your hoodie on your body. Why you a fuckin'
            wiseass?"

Alvin: "Well it was cold."

Officer: "You want me to smack you?"

Alvin: "You're gonna smack me?"

At this point every word that comes out of Alvin's mouth seems to bring about more rage from the officers. They are now shouting at him instead of talking. The sounds of grunts and rough, sudden movement become audible as the officers order Alvin to put his hands over his head and begin to frisk him.

Officer: "You want to go to jail?"

Alvin: "What for?"

Officer: "Shut your fuckin' mouth, kid, shut your fuckin' mouth!"

Alvin: "What am I gettin' arrested for?"

Officer: "For being a fuckin' mutt, you know that?"

Alvin: "That's a law? Being a fucking mutt?"

Officer: "Who the fuck do you think you're talking to?"

At this point, the officers pull Alvin's arms behind his back, and he asks why they are grabbing his arms. The officer responds, "I will break your fucking arm off right now." The audio gets muffled as the officers push Alvin forward aggressively, but one can hear them yelling orders at him with rage in their voices, threatening to punch him in the face and seemingly trying to force him to resist. As the audio cuts out, one can hear an officer yelling at Alvin with short breaths, "Take a fucking walk! You hear me, you fucking shit!"

Alvin had not committed any crime on the day in June when the recording was made, but for a second time he was stopped by local police officers who rode in squad cars with the words COUR-TESY, PROFESSIONALISM, AND RESPECT painted on the side doors. In the course of the interaction, this young man, the son of a police officer himself, was mocked, insulted, and abused, verbally and physically. Listening to the officers berate him evokes emotions similar to those I felt when watching the sickening video of Derrion Albert's murder: a quickening heart rate, a feeling of sadness, fear, and horror that lingered on even after I closed the video and attempted to move on. However, another emotion emerges more forcefully when listening to the recording of this young man's interaction with the police: an intense, visceral anger.

Residents of poor, segregated communities have felt this anger for the past several decades (and much longer, of course).[6] It has spread beyond these communities not because of any recent change in policing tactics or a major rise in police shootings, but rather because more and more interactions between police and residents have been recorded. Because someone was taping Tamir Rice's shooting, Eric Garner's arrest, and Walter Scott's murder, those of us who live outside the nation's ghettos have been given a glimpse into the way those inside the ghetto can be treated. These videos are not a fair representation of police interactions with residents, the majority of which are cordial and respectful.[7] But the scenes of a man being choked to death, another man killed while attempting to flee, or a twelve-year-old boy being shot while playing in a park reveal very clearly the extreme version of what is possible for young men of color in the United States.

In his book *Between the World and Me*, the writer Ta-Nehisi Coates describes the constant possibility of death at the hands of the law as "merely the superlative form of a dominion whose prerogatives include friskings, detainings, beatings, and humiliations." "All of this is common to black people," writes Coates. "And all of this is old for black people."[8]

But for most of the country, including many African Americans who have never lived in the ghetto, the images of police brutality are neither common nor old. They are jarring. They generate shock, stress, and anger for Americans who have an intellectual awareness of police violence but no visual, emotional awareness of what it looks like. For the last several decades, America's poor, racially and ethnically segregated neighborhoods have been the primary sites for a systematic policy of intensive policing and mass imprisonment, the two dominant features of the nation's policy approach toward urban poverty.[9] But now we have cameras in our cellphones, and it is visible to everyone.

The videos of police violence have resonated so powerfully because they come at a time when there is no crisis of crime in most of the country, when every other form of violence in society has subsided.[10] They come at a time when more than two million Americans are in prisons and jails, a number that has grown even as violence has fallen. And they come at a time when Americans' fear of being victimized has subsided, and their attitudes toward criminals have softened. There were years in the 1990s in which more than 30 percent of Americans thought crime and violence were the most important problems facing the United States. By the end of the 2000s, just 5 percent of Americans thought so.[11]

After two decades of falling violence, the draconian criminal justice system seems like a relic from a different era, and police violence feels more and more out of place. As protests against police brutality and mass incarceration continue in cities all over the country, it is worth stepping back and asking a question: How did we get to this point?

In the early morning hours of a July Sunday in 1967, police raided an unlicensed drinking club on the near west side of Detroit and attempted to arrest everyone inside. A crowd gathered. A bottle was thrown at the police. Looting began, and soon there was chaos, burning buildings, and reports of sniper shootings. Both the Michigan National Guard and federal troops were ultimately called in. Over forty people were killed, over 2,500 buildings were destroyed, and over 7,000 people were arrested.[12]

The riots in Detroit broke out just a few weeks after violence erupted in Newark, when a black taxi driver was arrested and beaten up on the way to the precinct. A false rumor spread that he had been killed by the police. A crowd gathered by the precinct office, and then came looting and absolute mayhem. Accounts of the Newark riots tell of white residents standing in armed patrols guarding their neighborhoods, and of officers from the Newark Police Department shooting randomly at black people all over the ghetto.

The riots in Newark came a year after Chicago exploded when a Puerto Rican man was shot by police during the city's first Puerto Rican Parade, and two years after Watts erupted in violence when an officer allegedly kicked a woman thought to be pregnant. The riots in Watts were broadcast on live TV, bringing surreal scenes of shootings, fires, and unbridled chaos to the nation. Smaller-scale rioting—which was still violent, destructive, and terrifying—had broken out in Brooklyn and Harlem, in Cleveland, Jacksonville, Milwaukee, Omaha, and Philadelphia, over the previous two years.

For two summers, Americans watched news reports showing police officers crouching and exchanging fire with hidden combatants on city streets, imagery that was eerily similar to the footage of soldiers in Vietnam. The nation was at war abroad, but the scenes from America's ghettos conveyed the clear message that the United States was also in the midst of a civil war.

A week after the Detroit riots, speaking from what used to be known as the White House "Fish Room," President Lyndon Johnson appointed Governor Otto Kerner of Illinois and Mayor

John Lindsay of New York as the chairman and vice-chairman of a presidential committee created to understand why America's cities were erupting in riots. The committee came to be known as the Kerner Commission. The president promised the commission's leaders that their investigation would face no interference and would not be influenced by politics. "We are looking to you not to approve our own notions," he told them, "but to guide us and to guide the country through a thicket of tension, conflicting evidence, and extreme opinions."[13] The president laid out three questions for the committee to answer: "What happened? Why did it happen? What can be done to prevent it from happening again?"

The eleven commission members—Democrats, Republicans, a police chief, a labor leader, a civil rights leader, the head of a defense firm, and the head of a state commerce department (the sole woman)—took the president at his word. They spent the next seven months carrying out interviews and site visits in the cities hit by riots, and they put together a report that ran over four hundred pages. Influenced by several cabinet members, President Johnson had suspected that a large-scale conspiracy was behind the riots. But the Kerner Commission found no evidence to support the idea that the riots were planned and orchestrated by either Communists or black militant organizations. Instead, it concluded that the unrest was the result of deep-seated frustration arising from continuing racial injustice and discrimination, political marginalization, blocked economic opportunities, and unrelenting segregation.

The answers to Johnson's three questions could not be found in a vast Communist conspiracy or even in the unlawful actions of those within the ghetto, the commission concluded. The answers could be found outside the ghetto. The most jarring sentences in the report made this conclusion crystal clear: "What white Americans have never fully understood—but what the Negro can never forget—is that white society is deeply implicated in the ghetto. White institutions created it, white institutions maintain it, and white society condones it."[14]

The riots that were the focus of the Kerner Commission were the most visible, destructive examples of a much larger crisis that had been unfolding in America's cities during the 1960s. The term *urban crisis* meant different things to different people but generally referred to a set of growing social problems that were most severe in the cities. Cities were the most visible settings for America's growing pollution problem. Cities were the places where shifts in the labor market, like the decline in low-skilled manufacturing jobs, took their greatest toll. Cities were the places left behind as a large-scale, long-term migration to the suburbs gathered momentum.

At the heart of the urban crisis was the question of how to understand, and confront, the economic dislocation, severe racial inequality, and simmering unrest that was concentrated in urban neighborhoods. President Johnson had envisioned a new, Great Society that would harness the nation's economic prowess and use it to relieve poverty, improve health, create great schools, and bring civil rights to all Americans. The nation's cities, particularly its primarily black ghettos, were the most glaring signs that Johnson's vision had failed. The president's failure became visible in Watts, Newark, and Detroit, then culminated in the wave of anger, grief, protest, destruction, and violence that spread through hundreds of American cities when Martin Luther King, Jr., was assassinated in 1968. When Johnson created the Kerner Commission, he was pleading for an answer to the crisis of urban poverty in the black ghetto.

The authors of the report traveled to cities where black communities had been ignored by white political leaders and brutalized by ruthless police departments. They heard residents who were emboldened by their successes in achieving basic civil rights but angered by their inability to find stable employment. They explained to the president that the riots were an outgrowth of relentless racial injustice and staggering inequality. The unrest could not be separated from the poverty, social disorder, disempowerment, and anger that had arisen because a segment of the population had been excluded from mainstream economic, political, and cultural life, unable to experience the prosperity enjoyed by much of the country in the 1960s.

The solution to the urban crisis, according to the authors of the report, was a policy agenda that relied on massive federal investment designed to integrate and empower marginalized segments of the population, most notably black Americans in urban ghettos. The authors outlined a comprehensive agenda for American cities that included billions of dollars in federal funding for schools, jobs, social services, income supports, and a mix of housing programs designed to confront racial segregation, improve housing in black neighborhoods, and allow black families to move more freely into a wider range of communities. The authors pointed out the folly of concentrating poverty in high-rise public housing projects. They conveyed the anger of young people who saw their siblings and neighbors being brutalized by officers who looked different from them and lived somewhere else. And they heard the pleas for work, the calls for decent wages, and the yearning for a chance to escape poverty.

The Kerner Commission report is a remarkable public document: a large-scale research project, an unflinching acknowledgment of racism in America, and a national bestseller. But its recommendations went nowhere. President Johnson had created the commission to explain the spread of urban unrest. When it completed its task, Johnson refused to accept, or even acknowledge, the report's conclusions. He simply ignored it.

Just a few weeks before he announced the formation of the Kerner Commission, Johnson had signed into law the Safe Streets and Crime Control Act of 1968. The act established $400 million in grants to strengthen law enforcement, provided forgivable loans and grants for officers to receive training and education, and allowed for federal funds to be used to bolster police salaries and to train officers "to ease tensions in ghetto neighborhoods." On the day he introduced the legislation, Johnson used his platform to push further beyond the stipulations of the legislation, asking every city to expand the size of its police force and to increase the salaries of officers: "I call upon every citizen in this Nation to support their local police officials with respect and with the resources necessary to enable them to do their job for justice in America."[15]

The new federal legislation, and the words used to introduce it, reveal an understanding of the central problem in America's ghettos very different from the one put forth in the Kerner Commission report. The core problem was not black disenfranchisement, continuing inequality, or racial injustice—the problem was crime. And the solution to the problem did not involve uncovering the root causes of poverty, expanding civil rights, or fighting injustices. The solution was to support the police, both with expanded resources and with a call for deference and respect.

Johnson's words were not anomalous. They reflected a shift in the national mood, and a shift in the way that politicians had begun to talk about the problem of urban violence.[16] In 1961 President Kennedy had declared a "total attack on delinquency" and passed legislation providing federal funding for organizations to administer a range of social programs for high-risk youth in urban neighborhoods. In a speech in 1962, FBI director J. Edgar

Hoover described urban crime as a fundamental threat to the nation, referring to city streets as "jungles of terror" and calling for "stiffer laws and a more stern policy toward these perverted individuals."[17] And by the time of the 1964 presidential election, the problem of urban unrest and violent crime was a major theme of discourse on the right. Republican presidential candidate Barry Goldwater campaigned on a platform explicitly linking racial unrest and the civil rights movement with social upheaval and violent crime.[18] Although Johnson was reelected easily in 1964, a slate of "law and order" candidates whose language resembled that of Goldwater were swept into office in the midterm elections of 1966.[19]

Over time, as public anxiety about urban violence grew, President Johnson's own rhetoric hardened. He argued that confronting poverty was not sufficient, that cracking down on crime was also necessary for the Great Society that he imagined.[20] In September 1965 he signed the Law Enforcement Assistance Act, a groundbreaking piece of legislation that expanded the purview of the federal government beyond "housing, employment, mental health, education, transportation, and welfare" and into the realm of law enforcement and criminal justice.[21] "We labor for that day when every man can satisfy his basic needs and those of his family; when every child has a chance to develop his mind and enlarge his spirit to the limits of his being; when the slow killers—want, ignorance, and prejudice—are finally contained," Johnson announced on the day he signed the legislation. "But if we reach that day, and still walk in terror through the public streets, our labors will have been futile."[22]

A narrative explaining the urban crisis as a problem of criminality and lawlessness, a problem unique to the urban ghetto, had taken hold in the minds of a growing segment of the American public and their political representatives. And the explanation of the urban crisis that focused on inequality and injustice was losing political salience.

By March 1968, when the Kerner Commission delivered its report to President Johnson, he was gearing up for a reelection campaign. The report he had commissioned blamed white Americans for urban unrest and implicitly suggested that the president's major legislative achievements, the programs that composed the War on Poverty, had failed to address the crisis in the nation's cities. Johnson's rejection of the Kerner Commission report can be viewed as nothing more than a political calculation in an election year, but his decision may have signaled something larger. It may have marked the demise of the idea that a policy agenda focused on empowerment, integration, and investment could be a politically viable solution to the problem of the urban ghetto.

If the president's response to the Kerner Commission report signaled the end of one narrative of the urban crisis, the run-up to the 1968 presidential election confirmed the rise of another. As the presidential election approached, the urban crisis escalated with riots that continued into the spring of 1968, after the assassination of Martin Luther King. News from Vietnam worsened, and opposition to the war intensified at home. President Johnson sensed declining support and rising antiwar sentiment within his own party and decided to end his campaign for reelection. Richard Nixon was elected president in November 1968, with 56 percent of the electoral vote. He rode to victory by linking the antiwar protesters and the urban rioters as partners in lawlessness, emblematic of the breakdown of social order. His administration began with an explicit focus on the urban crisis and with a declaration of the need for a coherent urban policy agenda. Over the course of his two terms in office, the content of the new policy slowly came into focus. It was characterized by the abandonment of poor urban neighborhoods and the punishment of their residents.

As president, Nixon rejected the effort to link the common challenges faced by cities and their suburbs, as proposed by moderate Republicans like HUD secretary George Romney. The Nixon administration viewed this type of metropolitan focus as a step toward "forced integration" and saw the problems of cities as local issues. Funding to cities was shifted into block grants to states as part of the administration's "New Federalism," reflecting a broader abdication of the federal government's role in responding to the challenges that cities faced.

By Nixon's second term, the policy of abandonment and punishment solidified. Declaring a moratorium on all federal housing programs, Nixon asserted that the urban crisis had ended. He pointed to improvements in air quality and housing conditions, the stabilization of city government finances, and the decline in "civil disorders," and proclaimed that "America is no longer coming apart." In a radio address delivered on March 4, 1973, Nixon announced to the nation that "the hour of crisis has passed."[23]

In fact, a new crisis in America's cities was just beginning. In the mid-1970s the national economy was entering a long period of stagnation in which urban labor markets would be decimated. Cities were losing middle-class residents and absorbing new immigrants without the resources or tax base to support an increasingly poor population. And the country was moving toward the most violent era of its modern history.

———

Two sets of stories, two narratives, emerged during the 1960s to explain the crisis that had arisen in the nation's cities (see Figure 7.1). The narratives can be visualized along two axes of urban policy: one spanning from punishment to justice, the other from investment to abandonment.

The first narrative explains the urban crisis as a product of

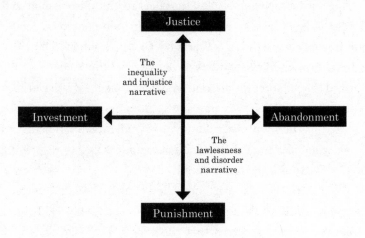

Fig. 7.1   The two narratives of the urban crisis

inequality and injustice. This narrative was crystallized in the Kerner Commission report, but it also provided the moral justification for the Civil Rights Act, the Voting Rights Act, and the Fair Housing Act. It was the narrative that led to President Johnson's War on Poverty, a set of programs designed to address several of the core challenges of the urban crisis, including joblessness, underresourced and low-quality schools, and political marginalization. This is the narrative that led the members of the Kerner Commission to propose a long-term policy agenda focused on the dual goals of justice and investment, aiming to address the brutal, discriminatory treatment of residents in the ghetto, to implement reforms designed to bring African Americans into positions of power, and to provide massive resources to improve the functioning of institutions and offer greater opportunities.[24]

The alternative narrative, which gathered support steadily over the course of the 1960s, argued that the urban crisis was explained not by inequality and injustice but rather by growing lawlessness and disorder. Those telling this story argued that urban neighborhoods should be abandoned, left on their own to deal with rising poverty and joblessness. Nixon justified it by asserting that the hour of crisis had passed, and his adviser Daniel Patrick Moynihan placed a label on it when he called for a period of "benign neglect."[25]

Instead of investing in neighborhoods and taking steps to bring about racial justice, the proponents of the lawlessness and disorder narrative argued that the solution to continuing urban unrest was to stand back, call off efforts to move toward racial justice, initiate the forceful takeover of the ghetto by the police, and expand incarceration. During his time in office, Nixon withdrew federal resources for urban neighborhoods, expanded federal support for law enforcement, and moved toward an increasingly punitive criminal justice system.

The model of abandonment and punishment that was put into place during the Nixon administration has undergone some adjustments but has remained mostly intact over time. President Carter bolstered funding for community development block grants, but President Reagan slashed funding for urban communities.[26] President Clinton oversaw an expansion of the earned income tax credit and implemented programs designed to lure businesses into distressed neighborhoods, but there was no fundamental shift in urban policy during Clinton's administration. His most lasting impact on cities came from the reforms of the welfare system and the destruction of public housing developments through the HOPE VI program.[27] President George W. Bush passed three of the largest tax cuts in the nation's history, provided federal support for faith-based social service programs, and otherwise mostly ignored the problem of urban poverty.[28]

On the other hand, the most consistent response to the challenges of urban crime, violence, and poverty has been punishment.

After a lull in criminal justice policy under Ford and Carter, President Reagan brought Nixon's nascent War on Drugs to fruition, and President Clinton expanded it further. Clinton added tens of thousands of new police officers to America's streets when he signed the Violent Crime Control and Law Enforcement Act of 1994, which provided grants encouraging states to implement reforms that required individuals convicted of violent crimes to serve at least 85 percent of their sentences. At the same time, states eliminated parole and established mandatory minimum sentences for drug offenses and violent crimes. On the axis ranging from punishment to justice, the Clinton administration pushed the nation further toward punishment.

The advent of President Barack Obama's administration provided hope that the long-standing model of abandonment and punishment would come to an end. It did not. Although his administration took steps to scale back the level of incarceration, President Obama's ambition to make urban poverty a national priority faded quickly in the early days of his presidency. He established the White House Office of Urban Affairs and talked about expanding some of the most innovative urban initiatives that had been proposed in a long time, including Promise Neighborhoods and Choice Neighborhoods. But overwhelmed by a financial crisis, an economic downturn, and an obstructionist Congress, Obama never carried out his vision for a new urban agenda. His urban programs were diluted and arrived with insufficient funding to generate transformative change. His signature piece of "urban" legislation was the Recovery Act, an enormous influx of around $800 billion that was spread out across America's families and communities. The stimulus was more successful than most acknowledge, but it shared a feature with most major urban policies implemented since the early 1970s: It was temporary.[29]

It didn't take long for President Donald Trump to undo many

of the changes in policing and criminal justice that Obama had worked to implement. Trump campaigned on a platform of law and order and appointed Jeff Sessions, one of the strongest advocates of tough criminal sentencing and unconditional support for law enforcement, as attorney general. Since taking office, Sessions has taken active steps to roll back the Obama administration's investigations into civil rights abuses by police departments, and he has ordered prosecutors to pursue the harshest charges available to them.[30]

These developments might lead one to conclude that Nixon's policy of abandonment and punishment is alive and well, that the United States will continue to rely on the police and the prison to manage the problems of urban poverty, economic dislocation, and violent crime. But this conclusion is premature. The election of Donald Trump has distracted attention from a movement that has been gathering momentum for a decade or longer. Away from the spotlight of presidential politics, a growing group of conservative politicians, activists, and organizations built a campaign to scale back the size of the criminal justice system. They have joined forces with critics of mass incarceration on the left to form a platform focused on policing and criminal justice reform and to move the country away from the idea that punishment can be a sustainable solution to the problem of urban poverty.

The model of abandonment and punishment that Nixon put into place more than forty years ago has proven remarkably durable, and it has undergone only superficial changes in the years since he left office. But despite the election of Donald Trump and the efforts of his attorney general, that model is slowly coming to an end.

The Heritage Foundation is one of the country's most prominent, influential conservative think tanks. I found myself there on a rainy day in December 2013, seated around a long oval table with a group of twenty or so researchers, policy makers, institutional leaders, and public intellectuals who had been invited to join a day-long discussion on the impact of incarceration and the future of criminal justice policy. In a scene that is possible only at an institution like the Heritage Foundation, every single person around the table was male.

Although the meeting lacked any gender diversity, it was intellectually and politically diverse. A few seats to my left sat John DiIulio, the academic whose dire predictions about rising violent crime had pushed policy makers toward some of the most punitive criminal justice policies of the 1990s. Across the table was Michael Jacobson, former president of the Vera Institute for Justice, who had worked for years to reduce the size of the criminal justice system and fought for fair, humane, fair criminal justice policies. To my right sat Robert Woodson, the leader of the extraordinary organization now called the Woodson Center, which has championed the role of faith-based organizations in the effort to confront violence. And on the other side of the table was Alfred Blumstein, the venerable criminologist who had been documenting and dissecting the rise and fall of violence for decades.

We spent several hours discussing what is known about how mass incarceration has affected families, how time in prison alters long-term prospects for stable employment, and how the impact of imprisonment lingers on to affect the next generation. The discussion ranged from empirical findings to policy options to social and moral values. Old, lingering tensions rose to the surface at a few points, and there were moments of disagreement, frustration, and anger. But there was one point of virtual consensus. Almost everyone in the room agreed, some eagerly and some begrudgingly, that the scale of incarceration in the United States was unsustainable. In a time of falling violence, the staggering number of incarcerated Americans seemed misguided to all of us, and no one contested the consequences of mass incarceration. From the academics to the policy wonks to the public intellectuals to the directors of nonprofits, everyone around the table acknowledged that something had to change.

After we adjourned, I made the short walk from the Heritage Foundation to D.C.'s Union Station in the rain. When I had walked the opposite direction in the morning, I thought that I would have to spend the day making the case for the damaging consequences of mass incarceration, arguing that the crime decline had changed the nature of the debate on criminal justice policy, and fending off attacks in the process. Yet I had faced few challenges throughout the day. The exchanges that had generated disagreement were about minor differences in the interpretation of evidence, not about major differences in values or goals.

Somewhere during the time that I walked to Union Station, stood in the long line for the train, and made my way back home to New York, it occurred to me: The era of the prison is coming to an end. In one day, I had listened to people whose views spanned the political spectrum make a collective case against mass incarceration, based on empirical evidence about its consequences, on moral judgments about its symbolism, and on philosophical assessments of its role in society. The question that had dominated the day was not whether we should continue to rely so heavily on the prison. It was what would replace it.

Five voices provide a hint as to the answer.

The first of these voices focuses on *justice*: "If the way we pursue reforms does not contribute to the building of a movement to dismantle the system of mass incarceration, and if our advocacy does not upset the prevailing public consensus that supports the new caste system, none of the reforms, even if won, will successfully disrupt the nation's racial equilibrium."[31] These words were written by Michelle Alexander, a civil rights lawyer and legal scholar who has become the most prominent voice attacking mass incarceration from the left. Her book, *The New Jim Crow,* reached a wider audience than any previous scholarship on incarceration, and it resonated with readers in a way that is extremely rare for an academic book.

Alexander built a case, methodically and persuasively, arguing that mass incarceration represents the latest in a series of institutions and policies designed to reinforce a racialized caste system in the United States.[32] Her argument meshes with the writings of Ta-Nehisi Coates, who points toward the systems of law enforcement and criminal justice as part of a broader structure built on the ideology of white supremacy.[33] The prison, according to both writers, is something more than a tool used to improve public safety. It is part of a system that is designed to maintain racial inequality.

Alexander envisions changes to criminal sanctions, to sentencing laws, and to the role of police within low-income communities of color. But her solution is not to chip away at the criminal justice system through reforms; rather, she calls for a nationwide reckoning, a movement to acknowledge the racial caste system that is supported by the prison and to dismantle it collectively. One could argue that the Black Lives Matter movement has heeded the call, mobilizing against police brutality and racially biased policing in cities throughout the country. The call for justice has been pushed into the mainstream.

The second of the five voices focuses on *redemption*: "These people have committed crimes, but they're still human beings, created in the image of God. Can we help them restore what's left of their lives?"[34] Tony Perkins began his professional life as a part-time police officer in Baton Rouge, but his career in law enforcement ended quickly. In the summer of 1992, the antiabortion activist group Operation Rescue descended on Baton Rouge in an attempt to shut down the city's Delta Women's Clinic through protest and civil disobedience. Perkins, who was also a reporter for a conservative local news station, used his media position to criticize his own police department's efforts to control the protests. He was suspended from the police force for his actions. When his suspension was over, he resigned.[35]

Perkins turned his local notoriety into a seat in Lousiana's House of Representatives. After two terms and an unsuccessful U.S. Senate bid, he became president of the Family Research Council, an organization with a mission "to advance faith, family and freedom in public policy and the culture from a Christian worldview."[36] Scaling back the prison system is a part of this mission. Perkins's stance on imprisonment is driven by his religious belief in the dignity of all human life and the sanctity of the traditional family. He has fought passionately against abortion, against the rights of transgender citizens, and against homosexuality. He is now fighting against mass imprisonment: "Our criminal justice system is one arena where unintended consequences can jeopardize family unity."[37]

The third voice, from someone who has fought against racial discrimination over a long career, focuses on *rights*: "I think the problem is that some police believe that their role is to control black and brown people."[38]

Barbara Arnwine is the former president and executive director of the Lawyers' Committee for Civil Rights Under Law, one of the most influential civil rights organizations in the country. At five-thirty in the morning on November 21, 2011, a SWAT team raided her home in Prince George's County, Maryland. The officers broke into the house, woke everyone inside, and held them "at gunpoint for three hours," according to Arnwine.[39]

Press accounts indicated that the officers were looking for Arnwine's nephew, who was linked to a robbery that had taken place weeks earlier. In the aftermath of the raid, Arnwine gave several interviews recounting the "outrageous" treatment of her family, and suggesting that "they had the wrong address." Reverend Jesse Jackson, Sr., was one of the people who interviewed Arnwine, expressing disbelief at what had transpired: "If it can happen to her it can happen to anyone."

In more than twenty-five years as the leader of the Lawyers Committee, Arnwine had fought against discrimination in employment and housing and worked tirelessly against voter suppression. In her last year in office, after going through this harrowing experience, she brought together the most prominent civil rights organizations around the issues of policing and criminal justice. The Lawyers Committee has worked to identify police departments that disproportionately target communities of color and to advocate for training programs to reduce bias, for independent monitoring of police activity, for policing reforms like body-worn cameras and dashboard cameras, and for an end to the type of militarized policing that its former leader experienced firsthand, in her own home.

After leaving her position at the Lawyers Committee, Arnwine founded the Transformative Justice Coalition (TJC), which "seeks to be a catalyst for transformative institutional changes that bring about justice and equality in the United States and abroad."[40] One of the eight focal areas of her new organization is the Criminal Justice Project, which aims to reduce the rate of incarceration for people of color. Another, which was developed "through the leadership of its [TJC's] President," is the Policing Reform Project, designed to "end police misconduct and killings by reducing racial bias, racial profiling, racial targeting, militarization and other inappropriate policing tactics."

The fourth voice, coming from one of the most influential figures on the right, focuses on *austerity*: "Spending more on education doesn't necessarily get you more education. We know that—that's obvious. Well, that's also true about national defense. That's also true about criminal justice and fighting crime."[41]

In the run-up to the 2012 elections, 95 percent of Republican members of Congress signed their name to a document containing the following pledge:

> I, _____, pledge to the taxpayers of the (_____ district of the) state of _____ and to the American people that I will: ONE, oppose any and all efforts to increase the marginal income tax rate for individuals and business; and TWO, oppose any net reduction or elimination of deductions and credits, unless matched dollar for dollar by further reducing tax rates.

They signed this pledge because of Grover Norquist, the founder of Americans for Tax Reform, an organization established to lobby against government taxes in any form. His offshoot organization, the Cost of Government Center, fights against government spending and advocates for fiscal restraint. Norquist has lobbied to have at least one public landmark in every county in the country named after President Ronald Reagan. He has been called "one of the most influential figures in the history of the U.S. tax code and the U.S. budget."[42] And he has become a major force arguing for reforms of policing and incarceration.

Joining with groups like Right on Crime, which emerged out of Texas, Norquist has been an early, active supporter of efforts by conservatives to highlight the enormous resources that federal and state governments devote to criminal justice and to argue for a different approach.[43] This approach includes reducing penalties for minor drug crimes, diverting offenders from the prison system, and focusing resources on reducing recidivism. It is no coincidence that these calls for reform led to early successes in red states like Texas, Georgia, and South Carolina. They are pitched as efforts to get the government out of citizens' lives, to make the criminal justice system more efficient, to reinsert the community into our criminal justice system, and to provide sinners with a chance at redemption. And all these reforms also serve a larger purpose: They are designed to save taxpayer dollars.

The fifth and final voice focuses on *liberty*. "It's hard to watch that video of [Eric Garner] saying 'I can't breathe, I can't breathe' and not be horrified by it. But I think there's something bigger than the individual circumstances. . . . It is also important to know that some politician put a tax of $5.85 on a pack of cigarettes so that [has] driven cigarettes underground by making them so expensive. But then some politician also had to direct the police to say, 'Hey we want you arresting people for selling a loose cigarette.' And for someone to die over breaking that law, there really is no excuse for it."[44]

Senator Rand Paul's (R-KY) comments on the death of Eric Garner in Staten Island reveal multiple layers of frustration: frustration with the actions of the officers who killed him, with the law that prohibited selling loose cigarettes, and with the decision makers who demand that the law is enforced. Senator Paul is the most prominent libertarian in the country, and a former Republican presidential candidate. He has turned those layers of frustrations into multiple pieces of proposed legislation, and he has been more active than just about any other national politician in the effort to scale back the carceral state.

Paul teamed up with Senator Patrick Leahy (D-VT) to sponsor the Justice Safety Valve Act, which gives judges more discretion to disregard mandatory minimum sentences in cases where the offense is not violent or the defendant has mental health issues. He partnered with Senator Cory Booker (D-NJ) to propose the

REDEEM Act, which would establish a process to allow juveniles and nonviolent offenders to seal or expunge their criminal records. And he joined with Senator Harry Reid (D-NV) to allow nonviolent offenders the right to vote when they complete their sentence. Senator Paul has worked to end the federal government's program to supply local police departments with military equipment, and to reform the government's capacity to take over private property through civil asset forfeiture.

The common thread is a focus on how the government has overstepped its bounds and impinged upon the liberty of American citizens. Twenty years ago this argument would have been impossible for a mainstream politician to make. At this point it's not particularly controversial.

Michelle Alexander, Tony Perkins, Barbara Arnwine, Grover Norquist, and Rand Paul may not think they have much in common, but their voices are part of a chorus of people and organizations that have been calling for criminal justice reform on the basis of justice, faith, austerity, rights, and liberty. They may not be working directly with one another, but they are part of a new compromise that is beginning to shape the next model of urban policy. In my diagram of urban policy narratives, the new compromise sits in a quadrant that has been unoccupied for the past fifty years.

On the spectrum from punishment to justice, the new compromise leans toward justice. The calls for justice come, in different forms and different words, from Michelle Alexander on the left and from Rand Paul on the right. They come from people who argue that the prison system is part of a racial caste system, and from those who argue that the scale of an imprisonment represents an overreach of the federal government, an affront to personal liberty, and a danger to the traditional family.

Although the election of President Trump is a major step backward for those calling for a shift away from punishment and toward justice, the sentiments expressed by Trump and Jeff Sessions do not align with the much broader movement to reform the criminal justice system and law enforcement, and to repair the relationships between the police and the residents they serve. Fewer politicians are calling for crackdowns on the drug trade, or for zero-tolerance measures to confront crime; few are arguing for more aggressive policing or harsher sentencing. Bipartisan coalitions have formed to develop ways to change the way law enforcement interacts with urban communities, with leadership from Republicans.[45] Many no longer see punishment as a solution to the problem of urban poverty, and the ideal of justice is now guiding criminal justice reform.

On the spectrum from abandonment to investment, however, the new compromise continues to lean toward abandonment (see Figure 7.2). Advocates for civil liberties have shared the same podium with fiscal hawks like Grover Norquist, melding the argument against the expansive criminal justice system with an argument against government taxation.[46] The new compromise that has taken hold represents a call for justice, but also represents a clear abdication of the government's role in low-income communities of color, a retreat from the nation's poorest urban neighborhoods.

The impact of this new movement has become visible in public policy. The Fair Sentencing Act, passed in 2010, addressed the most glaring example of racially biased punishment by reducing the disparities between sentences for crack versus powder cocaine. The severe penalties for the use of crack cocaine had long stood as the most notorious example of the way criminal justice policy had targeted black Americans in an explicit manner. The Second Chance Act, first passed in 2008 and renewed in 2015, was designed to give returning prisoners a better chance to integrate

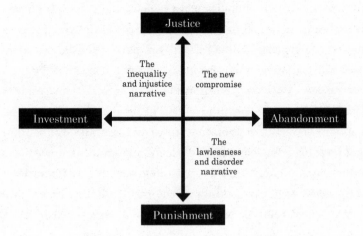

Fig. 7.2   Policy responses to the urban crisis: The new compromise

back into society by making it possible for some prisoners convicted of nonviolent offenses to have their records expunged. The law was renewed in 2015 with additional funding for the improvement and evaluation of prisoner reentry programs.

States have taken more aggressive steps to reduce the size of the incarcerated population. Texas has reformed its parole and probation system to reduce the rate at which former prisoners return to prison, and it has been a leader in the use of drug courts that divert low-level offenders away from prison. Connecticut has implemented a series of policy changes designed to make the state a "second chance society," to use the term coined by Governor Dannel Malloy. The state has reclassified the crime of drug possession from a felony to a misdemeanor, reformed the parole system, and proposed raising the age of criminal responsibility for most crimes from eighteen to twenty-one.

And dozens of states have passed legislation that allows local jurisdictions the chance to reform their criminal justice systems in ways that create savings, and to reinvest those extra resources in programs designed to serve former prisoners more effectively and reduce violence. These reforms are part of the Justice Reinvestment Initiative, a movement to convert a portion of the massive resources devoted to criminal justice into new investments designed to support communities.[47] The ideals behind this movement are powerful, and in some states and localities, the reforms that have been implemented have led to important improvements in the way returning prisoners are integrated into communities.[48]

However, the shortcomings of the Justice Reinvestment Initiative reflect a larger problem with the array of efforts at the local, state, and federal levels designed to reform a prison system that has grown to a size that no one could have imagined fifty years ago. The movement focuses entirely on the system of criminal justice and on the population of people who move through that system. It relies on resources that are saved by making the criminal justice system more efficient, and it uses these resources to reinvest in more effective programs to divert offenders from entering the prison and to better serve those leaving it. In some places, it has reduced the size of the incarcerated population and led to more effective programs for returning prisoners. But it is not designed to generate new resources for the communities where violence is concentrated, or for the institutions that are crucial to ensuring that children never become enmeshed in the criminal justice system.[49]

As with almost all reforms implemented over the past several years, this movement is guided by the goal of justice but ignores the need for new, substantial resources to build stronger neighborhoods. The details of the Justice Reinvestment Initiative illuminate the central problem with the new compromise: The shift away from punishment and toward justice has not come with an equally strong movement away from abandonment and toward investment.

Reducing the prison population, which has grown to a level that is internationally unprecedented, is a fundamental challenge for the United States. By itself, however, it is not a valid approach to reducing violence or confronting urban inequality. The communities that have seen a generation of young people swept into the criminal justice system are the communities that will have to absorb the rising number of returning men, and some women, from our jails and prisons. Most of these communities will see a stream of returning prisoners without strong, stable institutions that are necessary to enable them to reintegrate into their families, into the labor force, and into secure housing. If policy makers take steps to reduce the size of the imprisoned population without also providing massive resources for reintegration through strong local institutions, they will destabilize communities that are already fragile. They will amplify, not reduce, the costs of mass incarceration.

Similarly, changing the way police officers interact with residents in low-income communities of color is crucial to restoring legitimacy in one of the most important institutions in our society. But it is also essential to recognize the role that law enforcement has played in preserving social order and reducing violence. If the well-justified calls for policing reform drift into a broader movement to reduce the role of police in urban communities, we risk returning to a time when the poorest American neighborhoods were left on their own to deal with the challenges that come with concentrated poverty, a time when police departments were overwhelmed by the problem of violent crime and helpless to do anything about it. We risk drifting into a new era of rising violence.

As protesters have called for an end to police brutality, only minimal progress has been made in generating new investments to bolster community organizations that are crucial to stabilizing neighborhoods, to support resident groups that can begin to play a larger role in regulating behavior in public space, or to provide universal police training in areas like conflict de-escalation. As advocates have made the case for sentencing reforms and decarceration, there has been little progress in ensuring that every former prisoner has a legitimate opportunity to obtain training before he or she leaves prison, and to find a stable job, stable housing, and physical and mental health care upon exit from the prison system. There has been virtually no progress in supporting the institutions, and the communities, to which the nation's enormous prison population will return.

———

The new compromise represents a misunderstanding of the crisis in America's cities, and a misguided response. The crisis in our cities is not simply about the scale of incarceration or the brutality of policing. It is about the way the most marginalized groups within American society, segments of the population blocked from opportunity by hatred, discrimination, oppression, and public policy, are concentrated in the most disadvantaged neighborhoods of urban America.

This problem was visible as far back as 1830, when the French social scientist Alexis de Tocqueville observed that a growing segment of freed blacks and new immigrants at the margins of American society had become segregated in intensely poor sections of cities. The French visitor noted that the population of urban blacks was "condemned by the laws and by public opinion to a hereditary state of misery and degradation," and he considered the emergence of urban poverty to be a "danger which threatens the future security of the democratic republics of the New World."[50]

The urban crisis became impossible to ignore in the 1960s,

when riots spread across cities throughout the country and Kenneth Clark warned that "the dark ghettos now represent a *nuclear stockpile* that can annihilate the very foundations of America."[51] The problem grew more severe by the 1980s, when violent crime spiraled out of control, and it peaked in the 1990s: "The crime, poverty and physical and social deterioration of the inner cities is America's most obvious problem," wrote the journalist Nicholas Lemann in the *New York Times* back in 1994.[52]

The crisis in our cities at this moment is about much more than the prison system and the police. It is about how to deal with one of the most persistent problems in U.S. history, the problem of urban poverty. The challenge that now faces the nation is not, in my mind, how we can reform the systems of law enforcement and criminal justice so that they are less expansive, less oppressive, more just, and less expensive. *The challenge is to put forth a new model to respond to urban poverty and to reduce violent crime.*

And as we consider what the next grand model of urban policy should look like, we have to begin with a more immediate, more urgent set of challenges that discussions of criminal justice reform or urban policy often ignore: In an age of inequality, how do we fortify urban neighborhoods and ensure that they do not fall apart? While we seek ways to confront the rise of inequality itself, how do we act now to reduce the consequences of urban inequality? And most importantly: After years of relying on the police and the prison to deal with the problem of urban poverty through brute force, how do we ensure that a new set of guardians is prepared to look out over every urban neighborhood?

8

THE END OF WARRIOR
POLICING

The Jack Maple CompStat Center is something between a large conference room and a small auditorium. The room is on the eighth floor of the New York Police Department's headquarters at One Police Plaza, a huge building that is somehow tucked away behind an even larger municipal building next to lower Manhattan's City Hall Park. Outside the CompStat Center is a plaque honoring Jack Maple, the founder of CompStat. Maple was serving as deputy police commissioner at the time when he is said to have sketched out the four principles of CompStat on a napkin at Elaine's, the restaurant on the Upper East Side where New Yorkers like Woody Allen, Norman Mailer, and Police Commissioner William Bratton were regulars.[1]

He wrote just twelve words in total: (1) accurate and timely intelligence; (2) rapid deployment; (3) effective tactics; (4) relentless follow-up and assessment. These principles may seem basic in retrospect, but at the time they were revolutionary. Before the days of CompStat, police officers were dispatched across the city's streets without precise data on crime patterns to guide them, and they spent their time responding to crime rather than trying to prevent it. The department's resources were not tracked closely, and managers were not held accountable for outcomes in their precincts.[2]

Maple's principles were the foundation of a management system that began with precise data on where and when serious crimes occurred, then quickly deployed police resources to shut down the criminal activity. And then in meetings that became legendary, officers responsible for each beat within New York City came together and answered pointed questions about where crimes were taking place, what was being done to respond, which tactics were working and which were not, and what would be done differently. The new management system, which has been replicated in police departments and public agencies across the country, was designed to focus the entire department on a tangible outcome and to hold every officer accountable, live and in person, when any hint of rising crime occurred on their beats.

And it all happened in the room that would be named in Jack Maple's honor. The CompStat Center has towering ceilings with large monitors attached to all four walls. At one end is a row of tables with microphones reserved for the leaders of the police department, allowing them to see the entire room. Facing them, about forty feet away, is a single podium where officers have stood for years, on their own, faced their superiors, and attempted to explain why crime was rising or falling in the section of the city under their watch.

I visited the CompStat Center on the morning of April 6, 2016, after waiting for fifteen minutes in a security line that formed well outside the visitor's entrance at One Police Plaza. The large group of community leaders, government officials, and residents waiting in line were not there for a traditional CompStat meeting held by the NYPD. We were there for the first meeting of NeighborhoodStat.

NeighborhoodStat was dreamed up by Elizabeth Glazer, the director of the Mayor's Office of Criminal Justice. She arrived in the de Blasio administration in the summer of 2014, the same summer that Eric Garner was killed by the NYPD, protests against police brutality took place across the city, and the police union feuded publicly with the mayor. Although the protests and political drama dominated the headlines that summer, the more troubling development was a sharp spike in shootings that had taken place in a small number of housing developments around the city, places that remained extremely violent even as most of the city had become historically safe.

To respond to the spike in violence, Glazer and Mayor de Blasio developed the Mayor's Action Plan for Neighborhood Safety, or MAP. The MAP initiative consisted of a set of investments target-ing fifteen of the most violent housing developments in the city. Community centers stayed open later, lighting and security cam-eras were installed, the number of slots available for the youth summer employment program was increased, and meetings were planned to allow community residents the chance to develop and implement new ideas to keep their buildings safe.[3]

But NeighborhoodStat was the piece of the MAP initiative that excited Glazer the most. Her vision built on the one sketched out by Jack Maple more than twenty years earlier, with one major difference. When Maple drew up CompStat, New York City was one of the most dangerous places in the country. When Glazer put together NeighborhoodStat, crime in New York was at a historic low point. Her vision was not focused entirely on crime, as Maple's was. Her vision was focused on building stronger neighborhoods.

Glazer envisioned a system that would enable an entire com-munity to focus on the precise times and places where a broad range of community problems arose, including trash in public spaces, broken lights, truant kids, homeless people in need, and crews of drug dealers, as well as assaults, rapes, shootings, and other crimes. She envisioned a system that would change the way community resources were spent, one that would hold accountable public agencies like the department of sanitation and the New York City Housing Authority, as well as homelessness prevention agencies, tenants' associations, building managers, antiviolence organizations, police officers, and residents. The challenge addressed in NeighborhoodStat would be not only to deal with the problem of crime but also to find solutions to specific problems that weakened the entire community. And it would start by bringing every key actor within the community together in the room dedicated to Jack Maple.

On that morning in April 2016, Glazer's vision came to fruition. Roughly two hundred people packed into the CompStat Center for the first meeting of NeighborhoodStat, which focused on several housing developments in Brooklyn: Brownsville and Van Dyke, Red Hook, Boulevard, and Ingersoll Houses.

One by one the key representatives from each development came to the podium and answered questions about the state of the building and the neighborhood, while everyone in the room looked at maps showing statistics about each of the developments on the monitors overhead. A building manager was grilled about lobby doors that were frequently left open and unsecured, representatives from the sanitation department were asked about a pile of bulk trash that had grown outside one of the buildings, local service providers were asked what they were doing to understand the problem of domestic violence, and the president of a tenant association was asked why so few young people from her building had applied for summer jobs through the city.

There were uncomfortable moments when leaders of public

agencies had no answers for the pointed questions directed at them. But if they didn't have an answer, they were given action steps to move toward a solution, and they were told to report back.

And in the midst of the discussions of sanitation, summer jobs, and lobby doors, a group of officers from the NYPD emerged as central figures in each community. The officers had been handpicked to become a new kind of cop, called neighborhood coordination officers (NCOs). The NCOs were part of the police department's ambitious plan—which, it should be said, was mandated by a court order—to end the aggressive policing that had targeted poor communities of color, and to create stronger ties between residents in disadvantaged neighborhoods and the police. The task of the NCOs was not to make arrests but to get to know every person within the neighborhood and to understand the problems of the community from the inside out. Officers for the program were selected carefully, and those who spoke at the NeighborhoodStat meetings were personable, funny, and exhibited a genuine concern for the neighborhood and its residents.

And they knew their neighborhoods intimately. When one of the NCOs in the Red Hook complex was asked about violence, he listed three "crews" of young men that had been actively involved in violent activity within the developments. These three crews had been responsible for much of the violence around Red Hook in previous years, but to that point in 2016 they had worked out a tenuous peace. As he finished his question and answer session, the officer stopped and said that if a new beef began, he would need everyone's help in the community to make sure it didn't erupt into violence. Those sitting in the section of the room reserved for the representatives of Red Hook, who had greeted the officer at the beginning of the meeting with hugs and handshakes and smiles, nodded in agreement.

The initial meeting of NeighborhoodStat was overcrowded and

dragged beyond the allotted schedule. But as I left, I watched a resident seek out a public official from the department of sanitation to ask her what to do about an unkempt area around her complex. I saw a building manager assuring the leader of a tenant organization that he would find out why one of the doors on her building wasn't secured. And I saw the director of an antiviolence organization, a man who spoke up to express the anger felt by young men throughout the city, begin a conversation with an NCO from the same community.

Jack Maple's vision was still as powerful as it was when he first wrote it down on the famous napkin at Elaine's, but it had been revised. I walked out of the CompStat Center convinced that NeighborhoodStat should be the next model of policing in the United States.

_____

The last model of policing in New York City began with an essay titled "Broken Windows," perhaps the most influential piece of writing on American law enforcement in the past century.[4] The essay, which appeared in the *Atlantic Monthly* in 1982, was written by George Kelling and James Q. Wilson, both researchers who had spent a great deal of time studying and thinking about crime, policing, and how to make communities safer. Kelling in particular had taken part in several evaluations of policing tactics and strategies that were funded by the Police Foundation, which seeks to improve policing through experimentation and research. One of these evaluations was conducted in Newark, New Jersey.

The Newark "foot patrol" experiment was designed to assess whether taking officers out of patrol cars and asking them to patrol on foot would improve their capacity to control crime. Judging by the crime rate, the experiment didn't work. In the sections of the city where officers were switched to foot patrol, rates of criminal activity did not drop at all. What did change, however, were residents' perceptions of their neighborhoods. In the places where officers walked the streets, residents were less afraid of crime, felt better about the police, and thought their neighborhoods were getting safer even if the official crime rate suggested otherwise. Kelling walked alongside the officers on foot patrol to try to understand what officers were doing to make people feel more comfortable. "What foot-patrol officers did," he and Wilson concluded, "was to elevate, to the extent they could, the level of public order in these neighborhoods."

Kelling and Wilson argued that officers on foot patrol were able to get a feel for the informal rules that governed behavior in the community. Officers were able to understand who were the regulars and who were the strangers, what types of behaviors were tolerated and what types were discouraged, when was it necessary to let someone hang out and when was it necessary to move someone along. Maintaining order, according to the authors, had always been the most important function of the police. Sometime around the 1970s, however, the role of the police had become distorted, and this crucial element of policing was forgotten. Asking officers to patrol their beats by foot gave them the capacity to enforce a commonly understood set of norms, a local social order.

Kelling and Wilson then went further. Extending beyond the evidence from Newark, they put forth a theory of what happens when social order breaks down, and when signs of disorder begin to emerge. Their ideas came to be known as broken windows theory:

> A piece of property is abandoned, weeds grow up, a window is smashed. Adults stop scolding rowdy children; the children, emboldened, become more rowdy. Families move out, unattached adults move in. Teenagers gather in front of the corner store. The merchant asks them to move; they refuse. Fights occur. Litter accumulates. People start drinking in front

of the grocery; in time, an inebriate slumps to the sidewalk and is allowed to sleep it off. Pedestrians are approached by panhandlers.

At this point it is not inevitable that serious crime will flourish or violent attacks on strangers will occur. But many residents will think that crime, especially violent crime, is on the rise, and they will modify their behavior accordingly. They will use the streets less often, and when on the streets will stay apart from their fellows, moving with averted eyes, silent lips, and hurried steps. "Don't get involved." . . .

Such an area is vulnerable to criminal invasion. Though it is not inevitable, it is more likely that here, rather than in places where people are confident they can regulate public behavior by informal controls, drugs will change hands, prostitutes will solicit, and cars will be stripped. That the drunks will be robbed by boys who do it as a lark, and the prostitutes' customers will be robbed by men who do it purposefully and perhaps violently. That muggings will occur.

Their theory connecting small signs of disorder to violence and urban decline was anecdotal and speculative. Even so, it would change policing for the next several decades. One of the strongest advocates of broken windows theory was William Bratton, who in 1990 became chief of the New York City Transit Police and began to put Kelling and Wilson's ideas into action. Focusing on the process leading from small signs of disorder to major cycles of crime, he and his police force targeted even the most minor of violations. "Fare evasion and graffiti would no longer be considered too petty to address," Bratton wrote later. "In fact, we'd focus on them as vigorously as serious crimes like robberies, if not more so. Why? Because serious crime was more likely to occur in a lawless environment."[5]

Over time, the subway cars became free of graffiti, panhandlers became less aggressive, and the transit system became cleaner and safer.[6] Bratton left the Transit Police for a brief stint in Boston, then was brought back as commissioner of the New York Police Department in 1994. Alongside Mayor Rudy Guiliani, Bratton took broken windows policing to a new level. Motivated by the idea of cracking down on the "small stuff," the NYPD arrested New Yorkers for minor crimes at an accelerating rate. Crime was declining, yet the number of arrests for misdemeanors (minor crimes like jumping a subway turnstile or carrying small amounts of marijuana) more than doubled in New York City from 1990 to 2010, rising from fewer than 120,000 arrests to roughly 250,000. In 1993, the year before Bratton took over the police department, there were fewer than 1,500 arrests across the city for marijuana possession. In 2000, the NYPD made more than 50,000 arrests for the same crime.

Lower-level criminal courts in New York City became flooded with minor offenders. The result, according to Yale Law professor Issa Kohler-Hausmann, was a fundamental shift in the function of the criminal justice system.[7] Lower-level courts, instead of adjudicating guilt or punishment, were being used to "manage" minor offenders in the hope of keeping them under surveillance and occupied long enough to prevent more serious crimes. The logic of this approach was endorsed explicitly by Bratton himself: "A subway criminal arrested for a misdemeanor rather than a felony wouldn't be going to prison, but he wouldn't be victimizing anyone for a while, either."[8]

In New York City, the idea of "fixing broken windows" evolved into the practice of arresting every potential troublemaker in sight. Hundreds of thousands of New Yorkers were arrested for minor offenses, and over time hundreds of thousands more were stopped and questioned on the street. The rise in "reasonable suspicion" stops of New York City residents represented an advanced stage in the NYPD's attempt to dominate public spaces. Under

Mayor Michael Bloomberg and Police Commissioner Ray Kelly, the number of police stops rose from fewer than 100,000 to almost 700,000. And most of this activity was concentrated in the city's poorest, most segregated communities.

The model of policing developed in New York was replicated across the country.[9] Since 1990, as crime declined nationally, the arrest rate for major crimes like burglary, motor vehicle theft, robbery, aggravated assault, and murder plummeted as well.[10] Over the same period, the rate of arrests for possession of marijuana, a minor crime that is more closely tied to policing practices than to criminal activity, almost tripled.[11] The rise of drug arrests is a hallmark of the dominant model of policing in use for the past twenty years. Under this model, police took over public spaces and became a constant, sometimes menacing presence in low-income communities of color. Arrests and stops were the metrics of police success, and incidents of police violence, excessive force, or brutality were the by-products.

This model of city policing has stood firm for most of the past two decades. But in the NYPD and many police departments elsewhere, there are strong signs that it is coming to an end. In 2013 a federal judge found the NYPD's racially imbalanced use of stop, question, and frisk to be unconstitutional. Mayor de Blasio campaigned on a platform to end the use of stop, question, and frisk as a central strategy of policing and brought William Bratton back to New York to implement a new model of policing for a safer time. The same police commissioner who had made broken windows policing famous used his final tour of duty to change the culture of the NYPD. Misdemeanor arrests declined during Bratton's second stint as commissioner, which ended in 2016, and the number of "reasonable suspicion" stops of citizens by police officers dropped by 93 percent from its peak of 685,000 stops in 2011 to just over 46,000 in 2014.[12]

In his latest assignment in New York, Commissioner Bratton

committed to a new version of broken windows policing that limits the need for aggressive enforcement. "We expect to see nearly a million fewer enforcement contacts like arrests, summonses, and reasonable-suspicion stops when compared to their respective historic highs," he wrote. "The diminished need to use enforcement tools for every problem is in keeping with one of the most salient observations that Kelling and Wilson made about Broken Windows: 'The essence of the police role in maintaining order is to reinforce the informal control mechanisms of the community itself.'"[13]

These words are meaningful, even if they do not align with the vision of "broken windows" that Bratton himself put into place in New York City. His revised vision, however, may well be a guide to what policing can become after the era of violence.

How do we turn this vision into reality? The first step is to make sure that the efforts of police officers and their supervisors are aligned to achieve a goal that is broader than reducing crime. What made CompStat such a successful management tool was that the entire system was organized around a single outcome that was clear to everyone who entered the cavernous room named after Jack Maple: the crime rate. Incidents of major criminal activity were the sole focus of the tense forums that occurred every other week in the CompStat Center, and this focus led to undeniable improvements in the department's efficiency and effectiveness. But it is now clear that this singular focus on criminal incidents creates perverse incentives for police officers, encouraging them to take whatever steps necessary to show a drop in crime, while ignoring the perceptions of the community they were hired to serve.

Changing the behavior, tactics, and management of police officers requires changing the set of outcomes that police activity is organized to achieve. Police departments and the officers within them should be evaluated not only by the rate of crime or violence in a neighborhood or city but also through regularly collected surveys of residents' victimization, fear of crime, satisfaction with their community, and satisfaction with the police. An initial step in the effort to reform policing is to undertake a large-scale data collection project, one that moves beyond data on criminal complaints and arrests to include sensor data on shootings, administrative data on 911 calls and hospital admissions, and new data on community sentiment. If police officers are to play a new role in urban neighborhoods, they must have continuous data from every major city to assess how community conditions are changing. And that information must be used, in forums like NeighborhoodStat, to guide community-wide planning that includes the police.

A second, more challenging task is to reorient policing toward the goal of rebuilding trust between police and the communities they serve. In March 2015, President Obama's Task Force on 21st Century Policing put forth a document with compelling recommendations about how police departments can begin to rebuild trust and legitimacy.[14] The task force recommended that police departments provide training to make officers aware of how implicit racial bias influences the perceptions and behaviors of everyone, including police officers, as they interact with people of color; that departments take conscious steps to continuously incorporate community discussion and input into their procedures on a regular basis; that they focus on transparency in responding to high-profile incidents involving potential misconduct of officers; and that they seek out opportunities for positive, nonenforcement interactions between officers and residents. The list, which reflects a thoughtful, smart vision of a new form of policing, goes well beyond these suggestions to include fifty-nine total recommendations.

The real challenge lies in executing these recommendations. For the past few decades, a very different vision of policing has been carried out in America's neighborhoods. Officers who have been taught to dominate public spaces are now being taught to take a different approach, and it is naïve to think that the adaptation will be simple or quick. Communities that have seen the police as a menacing, occupying force will not be convinced to accept the new role of the police without suspicion. And each video showing an officer abusing, humiliating, or killing a citizen on the streets of urban America makes it more difficult to imagine the police as a force for stability and peace within urban communities.

If police officers are to become a different kind of urban guardian, they will need assistance. Funding is necessary to implement new training and to allow departments to hire new officers whose role is not to enforce the law but rather to build relationships with community residents. Community policing is an old idea that has come to mean many different things to different people—but the neighborhood coordination officers in New York City, whose explicit job description is to build stronger relationships between officers and residents, provide a model for what the next stage of neighborhood policing should look like.

The last step is to acknowledge the role that police have played in reducing violence, and to double down on proven methods of controlling violent crime without targeting entire communities. One of the most consistent findings about crime and violence is that a large share of criminal activity happens in a small number of places. A study of the precise street segments and intersections where crime occurs in Boston found that about 8 percent of all such "micro-places" account for about two-thirds of all street robberies.[15] Policing focused on "hot places" relies on close collaboration between community residents and police to identify the precise locations where, and times when, problems are likely to arise. Police resources and oversight are then directed toward those locations, and collaborative plans are made to address long-term problems like poor lighting, gang activity, graffiti, or vacant properties.[16] This approach, which falls under the umbrella of problem-oriented policing, rests on some of the strongest empirical evidence of effectiveness that has ever been generated on police tactics and strategy.

Criminal activity is not only concentrated in a small number of hot spots, it is carried out by a tiny group of people who are linked together in a tight network of victims and offenders. The sociologists Andrew Papachristos, Chris Wildeman, and Elizabeth Roberto analyzed data on gun violence in Chicago and found that more than 70 percent of all nonfatal gunshot victims were part of a violent network of individuals that made up just 6 percent of the community population.[17] Another study found that 40 percent of all firearm homicides occurred within a network containing just 4 percent of the population.[18] Living within a high-crime neighborhood of Chicago does not automatically mean that young people are at high risk of becoming involved with violence. Being a part of the narrow network of young people who are linked together by criminal activity, however, raises the odds of becoming a gunshot victim exponentially.

Engaging the group of people within a community who are at greatest risk of victimization has become one of the most effective methods of interrupting exchanges of violent activity that account for a large share of gun violence. This engagement can happen by training "interrupters" to reach out to young people in the aftermath of violence, before they take action to reciprocate.[19] It can happen by delivering a clear message to leaders of gangs or crews telling them that their entire network will be targeted if any member engages in gun violence.[20] And it can happen through call-in meetings, where individuals who are enmeshed within the criminal justice system are given a warning and an offer. The warning is unflinching: *If you continue to engage in firearm violence, you will face serious, uncompromising prosecution.* But the offer must be equally sincere: *If you choose a different path, you will be supported with all resources and assistance that the community and the state can muster.*[21]

Enforcement and outreach that are focused on hot spots and vulnerable people allow for a shift in the way the police interact with residents in high-crime neighborhoods. Instead of subjecting an entire community to intensive surveillance under a veil of suspicion, it is possible to target the very small number of places where an overwhelming share of violence occurs, and to focus resources on solving the problems in those places. It is possible to reach out to the people who are most likely to be victims and offer them resources that allow them to remain safe.

Police departments around the country have already implemented some of these ideas. The City of Fresno's police department implemented a survey to monitor residents' perceptions of, and attitudes toward, the police.[22] Chicago created a task force calling for an overhaul of the police department's tactics and culture, and it undertook a massive effort to train its officers in the principles of procedural justice.[23] The Washington State Criminal Justice Training Commission overhauled its law enforcement training curriculum: Officers who used to be required to stand silent and salute their instructors now have to initiate a conversation every time they cross paths, while addressing them with respect and a smile.[24] In Los Angeles, officers have begun training on how to de-escalate conflict, how to talk to residents respectfully, and when it's appropriate to curse and when it's not.[25] In a growing number of departments across the country, officers are being asked to change their role, to transform from warriors into guardians.[26]

All the best evidence indicates that police will be essential to

any effort to reduce violence. But even as we ask police departments to change the way they interact with communities, we
must recognize the limits of any agenda for neighborhood change
that relies primarily on reforms within police departments. For
the past two decades, law enforcement has been asked to take
over public spaces, to deal with the wide range of social problems
that become visible on city streets, and to control crime. Now that
police officers are being asked to step back from this role, it is
imperative that others step up and play a larger role in overseeing
urban communities. If there are no longer warriors on the street,
there must be a larger supply of guardians.

9

THE NEXT URBAN
GUARDIANS

The East Lake Golf Club is located about five miles east of downtown Atlanta.[1] The course has a grand history, built in 1908 and redesigned in 1913 by Donald Ross, one of the most prominent twentieth-century course architects. East Lake was the home course of golf legend Bobby Jones, who is said to have played his first and his last rounds of golf there. In 1963 the course hosted the Ryder Cup, a biennial tournament that pitted the best American golfers against the best British golfers in the world's most prominent international golf competition. Arnold Palmer was the captain of the winning American team in what may have been the greatest moment in the course's storied history.

Over the twenty years or so following that victory, however, the East Lake Golf Club and the community surrounding it began to change rapidly. At the time of the 1960 census, almost all of Atlanta's black population lived west of the city's downtown, and the neighborhoods around East Lake were just about entirely white. In the following decade, these neighborhoods experienced a swift, sudden racial turnover. The growing black population spread into the communities east of downtown, while the white population fled the prospect of integrated neighborhoods by moving northward or farther east. The neighborhoods immediately surrounding the golf club transitioned from almost completely white to predominantly black. By 1970 the neighborhood just north of the clubhouse had changed from 99 percent white to 90 percent black.

As the white population fled the adjacent neighborhoods, the golf community abandoned East Lake. The Atlanta Athletic Club, which owned the club, sold one of the site's two courses to real estate developers and moved to a site well north of the city, in Duluth, Georgia. A group of the club's members came together to buy the original clubhouse and the main course, but the course fell into disrepair over time.

The neighborhood surrounding the course fell apart as well. In 1970 a public housing project was built on the site of the second course and named East Lake Meadows. Like many public housing projects across the country, East Lake Meadows quickly deteriorated as federal funding for public housing was slashed. Apartments were not maintained, trash was not collected, and public spaces were taken over by gangs and drug distribution.

The decline of East Lake was replicated all over the United States as urban neighborhoods lost middle-class residents, and the government disinvested in central city neighborhoods that were struggling with large-scale job losses and growing fiscal challenges. What happened there is what happens wherever community institutions are not supported, housing is not maintained, and the basic investments in infrastructure, social services, and public institutions that most communities take for granted are withdrawn. The fall of East Lake, and the historic golf club located within it, is what happens to any place that is abandoned.

But the revitalization of the community, and the return to glory of the East Lake Golf Club, is a story about what can happen to a place when it is reclaimed. The reclamation began with Tom Cousins, a philanthropist who made his fortune in Atlanta real estate, building some of the city's most visible skyscrapers. Cousins, an avid sports fan, owned franchises in professional hockey, soccer, and basketball during his career. He purchased the NBA's St. Louis Hawks in 1968 and moved the team to Atlanta, where they remain to this day. Likely some combination of his devotion to Atlanta and his passion for sports drew him to East Lake. What he found there, at the borders of Atlanta's oldest golf course, shocked him. "It was almost beyond description," Cousins told an interviewer, describing the housing project that stood just a short distance from the tee box of the historic golf course's fourth hole: "Trash everywhere, windows broken out of the apartments, crime was rampant, no attempt to hide the drug dealing."[2]

Cousins developed an ambitious plan for the transformation of East Lake, seeking out partnerships with the mayor, the housing authority, and community leaders to make it happen. He established the East Lake Foundation to serve as a community institution around which the transformation of the neighborhood could be planned and implemented. He purchased the East Lake Golf Club, which was on the verge of bankruptcy, and imagined how a poor, mostly black community might be able to benefit from its proximity to an elite, exclusive, and historic golf course.

In the years that followed, both the golf course and the surrounding community began to transform. Cousins recruited one hundred colleagues in the business community to join the new East Lake Golf Club, asking each of them to make a $250,000 donation to the foundation. The main course was redesigned and became the home of a major PGA tournament. A second, public course was built specifically for golf instruction and physical education for young people in East Lake and throughout the city. A large share of the proceeds from the East Lake Golf Club went straight to the East Lake Foundation, which has provided a consistent source of funding and support for the neighborhood for the past twenty years.

As the golf club came back to life, the community was slowly rebuilt. East Lake Meadows, the notorious public housing project, was torn down as part of a larger effort to transform public housing in Atlanta led by the CEO of the housing authority at the time, Renee Glover. Glover's leadership and her willingness to partner with Cousins, the residents of East Lake Meadows, and others were essential to this effort. The master planning process with the residents of East Lake Meadows, who were led by their longtime tenants association president Eva Davis, took more than two years and was often difficult and controversial. But the key partners in the planning process developed trust with the residents of East Lake Meadows, who voted to build a new development rather than try to renovate the existing buildings. The stakeholders worked together to replace the housing project with over five hundred units of attractive mixed-income housing in a development named the Villages of East Lake. A high-quality charter school, Atlanta's first, was established to serve the community's students, generating dramatic improvement in academic performance. The community now features a YMCA, two early childhood education centers, a major grocery store, two banks, and other retail businesses.

In the time since Tom Cousins formed the East Lake Foundation, the community has transformed. Atlanta as a whole has experienced a sharp decline in violence, and serious violent crime has all but disappeared in East Lake. In 1992 alone, 221 violent crimes—aggravated assaults, robberies, and homicides—were reported in or around the East Lake Meadows housing project. Fifteen years later, in 2007, there were just 10 violent crimes in the new mixed-income housing development located on the same site.[3]

By any possible standard, the East Lake of the 1990s was a terrible, tragic place to raise a child. The East Lake of the present, on the other hand, is a great place to raise a child. Parents can send their children to early learning centers that are safe and nurturing settings, and to schools that provide high-quality instruction and set high expectations. Children raised in East Lake have somewhere safe to go after school, they have green space on which to play, and they can walk through the school hallways and neighborhood streets without worrying about the constant threat of violence.

The story of East Lake, Atlanta, does not provide a simple template for community transformation. There was controversy along the way, and some of the original residents had their lives uprooted against their will. Urban policy makers and advocates might object to the idea of tearing down public housing, building charter schools, or planning the redevelopment of a neighborhood around a golf course. But the central lesson from East Lake is not about a white philanthropist, an exclusive golf course, the demolition of public housing, or the establishment of charter schools. The lesson is that community change can be sustained only if it is planned and carried out by a well-run, well-resourced organization led by people who make a long-term commitment to the community and all its residents. When a process of change is planned around a strong, stable organization, like the East Lake Foundation, community transformation becomes possible.

Tom Cousins built on his experience in Atlanta to develop a model that he is trying to replicate in other cities. He has teamed with philanthropists like Warren Buffett, and dynamic leaders like former Atlanta mayor Shirley Franklin, to build a national organization, Purpose Built Communities, which is trying to take the example of East Lake to scale.

Purpose Built Communities is working directly with sixteen communities scattered across the country and is beginning planning with many more. Its model focuses on the development of mixed-income housing, a "cradle to college education pipeline" designed to provide high-quality learning environments from birth to college graduation, and "community wellness," which encompasses health, jobs, and safety. In truth, none of this is all that innovative or unique. Hundreds of community groups have tried to build housing, improve schools, and improve community health, with varying degrees of success. What is unique about the Purpose Built model is the establishment of a single organization responsible for designing a plan for the transformation of a community, then implementing and overseeing it. Within the Purpose Built network, this organization is referred to as the "community quarterback."

The community quarterback is an institution that makes a long-term commitment to the community. Once established, it must have sufficient resources and support to ensure that when times are tough or budgets are tight, it will continue to push forward the vision of change.

For decades, planners and advocates have argued that successful community development has to be organized around an "anchor institution," some large, stable institution with resources and stakeholders behind it. The idea of the community quarterback is different. It has a mission to oversee public spaces, to take care of everyone within them, and to make sure the neighborhood does not begin to fall apart. The community quarterback, in whatever form it takes, looks beyond the people who walk through its doors, and looks out over the community as a whole.

For anyone focused on building strong communities, a first step is to tour every single neighborhood within a city and ask a straightforward set of questions to anyone who will answer:

Who runs this street? Who looks out for the kids on this block? To whom can you turn when you need help, when there is a problem, when someone close to you is in danger? When you walk down the street as the sun goes down, who is in charge of that space?

The answer may be a group of longtime residents, the police, the pastor of a church, or the director of a youth organization. In some places there may not be anyone who looks out over the street, and in others it might be a group of teenagers who spend their time outside, unsupervised. These are often the streets where older residents retreat inside their homes, where children are told to play inside, where violence can flourish. These are the streets that have to be identified in every American city, the places where a community quarterback is essential.

The specific tasks of the community quarterback will vary from neighborhood to neighborhood. In places where residents are returning from prison, the institution must provide the resources required for their successful transition back into the community. In neighborhoods where crime is falling and housing prices are soaring, the community quarterback can take the lead in developing affordable housing or establishing community land trusts, which remove housing from the private market and preserve it, at an affordable price, for longtime residents. And in every neighborhood struggling with violence, the institution must provide safe, nurturing spaces for parents and their children.

Purpose Built Communities, which has created community quarterbacks from scratch, has developed the most ambitious model. Other models are out there, however. In many cities, community schools have been formed with the explicit goal of making the school building a resource used by everyone within a neighborhood rather than only the children enrolled.[4] Other community-minded organizations operate out of a single home. Community Renewal International is a faith-based organization that has set out to transform distressed neighborhoods by providing simple spaces from which to build community life.[5] The organization's "friendship houses" and "haven houses" are homes where community coordinators and volunteers live with their families. The houses serve as a hub for the neighborhood, offering social services, courses, and chances for neighbors to come together in a welcoming environment.

In the Dudley Triangle of Roxbury, Boston, the process of change began when residents were asked to come together to envision the type of neighborhood in which they wanted to live. They imagined being able to walk freely through the streets of their community and finding businesses nearby, churches, shops, good schools, and safe public spaces where neighbors could interact with each other. They sought to change their neighborhood from a dangerous, run-down, anonymous set of streets into an urban village, where the streets were clean and safe, where people knew their neighbors and looked out for each other.[6]

The Dudley Street Neighborhood Initiative (DSNI) began to turn this vision into reality. The organization formed a land trust and designed and built affordable homes for community residents. Young people from the neighborhood were given jobs in the community gardens and a greenhouse that the organization built, raising produce that was eaten by families in the neighborhood, donated to local shelters, and sold to urban farmers' markets. The DSNI waged campaigns to clean up abandoned lots, build new community centers, and stop outsiders from dumping trash on the streets. And the neighborhood slowly changed, through hours upon hours of time spent deliberating in community meetings, knocking on doors to gather support, navigating the city's bureaucracy, raising funds, and cultivating engagement and buy-in from all residents. "We're re-creating our neighborhood into the kind of village we want it to be," said Julio Henriquez, a DSNI board member.

Over time their work paid off. Residents got to know each other and took ownership over the streets of their neighborhood. Violence fell, and the feel of the neighborhood shifted. Robert Putnam, a political scientist at Harvard who has documented the erosion of American community life, took an interest and talked to community leaders about the work being done in the Dudley Triangle. He asked "Gino" Teixeira, the owner of the Ideal Sub Shop, how the neighborhood had changed over time. When Teixeira opened up his shop in the mid-1980s, he said, the neighborhood was a prototypical example of urban blight. "There was trash all over the place . . . abandoned cars, refrigerators, washing machines, you name it," Teixeira told Putnam and his colleagues. "And the drug dealers used to sell drugs right in front of the store, across the street, all over the place. . . . People used to be afraid to talk with each other." Almost twenty years later, his sub shop brims with activity. "This place is always full. . . . People aren't afraid to come in anymore."

Institutions like the Dudley Street Neighborhood Initiative can be found in many U.S. communities, but they are missing in others. Identifying the neighborhoods that lack a community quarterback is not simple, and generating the resources to create one in every community is not cheap. But the urban history of the 1970s through the 1990s demonstrates what happens when core community institutions wither away. If we want to avoid reliving that period of urban history, a first step is to ensure that a single organization is responsible for overseeing every low-income community across the country.

———

The second step, inspired by the words of urbanist Jane Jacobs, is to engage the people who have the greatest capacity to control violence. In a famous passage from her classic book *The Death and Life of Great American Cities,* Jacobs provided a perspective on urban crime, violence, and social order that is often forgotten: "The first thing to understand is that the public peace of cities is not kept primarily by the police, necessary as the police are. It is kept primarily by an intricate, almost unconscious, network of voluntary controls and standards among the people themselves, and enforced by the people themselves."[7]

Jacobs developed her theory about the foundations of social order within the city by watching urban life of the late 1950s unfold outside her apartment in the West Village in Manhattan. She saw how neighbors kept track of children, how storekeepers watched over sidewalks, and how complete strangers easily moved into and out of everyday street life on her block. The ideas in her book expanded discussions of public safety beyond the police, and beyond the kinds of organizations that I have highlighted as essential to safe communities. She focused on the capacity of people to regulate behavior in public space, and her ideas have now been confirmed, and refined, by decades of social science.

Robert Sampson, an urban sociologist and criminologist at Harvard, has spent much of his career gathering evidence and refining theories on how urban communities function, and on how social order emerges and erodes. To understand why violence arises in some communities and not others, he argues, it is not enough to know a community's level of poverty. It is essential to understand how residents think about each other and about their common environment, to consider the implicit understandings that community members share, and to gauge the level of collective commitment to public space. His research captures these dimensions of community life by asking residents about the types of activities that are considered acceptable in public spaces; about their willingness to intervene when a group of youths are fighting or a child is skipping school; about the level of trust among residents;

and about their willingness to organize when there is a threat to the neighborhood, like a proposal to shut down a community center or a fire station.[8] These forms of social cohesion, trust, and shared commitment to the community are the core elements of what Sampson refers to as "collective efficacy."

In several major research projects that have taken decades to carry out, Sampson and many collaborators have uncovered a remarkably consistent pattern in urban neighborhoods. Communities with high levels of collective efficacy, whether they are in Chicago or Stockholm, tend to have low levels of violence.[9] When social cohesion and trust within a community break down, violence tends to emerge. This connection helps explain why violent crime is more likely in neighborhoods where poverty is concentrated. It is not simply that poverty itself leads to areas of violent crime, but rather that concentrated poverty tends to slowly tear apart the social fabric of neighborhoods. In very poor neighborhoods, residents are more likely to retreat from public life and avoid their neighbors, and public spaces are more likely to be taken over by the threat of violence.

How, then, can the social fabric of a community be woven back together? How can residents begin to retake public space?

In 1998, the economists Philip Cook and Jens Ludwig conducted a survey in which they asked Americans how much they would pay in additional taxes to support a social program that was proven to be effective in reducing gun violence.[10] They began by asking respondents whether they would be willing to pay anywhere from $50 to $200 for such a program. Depending on the response, the figure was then doubled or halved to assess whether a higher or lower figure changed the answer.

The results offer a hint of the value that Americans attach to public safety. The average American was willing to pay $239 in extra taxes for a program that would reduce gun violence by 30 percent. Three out of four expressed a willingness to pay at least $50 in additional taxes to support the program. On the basis of these estimates, Cook and Ludwig were able to calculate the total "social" costs of gun violence, as reflected by how much Americans were willing to pay to reduce it. In 1998 the social costs of gun violence came to about $80 billion per year. By the same measure, every single shooting that could be prevented was worth over $1 million to Americans.[11]

Cook and Ludwig's calculations tell us just how much social value is created by any successful effort to prevent or reduce violence, but they also force us to consider a more complicated set of issues: Who bears the costs of those efforts? And who experiences the benefits?

Clearly, residents of violent neighborhoods benefit the most from living in stronger, safer communities. In their classic book on urban development, *Urban Fortunes,* John Logan and Harvey Molotch called this "use value": the value of a place as derived by the people who spend their daily lives there; the value of a place as it exists outside a market of exchange.[12]

Programs designed to engage residents in projects to transform their own neighborhoods are always described in terms of their potential impact on use values. Yet the benefits of any collective effort designed to transform a neighborhood extend well beyond that neighborhood's residents. Community transformation creates not just better places to live but also what Logan and Molotch call "exchange value," the value attached to a property or a place as it exists on the market. When community residents come together to fight crime or to clean up a park, property owners and local businesses benefit as the exchange value of their investment rises.[13] The city benefits as well, because declining crime leads to rising property taxes, an influx of residents and investment, and savings in public expenditures.[14] A conservative estimate of the direct costs to city and state governments for each violent crime that occurs is $10,000.[15] This figure includes the costs of paying the police and fire departments, prosecuting defendants in the judicial system, and housing and monitoring all individuals who enter the corrections system. It means that if residents of a community came together and found a way to prevent just ten serious assaults in a year, they would save taxpayers roughly $100,000. But the indirect, "social" cost of violent crime is truly staggering: Based on figures from Cook and Ludwig, preventing those same ten serious violent crimes would be worth millions of dollars to the American public.

Government officials, nonprofit community groups, and academics consistently ask residents of violent communities to work together to reduce violence, in the firm belief that they have tremendous untapped capacity to prevent violent crime. Programs relying on community engagement tend to draw in a small number of residents with a remarkable commitment to the neighborhood, people who work tirelessly for the collective good. These programs may generate positive changes and bring residents together for feel-good events designed to strengthen the community—but over time, programs that rely on residents' time and effort tend to run out of steam, and we wonder why.[16]

Maybe the answer is obvious: (1) organizing to confront violence takes lots of time and effort; (2) this time and effort usually is not compensated; and (3) much of the value derived from the effort goes to people outside the community. The solution may be equally obvious: If residents have the greatest capacity to oversee public spaces in their own neighborhoods, then perhaps it is time to fully acknowledge the value that they generate when they work to control violence. If in some communities relationships between law enforcement and residents are so damaged that the police are ineffective, then perhaps it is time to develop alternative, complementary approaches to generating informal social control. Perhaps it is time to create a new entity to "protect and serve" residents, one that is created from the community, and one that is compensated for performing the enormously valuable work of keeping the city safe.

In parts of England and Wales, they are called community wardens. In France they are social mediation agents, in Belgium they are prevention and security agents, and in South Africa they are community peace workers.[17] But perhaps the best example comes from Perth, in Western Australia, where the Nyoongar Patrol can be found each night walking city streets, looking out for people in need of assistance, and doing whatever they can to keep the streets safe.

The Nyoongar are an Aboriginal people located in the south and west parts of the country, and like other Aboriginal groups, they have suffered unimaginable violence, brutality, injustice, and humiliation over the course of the past two hundred years at the hands of the Australian government and its police forces. The plight of Aboriginals in the Australian criminal justice system drew national attention in the 1980s, after a series of disturbing incidents in which Aboriginal people died while in the custody of police or in jail. A royal commission established to investigate Aboriginal deaths in the prison system found no evidence that prison staff intentionally killed any of the ninety-nine people who died while in custody throughout the 1980s, but it did find many deaths that were explained by harsh prison conditions or general neglect among prison staff.[18] The report's authors proposed a wide range of reforms to improve conditions and standardize protocols for care in the prison system, but they also made a broader point: Aboriginals were no more likely to die in custody than white Australians. The alarming number of deaths while in custody could not be explained by the mistreatment of Aboriginals once they were behind bars; rather, it was explained by the overrepresentation of Aboriginals in prison.

The authors concluded that the only way to end the injustice experienced by Aboriginals in custody was to change the way police interact with Aboriginal people and to reduce their contact with the criminal justice system. They put forth hundreds of recommendations designed to confront the multiple disadvantages faced by the Aboriginal population and to begin a "process of reconciliation." And they proposed a new approach to policing Aboriginal communities, one that was led by members of the community itself.

The royal commission's report called for government funding to support programs like the Julalikari Night Patrol, which was established in the Northern Territory as a novel form of community policing. The goal of the night patrol was to allow local leaders to look after their own people and make sure they were safe, to establish a buffer between Aboriginal people and the police, to provide help and get community members off the streets before they were at risk of being arrested. "Aboriginal patrols operate on the basis of *cultural* authority which they derive from their embedded position within the Aboriginal domain," writes law professor Harry Blagg, who has documented the theory and progress of indigenous night patrols in extensive detail. "Their role is largely preventive and focuses on early intervention to forestall potential crises through direct mediation and by drawing on 'insider' cultural knowledge."[19]

Since the royal commission's report was published, hundreds of patrols have been established across Australia. Many are supported by government funding, and they are considered crucial programs in Australia's efforts to control crime and to repair relationships between the Aboriginal people and the government.

In March 2017, I traveled to Perth to observe the work of the Nyoongar Patrol in person. I spent hours talking with the leadership and staff from Nyoongar Outreach Services, which operates the night patrol out of a beautiful office building, with updated conference rooms for team planning, whiteboards with schedules for the night, and a large garage holding a fleet of shiny white vans with the organization's logo on the sides. The headquarters does not have the feel of a struggling social service agency; it has the atmosphere of a startup, where every member of the team is energized and motivated by a common mission.

When I met the patrol staff on a breezy Friday evening, they were preparing for a lively night. Because every single member of the patrol is of Aboriginal descent, they have extensive networks in the community and already knew of ongoing feuds and several house parties that teenagers had planned for the evening. After an hour of debriefing, the patrol teams fanned out to their designated sections of the city.

I joined a team led by Annie and Rachel, two extraordinary women who were remarkable to watch in action. I looked on as they tried to calm a shirtless man who was drunk and belligerent in front of a crowded bar. I saw them talk to a man who looked unwell, lying on a bench in the middle of a city plaza, and stay with him as the emergency medical technician asked him questions and eventually took him to get treatment. I watched as they greeted dozens of teenagers who approached us over the course of the night with smiles on their faces. And as midnight passed and we continued to walk the streets of Perth into the early hours of Saturday morning, I saw them maintain their energy and their empathy as they found ways to provide assistance to people who were still out on the streets, often on their own, sometimes desperate for help.

The challenges that emerge over the course of a shift change on a nightly basis, but the overarching goal of the patrol teams is to maintain a presence in the public spaces where young people hang out, to search for Aboriginal people who look as if they could use some help, and to give anyone who is causing trouble the chance to cool off or to go home before the police get involved. At times the patrol team's intervention comes with a stern warning, but usually it comes with a warm smile.

Annie, Rachel, and the staff from the Nyoongar Patrol are extremely good at what they do, and there is a reason for that. They are professionals. They go through extensive training, they come together each day to plan their shift, they meet with the police and with youth center staff on a nightly basis, and they walk the streets in sharp uniforms and clean, recognizable vans. Every member of the patrol staff cares deeply about the work they are doing. They are valued by everyone in the community, and they have the resources they need to be successful.

As I walked the streets of Perth with Annie and Rachel, I imagined a program that would employ residents of American neighborhoods to oversee public spaces in ways designed to improve community life, while working to control crime and violence. A program with staff hired from the community and trained to find help for people who are hurt, in trouble, in the midst of a domestic dispute, or simply in need of help. A program that would serve as a buffer between residents and the police, with staff trained to de-escalate conflicts and calm everyone down before the police are called.

I imagined what the most disadvantaged American neighborhoods would look like if they were overseen not only by police but also by "community advocates," people who have the greatest stake in keeping their own streets, and their own children, safe. I wondered how the atmosphere of city streets would change if community leaders were out in public spaces, enforcing common standards of behavior and helping residents in need, and paid wages commensurate with the value they generate for the community and the entire city.

Throughout the United States, one can find many examples of informal groups of residents who organize themselves into neighborhood watches or even citizens patrols.[20] But these groups are entirely different from the Nyoongar Patrol. Few of the U.S. groups are composed of true community advocates, residents whose job is to oversee public spaces and make sure every resident is safe, cared for, and welcomed. Nowhere are these groups seen as a priority for public investment, and nowhere are they seen as a potential solution for the crisis of legitimacy that has engulfed law enforcement.

During the long night I spent on the streets of Perth, I saw what happens when members of a highly disadvantaged group see friendly faces of authority on the street rather than combatants. Social problems and conflicts don't go away in their presence, but the space becomes more welcoming and safer. In places where violence has reached a crisis point, where residents are unwilling to talk with law enforcement, a new type of security force is needed. We have relied on warriors to control urban streets for the past several decades; it's now time to turn the streets over to advocates.

10

A WAR ON VIOLENCE

I have presented a substantial amount of evidence for the reader to digest, with complexities and caveats throughout. But the core argument of this book boils down to four key points.

The decline in violence is real, and it has transformed American city life. After a period in which the problem of violence dominated urban America, we are now living in the safest period of U.S. history. Violence has fallen in almost every city, and it has been cut by half or more in many of the largest urban centers. Although the national homicide rate rose in 2015 and 2016, the problem of urban violence is nothing like it was in the early 1990s. The decline in violence has redefined city life and transformed the experience of urban poverty.

Violence fell because an array of different groups mobilized to take over city streets. Although a range of factors likely contributed to the crime decline, the transformation of public space is the most important change that has taken place since the early 1990s. City neighborhoods, which for decades were abandoned and left on their own, are now overseen by police officers, private security, and cameras. And while the expanding reach of the criminal justice system is the most visible and most controversial change that has taken place in U.S. cities, it wasn't the police alone that became a more dominant presence in urban neighborhoods. At the peak of the era of violence, community residents and organizations mobilized to confront violence, and they played an important role in reducing crime. The changes that have taken place since the early 1990s are not uniformly positive or negative, but they reveal what happens when abandoned public spaces are reclaimed.

The decline in violence has led to stunning benefits for the most disadvantaged segments of American society, most notably young African American males. Every segment of the population has experienced a decline in violent victimization, but the most disadvantaged groups of Americans have benefited the most. The drop in the homicide rate is one of the most important public health breakthroughs of the past several decades, saving tens of thousands of black lives and reducing the racial gap in life expectancy. Schools have become safer places to learn, and academic performance has improved the most in the places that have become safest. The decline in violence has not reversed the rise of inequality in the United States, but it has changed its form and reduced its consequences. The crime drop has led to neighborhoods that are less segregated by income, and it has given children from poor families a better chance to rise up out of poverty as they reach adulthood.

The strategies that have been used to confront the dual problems of urban poverty and violent crime have also brought great costs. Since the late 1960s, the dominant approach to dealing with the challenges of urban poverty and violent crime has been to disinvest in low-income communities and to invest in the police and the criminal justice system—a strategy of abandonment and punishment. This approach has contributed to the crime drop but it has also led to widespread injustice, abuse, and anger. A diverse set of political groups from the left and the right has now come together to end this long-standing model of urban policy. They have moved discussions of criminal justice policy away from the goal of punishment, and toward the goal of justice. But there has been no movement away from abandonment and toward investment.

These are the lessons from the data presented throughout the book. The question that remains is: What comes next?

The last model of urban policy, which has been in place for fifty years, came together at a time when cities were on the decline. Middle-class families were leaving central cities and heading to the suburbs. Environmental damage was becoming visible in the form of polluted city air and water. City governments were going bankrupt. Violent crime was rising quickly.

The next urban agenda will be debated during a complex, tumultuous time in the recent history of urban America, but one that offers reasons for hope and optimism. After decades of suburbanization, central cities have begun to attract new populations. Instead of being viewed as the setting for society's problems, cities have come to be seen by many as part of the solution to challenges like climate change, economic stagnation, and innovation.[1] And for a brief moment in 2014, American cities were as safe as they had been at any point in U.S. history.

As this book goes to print in the winter of 2017, that moment may be passing us by, and the opportunity may be fading. Despite the positive change that has unfolded in urban America, the fundamental problems that became visible during the urban crisis of the 1960s have not been resolved. Urban inequality is more severe than it has been in forty years. Protest has erupted in black communities across the country after incidents of police violence; most of the protest has been peaceful, but at times it has turned deadly. And as the unrest has spread, we have seen ominous signs of an increase in violent crime, early signals that the level of violence may have reached its low point and is now on the rise.[2]

This is the context in which the next model of urban policy will take shape. What will it look like? As others continue to make the important case for an urban agenda focused on justice, urbanists must argue forcefully for a complementary agenda that focuses on investment. I laid out my ideas for what this agenda should look like in my last book, *Stuck in Place,* where I made a case for a "durable" policy agenda. By durable policy, I mean interventions, investments, policies, and programs that are designed to be sustained over time, to reach multiple generations of family members, and to be implemented at a scale that makes it possible to transform the lives of families and their communities.[3] The call for durable urban policy is a reaction to a historical pattern in which promising investments in urban neighborhoods have come and gone, implemented for short time frames with resources inadequate to generate transformative change. And yet urban poverty tends to persist over long periods and to be passed on across generations. Multigenerational urban poverty cannot be addressed with point-in-time interventions or influxes of funding that fade away after a few years. If public policy is going to address urban inequality, that policy must be durable.

Ideas for the content of such an agenda have come from other scholars and policy experts who have put forward compelling arguments for ways to create and preserve affordable housing, to connect residents of distressed communities to neighborhoods and cities of opportunity, to confront persistent joblessness, to support working parents, to bolster the wages of workers at the bottom end of highly stratified urban labor markets, and to ensure that children have access to high-quality daycare, schools, tutors, and

mentors as they advance toward college and the labor force.[4] The
central challenge is to turn these ideas into a movement for durable urban investment. Developing this movement means breaking
ties with those who seek to combine reforms of the criminal justice system with cutbacks in funding for urban neighborhoods. It
means combining arguments for reforms of sentencing policy with
arguments for reforms of housing policy, such that a decent, affordable home is available to every U.S. resident. It means reframing
the movement against aggressive, violent, racially biased policing
and mass incarceration into a movement against urban inequality.
And it means expanding the focus of this movement in a way that
places emphasis not only on justice but also on investment.

I continue to believe that the principles of durable urban policy
should guide this effort to confront urban inequality. But that is
the long game. Since I published my last book, it has become clear
that urbanists must do more than advocate for a grand vision of
federal policy and wait for it to materialize. I am not optimistic
about the prospects for a large-scale federal agenda to address
urban inequality, but I am hopeful about the prospects for a multilevel, multisector agenda to fortify urban neighborhoods and
confront violence right now. We are at a unique moment in the
nation's history in which most politicians across the political spectrum recognize the need for a new approach to confronting urban
violence. Americans have made clear their willingness to spend
substantial resources to reduce violent crime and to create safe
communities and cities. And one by-product of rising inequality is
the proliferation of philanthropists who have the capacity to make
investments at a scale that can transform entire communities. It
is not difficult to imagine an agenda around strong, safe communities that spans the public, private, and nonprofit sectors and that
has support across the political spectrum.

To get there, we must move beyond the narrow call for reforms of policing and the criminal justice system. The nation is at risk of experiencing a new wave of rising violence. It has already begun in a small number of cities, but it could happen in many more. And the evidence I have presented over the course of this book suggests that if violence begins to rise, the consequences of urban inequality will become much more severe.

The specific proposals I have laid out are meant to underscore a larger point: As a nation, we need to fight a new, urgent war on violence. Not a war on crime that is waged through the police and the prison. Not a war on drugs that is waged through feel-good public service announcements and brutal enforcement on the streets. At this moment, we need to fight a war on violence, and we need to do so in a way that is entirely different from the past. The police play a crucial role in the effort to maintain social order, but their role has to shift. The residents and institutions that look out over city streets must be supported on the front lines, as these urban guardians have the greatest capacity to create safe, strong urban communities.

The calls for justice that have dominated recent debates about policing, poverty, and crime are well justified and are crucially important to developing effective reforms of law enforcement and the criminal justice system. But the war on violence—with all its tremendous physical, emotional, social, educational, and financial costs—starts with investment.

NOTES

ACKNOWLEDGMENTS

1   Patrick Sharkey and Robert Sampson, "Violence, Cognition, and Neighborhood Inequality in America," in *Social Neuroscience: Brain, Mind, and Society*, ed. Russell Schutt, Matcheri S. Keshavan, and Larry J. Seidman (Cambridge, Mass.: Harvard University Press, 2015).

2   Patrick Sharkey and Gerard Torrats-Espinosa, "The Effect of Violent Crime on Economic Mobility," *Journal of Urban Economics* (2017).

3   Michael Friedson and Patrick Sharkey, "Neighborhood Inequality After the Crime Decline," *Annals of the American Academy of Political and Social Science* 660 (2015): 341–58.

4   Patrick Sharkey and Michael Friedson, "The Impact of the Homicide Decline on Life Expectancy of African American Males," *Demography* (2018).

5   Patrick Sharkey, Gerard Torrats-Espinosa, and Delaram Takyar, "Community and the Crime Decline: The Causal Effect of Local Nonprofit Formation on Violent Crime," *American Sociological Review* (2018).

PREFACE

1   For South Bronx culture, baseball, and politics of the summer of 1977, see Johnathan Mahler, *Ladies and Gentlemen, the Bronx Is Burning: 1977, Baseball, Politics, and the Battle for the Soul of a City* (New York: Macmillan, 2006). The commentary from the broadcast is available on YouTube: https://www.youtube.com/watch?v=bnVH-BE9CUo.

2   For more on the South Bronx in this period, see Randol Contreras, *The Stick-Up Kids: Race, Drugs, Violence, and the American Dream* (Berkeley: University of California Press, 2012); and Joe Flood, "Why the Bronx Burned," *New York Post*, May 16, 2010.

3   Mahler, *Ladies and Gentlemen.* See also Martin Gottlieb and James Glanz, "The Blackouts of '65 and '77 Became Defining Moments in the City's History," *New York Times*, August 15, 2003.

4   Lee Dembart, "Carter Takes 'Sobering' Trip to South Bronx," *New York Times*, October 6, 1977; and Manny Fernandez, "When Presidents Visited the South Bronx," *New York Times*, October 5, 2007.

5   Tom Wolfe, *The Bonfire of the Vanities* (New York: Macmillan, 1987).

6   Fernandez, "When Presidents."

7   Contreras, *Stick-Up Kids*, p. xv. For a description of the experiences of gang members in the Bronx and elsewhere in New York City, see Martin Sanchez-Jankowski, *Islands in the Street* (Berkeley: University of California Press, 1991). His account of a gang member's decision to attack another on the Grand Concourse, which borders Franz Sigel Park, is on page 151.

8   Ibid., pp. 74–75.

9   Marc Feinman, "The New York Transit Authority in the 1980s," at http://www.nycsubway.org/wiki/The_New_York_Transit_Authority_in_the_1980s.

10   Dennis Hevesi, "Yankee Official Resigns in Dispute over Racial Remarks," *New York Times*, July 24, 1994.

11   Ira Berkow, "Flash: It Is Safe at Yankee Stadium," *New York Times*, July 25, 1994.

12   The same gap between night and day game attendance held true across the East River in Queens, where the New York Mets played.

13   The gap between night and day game attendance for both Yankees and Mets games just about disappeared by the mid-2000s, the last few years before both teams opened up new stadiums.

14   Al Baker, J. David Goodman, and Benjamin Mueller, "Beyond the Chokehold: The Path to Eric Garner's Death," *New York Times*, July 14, 2014.

15   A bystander called 911 to report that a man was carrying a gun and pointing it at people in a Walmart store. Police responded and fatally shot the suspect, who was carrying a BB gun he had picked up from a store shelf. The bystander later retracted his claim that the victim had been pointing the gun at people. See Ilahe Izadi, "John Crawford's Family Sues Walmart, Ohio Town for Wrongful Death," *Washington Post*, December 14, 2014.

16   Rachel Clarke and Christopher Lett, "What Happened When Michael Brown Met Officer Darren Wilson," CNN.com, November 11, 2014.

17   Kate Mather and Joel Rubin, "Ezell Ford's Shooting Violated LAPD Policy, Police Commission Rules," *Los Angeles Times,* June 27, 2015.

18   Tom McCarthy, "Video Shows Boy, 12, Shot 'Seconds' After Police Confronted Child," *Guardian,* November 26, 2014.

19   Michael Martinez, "South Carolina Cop Shoots Unarmed Man: A Timeline," CNN.com, April 9, 2015.

20   Richard Perez-Pena, "Six Baltimore Officers Indicted in Death of Freddie Gray," *New York Times,* May 21, 2015; Scott Calvert, "Baltimore Prosecutors Say Freddie Gray Arrest Was Illegal Before Finding Knife," *Wall Street Journal,* May 19, 2015.

21   I discuss the literature on the effects of policing and incarceration in Chapter 3.

22   The impacts of parental incarceration on children are reviewed in Sara Wakefield and Christopher Wildeman, *Children of the Prison Boom: Mass Incarceration and the Future of American Inequality* (New York: Oxford University Press, 2014).

1. THE END OF THE ERA OF VIOLENCE

1   Uniform Crime Reporting Data Tool, "Uniform Crime Reports, 1960–2014," FBI, U.S. Department of Justice (2015), at http://www.ucrdatatool.gov. The term *homicide* refers to all crimes classified as murders and nonnegligent manslaughters.

2   The most extensive analysis designed to correct for bias in official estimates of homicide rates in the early twentieth century is Douglas Lee Eckberg, "Estimates of Early Twentieth-Century U.S. Homicide Rates: An Econometric Forecasting Approach," *Demography* 32, no. 1 (1995): 1–16.

3   For the best discussion of how the crack trade likely influenced trends in violent crime from the 1980s through the 1990s, see Alfred Blumstein and Joel Wallman, eds., *The Crime Drop in America* (Cambridge, U.K.: Cambridge University Press, 2006).

4   Centers for Disease Control and Prevention, "Homicide Rates Among Persons Aged 10–24 Years—United States, 1981–2010," *Morbidity and Mortality Weekly Report,* July 12, 2013, at http://www.cdc.gov/mmwr/preview/mmwrhtml/mm6227a1.htm?s_cid=mm6227a1_w.

5   William J. Bennett, John J. DiIulio, and John P. Walters, *Body Count: Moral Poverty—And How to Win America's War Against Crime and Drugs* (New York: Simon and Schuster, 1996), p. 43.

6   This argument is laid out most forcefully in ibid. See also John J. DiIulio, Jr., "The Coming of the Super-Predators," *Weekly Standard,* November 22, 1995. For a short retrospective, see "The 'Superpredator Scare," at http://www.nytimes.com/video/us/100000002807771/the-superpredator-scare.html.

7   DiIulio, "Coming of the Super-Predators."

8   John J. DiIulio, "How to Stop the Coming Crime Wave," Manhattan Institute (1996).

9   I should note that some criminologists did not share the view that the rate of violent crime was about to increase. Franklin Zimring cautioned against the sensational language used by DiIulio and critiqued his demographic projections, which were based on a series of dubious assumptions. See Franklin E. Zimring, "Crying Wolf over Teen Demons," *Los Angeles Times,* August 19, 1996.

10   Quoted in Fox Butterfield, "Serious Crimes Fall for Third Year, but Experts Warn Against Seeing Trend," *New York Times,* May 23, 1995.

11   Franklin E. Zimring, *The Great American Crime Decline* (New York: Oxford University Press, 2006).

12   Steven Levitt and Stephen Dubner, *Freakonomics* (New York: William Morrow, 2005); and John Donahue and Steven D. Levitt, "The Impact of Legalized Abortion on Crime," *Quarterly Journal of Economics* 116, no. 2 (2001): 379–420.

13   The rate of 4.4 homicides per 100,000 residents is the adjusted figure reported by the FBI in the 2015 version of "Crime in the United States," at https://ucr.fbi.gov/crime-in-the-u.s/2015/crime-in-the-u.s.-2015/tables/table-1.

14   See Eckberg, "Estimates"; and Roger Lane, *Murder in America: A History* (Columbus: Ohio State University Press, 1997). For a concise blogpost on the history of homicide in the United States, see Claude Fischer, "A Crime Puzzle: Violent Crime Declines in America," *Berkeley Blog* (2010), at http://blogs.berkeley.edu/2010/06/16/a-crime-puzzle-violent-crime-declines-in-america.

15   Poll results are reported in Peter Moore, "Poll Results: Government Statistics," YouGov.com (2014), at https://today.yougov.com/news/2014/05/08/poll-results-government-statistics.

16   This poll was taken in October 2011 by the Gallup organization. One question asked was "Have you, personally, EVER been the victim of a crime where you were physically harmed, or threatened with physical harm?" Twenty percent responded that they had, 80 percent that they had not. "Crime," Gallup.com (2011), at http://www.gallup.com/poll/1603/crime.aspx.

17   My favorite example of this came on November 2, 2015, when more than half a million daily readers of the *New York Post* were greeted with a startling headline: "Killings in NYC Spike." Those who stopped there might have been surprised to learn of a rising tide of violence in a city where the level of violent crime had dropped to historical lows. Those who read on, however, would find that the article focused on a single week: "The NYPD recorded seven slayings during the week that ended at midnight Saturday, sources said. That compares to just two killings that took place during the same time period in 2014, for a

350 percent spike." Tina Moore and Kenneth Granger, "Killings in NYC Spike," *New York Post,* November 2, 2015; and Ted Chiricos, Kathy Padgett, and Marc Gertz, "Fear, TV News, and the Reality of Crime," *Criminology* 38, no. 3 (2000): 755–86.

18   As an example, in the early 1990s about 15 out of every 1,000 articles in the *New York Times* contained the term *homicide.* By the end of the 2000s, when the actual rate of homicides had been cut in half, only 7 or 8 out of every 1,000 articles contained the term. Trends in the keywords *crime, murder,* and *homicide* found in *Times* articles all show the same pattern of change, which corresponds with actual levels of national crime fairly closely. See Alexis Lloyd, "Chronicle: Tracking the New York Times Language Use over Time," *New York Times,* July 23, 2014.

19   Kenneth Olmstead et al., "How Americans Get TV News at Home," Pew Research Center (October 11, 2013).

20   Danilo Yanich, "Crime, Community and Local TV News: Covering Crime in Philadelphia and Baltimore," Center for Community Development and Family Policy, University of Delaware (1998), at http://www1.udel.edu/ccrs/pdf/CrimeCommunity&TVNews.pdf.

21   Steven Pinker, *The Better Angels of Our Nature: Why Violence Has Declined* (New York: Viking, 2011).

22   "The Nation's Two Measures of Homicide," Bureau of Justice Statistics, U.S. Department of Justice (2014), at http://www.bjs.gov/content/pub/pdf/ntmh.pdf.

23   To understand the inherent problem with using the official crime rate as the only way to measure changes in actual crime and violence, it is useful to remember Goodhart's Law. In 1975 Charles Goodhart, a professor at the London School of Economics, delivered a lecture on monetary policy at a conference held at the Royal Bank of Australia. During his presentation, Goodhart put forward an idea that would become influential well beyond economics. "As soon as the government attempts to regulate any particular set of financial assets," he told his audience, "these become unreliable as indicators of economic trends." Goodhart's claim was about monetary policy, but his larger point was that whenever the attention of any individual, firm, agency, or organization becomes fixated on one particular measure of performance, that measure inevitably becomes tainted and no longer operates the same way or carries the same meaning. For instance, when a teacher's performance is evaluated based on how many of his students pass a standardized test, that teacher has a strong incentive to shift his focus toward the students who are on the "bubble" of passing or not passing. The students who have very little chance of passing may get little attention, even

if they need the most help. So the proportion of students who pass the test is no longer a good measure of how well that teacher is serving his students. Years after Goodhart's presentation in Australia, the anthropologist Marilyn Strathern restated his law in a more general way: "When a measure becomes a target, it ceases to be a good measure." See Alec Chrystal and Paul D. Mizen, "Goodhart's Law: Its Origins, Meaning and Implications for Monetary Policy," in *Central Banking, Monetary Theory and Practice: Essays in Honour of Charles Goodhart,* ed. Paul D. Mizen (Cheltenham, U.K.: Edward Elgar, 2003); Jennifer Jennings, "Below the Bubble: Educational Triage and the Texas Accountability System," *American Educational Research Journal* 42, no. 2 (2005): 231–68; and Marilyn Strathern, "'Improving Ratings': Audit in the British University System," *European Review* 5, no. 3 (1997): 305–21.

24   David Bernstein and Noah Isackson, "The Truth About Chicago's Crime Rates," *Chicago Magazine,* April 2014; David Bernstein and Noah Isackson, "The Truth About Chicago's Crime Rates: Part 2," *Chicago Magazine,* May 2014; and David Bernstein and Noah Isackson, "One Year Later: New Tricks," *Chicago Magazine,* May 2015.

25   Office of Inspector General, "Chicago Police Department Assault-Related Crime Statistics Classification and Reporting Audit," City of Chicago (April 2014), at http://chicagoinspectorgeneral.org/wp-content/uploads/2014/04/OIG-Crime-Stats-Audit.pdf.

26   Bernstein and Isackson, "Truth About Crime Rates Part 2."

27   Investigative studies of police reporting have been carried out in different cities over time, often uncovering underreporting or misreporting of violent crime. See Clayton J. Mosher, Terance D. Miethe, and Timothy C. Hart, *The Mismeasure of Crime* (Beverly Hills, Calif.: Sage Publications, 2010).

28   David Bernstein and Noah Isackson, authors of the *Chicago Magazine* articles, uncovered a series of episodes, occurring at various points over the past century, where the Chicago Police Department was alleged to have altered or underreported the level of crime in the city.

29   Chicago has been a leader in the effort to make city data transparent to and usable by city residents. The city's former chief data officer described his experience working to bring the open data movement to Chicago in Brett Goldstein, "Open Data in Chicago: Game On," in *Beyond Transparency: Open Data and the Future of Civic Innovation,* ed. Brett Goldstein and Lauren Dyson (2013), at http://beyondtransparency.org.

30   See Mosher, Miethe and Hart, *Mismeasure of Crime.* Although homicide is the most reliable measure of crime, every other type of crime has fallen as well, and

by a similar degree. From 1992 to 2014, when homicide fell by 52 percent, the rate of all violent crimes declined by 50 percent. Over the same time period, forcible rape is down by 38 percent, burglary is down by 54 percent, and motor vehicle theft is down by 66 percent. See Uniform Crime Reporting Data Tool, "Uniform Crime Reports, 1960–2014," FBI, U.S. Department of Justice (2015), at http://www.ucrdatatool.gov.

31   Data from coroners' reports are likely to contain substantial bias, particularly in the first half of the twentieth century. See Margaret A. Zahn and Patricia L. McCall, "Trends and Patterns of Homicide in the 20th-Century United States," in *Homicide: A Sourcebook of Social Research,* ed. M. Dwayne Smith and Margaret A. Zahn (Thousand Oaks, Calif.: Sage Publications, 1999).

32   An analysis of the homicide rate based on data from the FBI Uniform Crime Reports and the Vital Statistics system found that since 1950 the two sources correlate at 0.98. See John J. Donohue and Justin Wolfers, "Uses and Abuses of Empirical Evidence in the Death Penalty Debate," *Stanford Law Review* 58, no. 3 (2005): 791–845.

33   "Data Collection: National Crime Victimization Survey (NCVS)," Bureau of Justice Statistics, U.S. Department of Justice (2015), at http://www.bjs.gov/index.cfm?ty=dcdetail&iid=245#Publications_and_products.

34   UN Office on Drugs and Crime, *Global Study on Homicide 2013* (Vienna: UN Office on Drugs and Crime, 2013).

2. THE NEW AMERICAN CITY

1   I described some of the major trends in urban social, economic, and demographic change in the 1960s and 1990s in Patrick Sharkey, *Stuck in Place: Urban Neighborhoods and the End of Progress Toward Racial Equality* (Chicago: University of Chicago Press, 2013). The books that have had the greatest influence on my reading of this period are Kenneth T. Jackson, *Crabgrass Frontier: The Suburbanization of the United States* (New York: Oxford University Press, 1985); Douglas S. Massey and Nancy A. Denton, *American Apartheid: Segregation and the Making of the Underclass* (Cambridge, Mass.: Harvard University Press, 1993); Thomas J. Sugrue, *The Origins of the Urban Crisis: Race and Inequality in Postwar Detroit* (Princeton, NJ: Princeton University Press, 1996); and William Julius Wilson, *The Truly Disadvantaged: The Inner City, the Underclass, and Public Policy* (Chicago: University of Chicago Press, 1987).

2   Elijah Anderson, *Code of the Street: Decency, Violence, and the Moral Life of the Inner City* (New York: Norton, 1999).

3   Ibid., p. 23.

4   Elijah Anderson, "The Code of the Streets," *Atlantic Monthly*, May 1994.

5   Anderson, *Code of the Street,* p. 44.

6   Wilson, *Truly Disadvantaged*; and William Julius Wilson, *When Work Disappears* (New York: Alfred A. Knopf, 1996).

7   Loïc Wacquant, *Urban Outcasts: A Comparative Sociology of Advanced Marginality* (Cambridge, U.K.: Polity, 2008), p. 210; Loïc Wacquant and William Julius Wilson, "The Cost of Racial and Class Exclusion in the Inner City," *Annals of the American Academy of Political and Social Science* 501, no. 1 (1989): 8–25.

8   Eric Klinenberg, *Heat Wave: A Social Autopsy of Disaster in Chicago* (Chicago: University of Chicago Press, 2003), p. 56.

9   Mary Pattillo, *Black Picket Fences: Privilege and Peril Among the Black Middle Class* (Chicago: University of Chicago Press, 1999), p. 6.

10   Ta-Nehisi Coates, *The Beautiful Struggle: A Father, Two Sons, and an Unlikely Road to Manhood* (New York: Random House, 2008), pp. 29–30.

11   Ta-Nehisi Coates, "Beyond the Code of the Streets," *New York Times*, May 4, 2014.

12   Victor Rios, *Punished: Policing the Lives of Black and Latino Boys* (New York: New York University Press, 2011).

13   Martin Sanchez-Jankowski, *Islands in the Street* (Berkeley: University of California Press, 1991), p. 149.

14   Ibid.

15   This term comes from Jill Leovy's riveting book on the investigation of homicide in Los Angeles, *Ghettoside: A True Story of Murder in America* (New York: Random House, 2015), p. 33.

16   Philippe Bourgois, *In Search of Respect: Selling Crack in El Barrio* (New York: Cambridge University Press, 1995), p. 34.

17   Ibid.

18   Richard Curtis, "The Improbable Transformation of Inner-City Neighborhoods: Crime, Violence, Drugs, and Youth in the 1990s," *Journal of Criminal Law and Criminology* 88, no. 4 (1998): 1233–76.

19   The sociologist Derek Hyra conducted four years of ethnographic fieldwork focusing on neighborhood change in Shaw. His findings, which focus on the relationships between gentrification and social integration, cultural change, and political influence, are summarized in Derek Hyra, *Race, Class, and Politics in the Cappuccino City* (Chicago: University of Chicago Press, 2017). See also Hyra, "The Back-to-the-City Movement: Neighbourhood Redevelopment and Processes of Political and Cultural Displacement," *Urban Studies* 52, no. 10

(2015): 1753–73; and Hyra, "Making the Gilded Ghetto: Black Branding," International Conference on Contested Cities (2016), at http://contested-cities.net/working-papers/2016/making-the-gilded-ghetto-black-branding.

20   Shaw's population dropped as well, although it is difficult to specify by how much. The boundaries of the Shaw neighborhood do not align neatly with any particular political or administrative boundary, so population estimates vary depending on the boundaries used to define Shaw. According to Neighborhood Info DC, the population located within Advisory Neighborhood Commission #1B (covering U Street, Cardozo, Howard University, Pleasant Plains, LeDroit Park, and Shaw) declined slightly through 2000, then rose by 16 percent to 24,000 by 2010. The Howard University/Le Droit Park/Cardozo/Shaw neighborhood cluster also experienced the same trend in population. Using either definition of the neighborhood boundaries, the population of black residents in and around Shaw dropped from over 75 percent to under 50 percent from 1980 to 2010. See http://www.neighborhoodinfodc.org.

21   For a detailed history of the O Street Market, see Marc Fisher, "O Street Market: Symbol of Violence Becomes a Marker for D.C.'s Resurgence," *Washington Post*, November 19, 2013.

22   The district's homicide rate rose from 24 murders for every 100,000 residents in 1985 to 78 murders for every 100,000 residents in 1990, and it remained above 70 until 1995. Uniform Crime Reporting Data Tool, "Uniform Crime Reports, 1960–2014," FBI, U.S. Department of Justice (2015), at http://www.ucrdatatool.gov.

23   For estimates on international homicide rates, see "Global Study on Homicide 2013," UN Office on Drugs and Crime (2013).

24   Quoted in Fisher, "O Street Market."

25   The tally of homicides reached a low of 88 murders in 2012, rose to 162 in 2015, and fell back to 135 in 2016.

26   See Hyra, "Making the Gilded Ghetto." Hyra describes the importance of the municipal building and subsequent changes in the neighborhood in an interview by the Urban Institute (November 15, 2010), at https://www.youtube.com/watch?v=sJ6oSXEd7Og.

27   Fisher, "O Street Market."

28   Hyra, "Making the Gilded Ghetto."

29   Homicide rates are shown for 181 cities with at least 100,000 residents in the 1990 Census and with complete data from the FBI Uniform Crime Reports. Homicide rates from 1993 are averages over 1991 to 1993. Homicide rates from 2014 are averages from 2012 to 2014.

30   Michael Friedson and Patrick Sharkey, "Neighborhood Inequality After the Crime Decline," *Annals of the American Academy of Political and Social Science* 660 (2015): 341–58. Only a few other studies have analyzed trends in crime at a very local level in Boston, Cleveland, Denver, and Seattle. See Ingrid Gould Ellen and Katherine O'Regan, "Crime and U.S. Cities: Recent Patterns and Implications," *Annals of the American Academy of Political and Social Science* 626, no. 1 (2009): 22–38; Anthony Braga, David Hureau, and Andrew Papachristos, "The Relevance of Micro Places in Citywide Robbery Trends: A Longitudinal Analysis of Robbery Incidents at Street Corners and Block Faces in Boston," *Journal of Research in Crime and Delinquency* 48, no. 1 (2011): 7–32; and Anthony Braga, Andrew Papachristos, and David Hureau, "The Concentration and Stability of Gun Violence at Micro Places in Boston, 1980–2008," *Journal of Quantitative Criminology* 26, no. 1 (2010): 33–53. Ruth D. Peterson and Lauren J. Krivo took on the enormous task of gathering neighborhood-level data in dozens of cities across the country in order to write their excellent book *Divergent Social Worlds: Neighborhood Crime and the Racial-Spatial Divide* (New York: Russell Sage Foundation, 2010). However, the data they collected covered only a single year and thus did not allow for analyses of change over time.

31   Friedson and Sharkey, "Neighborhood Inequality."

32   Alice Goffman, *On the Run: Fugitive Life in an American City* (Chicago: University of Chicago Press, 2014).

33   John R. Logan and Charles Zhang, "Global Neighborhoods: New Pathways to Diversity and Separation," *American Journal of Sociology* 115, no. 4 (2010): 1069–109.

34   Lance Freeman, *There Goes the Hood: Views of Gentrification from the Ground Up* (Philadelphia: Temple University Press, 2011); Hyra, *Cappuccino City*. For a brilliant book documenting class-based change within a predominantly black neighborhood of Chicago, see Mary Pattillo, *Black on the Block: The Politics of Race and Class in the City* (Chicago: University of Chicago Press, 2008).

35   Edward Glaeser and Jacob Vigdor, "The End of the Segregated Century," Manhattan Institute (2012); Logan and Zhang, "Global Neighborhoods."

36   On the growth of deep poverty since welfare reform, see Kathryn J. Edin and H. Luke Shaefer, *$2.00 a Day: Living on Almost Nothing in America* (New York: Houghton Mifflin Harcourt, 2015). On the desperate challenges faced by the urban poor in Milwaukee as they attempt to find stable, affordable housing, see Matthew Desmond, *Evicted: Poverty and Profit in the American City* (New York: Broadway Books, 2016).

37   John Gurda, *The Making of Milwaukee* (Milwaukee, Wis.: Milwaukee County

Historical Society, 1999); and John Gurda, *Milwaukee: City of Neighborhoods* (Milwaukee, Wis.: Historic Milwaukee, Inc., 2015).

38   Ashley Luthern, "Duo Stands Trial, Accused of Milwaukee Retaliation Killing," *Milwaukee Journal Sentinel,* March 11 2015.

39   For details of the investigation, see Wisconsin Division of Criminal Investigation, "Case Report Case/Report Number: 14-2252/25 Summary Report of Investigation" (2015), at https://www.doj.state.wi.us/sites/default/files/14-2252-25.pdf.

40   Don Behm, "Milwaukee Faces Daunting Costs with Lead Water Pipes," *Milwaukee Journal Sentinel*, January 27, 2016.

41   Over the course of 2016, the number of homicides in Milwaukee remained just about as high as it was the year prior. In August 2016, four months after I visited, a well-known man in the Sherman Park neighborhood was killed as he fled from an officer. The man was carrying a gun as he fled and was shot once while holding the gun. He threw the gun over a fence and was shot again, and killed, while unarmed. The officer was fired and would later be charged with homicide. Riots broke out in the neighborhood overnight.

42   As an example, see Heather Mac Donald, "The Nationwide Crime Wave Is Building," *Wall Street Journal*, May 23, 2016.

43   As an example, leaders of the largest foundations in Chicago convened an emergency meeting in mid-2016, inviting policy makers and researchers to develop ideas for how to respond to the surge in violence. They offered immediate resources to community groups who proposed the most innovative ideas to quell the violence.

3. THE TRANSFORMATION OF URBAN SPACE

1   For information about the history of the BID, reports on finances, trends within the district, and so forth, see the Hollywood Entertainment District's website, http://onlyinhollywood.org/hollywood-bid. Data on the budget, arrests, and interactions with the Los Angeles Police Department come from "One Voice. One Vision. One Hollywood. 2015 Annual Report of the Hollywood Property Owners Alliance," Hollywood Entertainment District (2015), at http://onlyinhollywood.org/wp-content/uploads/2014/03/2015HPOA_AnnualReport_web.pdf.

2   Philip J. Cook and John MacDonald, "Public Safety Through Private Action: An Economic Assessment of BIDS," *Economic Journal* 121, no. 552 (2011): 445–62.

3   This claim is on the front page of the district's website, http://onlyinhollywood.org/hollywood-bid.

4   Lawrence E. Cohen and Marcus Felson, "Social Change and Crime Rate
     Trends: A Routine Activity Approach," *American Sociological Review* 44 (1979):
     588–608. Some of the more prominent refinements and critiques of the theory
     are reviewed in Ronald V. Clarke, "Situational Crime Prevention," *Crime and
     Justice* 19 (1995): 91–150; Pamela Wilcox, Kenneth C. Land, and Scott Hunt,
     *Criminal Circumstance: A Dynamic Multicontextual Criminal Opportunity
     Theory* (New York: Walter de Gruyter, 2003); and Per-Olof H. Wikström et al.,
     *Breaking Rules: The Social and Situational Dynamics of Young People's Urban
     Crime* (New York: Oxford University Press, 2012).

5   Since the development of routine activities theory, an enormous literature has
     emerged focusing on environmental factors that affect crime and on situations
     that make a criminal act more likely. This shift in perspective is found in
     "opportunity" theories of crime, rational choice theories of crime, situational
     crime prevention approaches, and even approaches that focus on characteris-
     tics of the built environment, which fall under the name of "crime prevention
     through environmental design" (CPTED). Environmental and situational theo-
     ries of crime have become much more detailed and sophisticated over time, with
     debates centering on the precise triggers of criminal behavior and the array of
     factors that make a criminal act more or less difficult to carry out. It has also
     spawned a policy-oriented wing of criminology focused on techniques to alter
     social settings so as to make criminal activity less common. Some useful reviews
     of this literature can be found in Marcus Felson, *Crime and Everyday Life,* 2nd
     ed. (Thousand Oaks, Calif.: Pine Forge Press, 1998); John E. Eck and David L.
     Weisburd, "Crime Places in Crime Theory," in *Crime and Place, Crime Preven-
     tion Studies,* ed. John E. Eck and David L. Weisburd (Monsey, N.Y.: Criminal
     Justice Press, 1995), vol. 4; Ronald V. Clarke, "Situational Crime Prevention:
     Theoretical Background and Current Practice," in *Handbook on Crime and
     Deviance,* ed. Marvin Krohn, Allan Lizotte, and Gina Hall (New York: Springer,
     2009); and Derek B. Cornish and Ronald V. Clarke, *The Reasoning Criminal*
     (New York: Springer-Verlag, 1986).

6   Many newspaper and magazine articles have reviewed some of the most counter-
     intuitive theories of the crime decline. One of the better reviews is Dana Goldstein,
     "10 (Not Entirely Crazy) Theories Explaining the Great Crime Decline," Marshall
     Project (November 24, 2014), at https://www.themarshallproject.org/2014/11/24/
     10-not-entirely-crazy-theories-explaining-the-great-crime-decline#.A7mIRfdIS.
     For a more comprehensive review of the evidence behind many of these theories,
     see Franklin E. Zimring, *The Great American Crime Decline* (New York: Oxford
     University Press, 2006).

7   John Schwartz, "U.S. to Drop Color-Coded Terror Threats," *New York Times*, November 24, 2010.

8   "Homeland Security Advisor System: Task Force Report and Recommendations," Homeland Security Advisory Council, U.S. Department of Homeland Security (2009).

9   Jonathan Klick and Alexander Tabarrok, "Using Terror Alert Levels to Estimate the Effect of Police on Crime," *Journal of Law and Economics* 48, no. 1 (2005): 267–79.

10   Thomas B. Marvell and Carlisle E. Moody, "Specification Problems, Police Levels, and Crime Rates," *Criminology* 34, no. 4 (1996): 609–46; and Steven D. Levitt, "Using Electoral Cycles in Police Hiring to Estimate the Effect of Police on Crime: Reply," *American Economic Review* 92, no. 4 (2002): 1244–50.

11   Klick and Tabarrok, in "Using Terror Alert Levels," attempt to adjust for effects of decreased tourism on crime by adjusting for subway ridership, which can be seen as a proxy for tourism levels.

12   For an excellent review of what we know about the relationship between the volume of police and crime, see Aaron Chalfin and Justin McCrary, "The Effect of Police on Crime: New Evidence from U.S. Cities, 1960–2010," National Bureau of Economic Research, Working Paper no. 18815 (February 2013).

13   William N. Evans and Emily G. Owens, "COPS and Crime," *Journal of Public Economics* 91, no. 1 (2007): 181–201.

14   Rafael Di Tella and Ernesto Schargrodsky, "Do Police Reduce Crime?: Estimates Using the Allocation of Police Forces After a Terrorist Attack," *American Economic Review* 94 (2004): 115–33.

15   Mirko Draca, Stephen Machin, and Robert Witt, "Panic on the Streets of London: Police, Crime, and the July 2005 Terror Attacks," *American Economic Review* 101 (2011): 2157–181.

16   Although Levitt's original study contained a coding error, his basic finding held up when the error was corrected and when he used different approaches to uncovering natural experiments that led to fluctuations in the number of officers on the street. For a critique of his original paper, see Justin McCrary, "Using Electoral Cycles in Police Hiring to Estimate the Effect of Police on Crime: Comment," *American Economic Review* 92, no. 4 (2002): 1236–43. For Levitt's response, see Steven D. Levitt, "Using Electoral Cycles in Police Hiring to Estimate the Effect of Police on Crime: Reply," *American Economic Review* 92, no. 4 (2002): 1244–50.

17   Evans and Owens, "COPS and Crime."

18   Although this chapter focuses on the raw presence of police, some criminolo-

gists have argued that new strategies of policing are a key reason for the crime drop, most forcefully Franklin E. Zimring, *The City That Became Safe: New York's Lessons for Urban Crime and Its Control* (New York: Oxford University Press, 2011). See also Oliver Roeder, Lauren-Brooke Eisen, and Julia Bowling, "What Caused the Crime Decline?" Brennan Center for Justice (2015), at https://www.brennancenter.org/publication/what-caused-crime-decline. Levitt, on the other hand, argues that changes in policing tactics likely did not contribute greatly to the crime decline. See Steven D. Levitt, "Understanding Why Crime Fell in the 1990s: Four Factors That Explain the Decline and Six That Do Not," *Journal of Economic Perspectives* 18, no. 1 (2004): 163–90.

19   Kevin Strom et al., "The Private Security Industry: A Review of the Definitions, Available Data Sources, and Paths Moving Forward," Bureau of Justice Statistics, U.S. Department of Justice (2009), at https://www.ncjrs.gov/pdffiles1/bjs/grants/232781.pdf.

20   The use of camera technology increased in the 1990s with support from the 1994 Crime Bill, then was bolstered again in the early 2000s through grants from the Department of Homeland Security.

21   Aundreia Cameron et al., "Measuring the Effects of Video Surveillance on Crime in Los Angeles," California Research Bureau, CRB-08-007 (May 5, 2008), at https://www.library.ca.gov/crb/08/08-007.pdf.

22   Ted Cox, "Number of Chicago Security Cameras 'Frightening,' ACLU says," DNAInfo (May 9, 2013), at https://www.dnainfo.com/chicago/20130509/chicago/rahm-boosts-number-of-security-cameras-frightening-number-aclu.

23   The crack epidemic had already begun to die down when the largest number of new police officers hit city streets, but law enforcement resources played a central role in shutting down drug dealers who operated in public spaces. For instance, "visible" homicides committed outdoors and typically related to the drug trade began to decline in New York City at times when the police department engaged in more aggressive enforcement of drug dealing in public space. See Jeffrey Fagan, Franklin E. Zimring, and June Kim, "Declining Homicide in New York City: A Tale of Two Trends," *Journal of Criminal Law and Criminology* 88, no. 4 (1998): 1277–324. See also Richard Curtis, "The Improbable Transformation of Inner-City Neighborhoods: Crime, Violence, Drugs, and Youth in the 1990s," *Journal of Criminal Law and Criminology* 88, no. 4 (1998): 1233–76.

24   Bruce Western, *Punishment and Inequality in America* (New York: Russell Sage Foundation, 2006).

25   For a history of the politics of criminal justice policy, see David Dagan and

Steven M. Teles, *Prison Break: Why Conservatives Turned Against Mass Incarceration* (New York: Oxford University Press, 2016). On the history of black community support for punitive policy in New York, see Michael Javen Fortner, *Black Silent Majority: The Rockefeller Drug Laws and the Politics of Punishment* (Cambridge, Mass.: Harvard University Press, 2015). On the role of black lawmakers in pushing through sentencing laws that contributed to the expansion of the prison system, see James Forman, Jr., *Locking Up Our Own: Crime and Punishment in Black America* (New York: Farrar, Straus and Giroux, 2017).

26 The Sentencing Project is one of the few organizations that fought the rise of incarceration well before mass imprisonment became well known to politicians and the public. A report co-written by its executive director reviewed available evidence and concluded that the rise of incarceration accounted for about a quarter of the decline in crime since the 1990s. See Ryan S. King, Marc Mauer, and Malcolm C. Young, "Incarceration and Crime: A Complex Relationship," Sentencing Project (2005), at http://www.sentencingproject.org/wp-content/uploads/2016/01/Incarceration-and-Crime-A-Complex-Relationship.pdf.

27 Jeremy Travis, Bruce Western, and Steve Redburn, eds., *The Growth of Incarceration in the United States: Exploring Causes and Consequences* (Washington, D.C.: National Academies Press, 2014).

28 I first read about Juanita Tate and her organization in Alexander von Hoffman, *House by House, Block by Block: The Rebirth of America's Urban Neighborhoods* (New York: Oxford University Press, 2003), and I began to research her work. Sadly, she passed away shortly after von Hoffman's book was published.

29 "Concerned Citizens of South Central Los Angeles," http://ccscla.org.

30 Interest in the relationship between community groups and crime was substantial in the 1960s and 1970s, when investment in community organizations was a major approach to confronting the challenges in poor urban neighborhoods. But this research focused mostly on specific initiatives to fight crime at the neighborhood level. After the enthusiasm for community approaches to crime waned, community organizations quietly began to emerge in the 1990s. For a review of the early work on community organizations and crime, see Dennis P. Rosenbaum, "Community Crime Prevention: A Review and Synthesis of the Literature," *Justice Quarterly* 5, no. 3 (1988): 323–95; and Wesley G. Skogan, "Community Organizations and Crime," *Crime and Justice* 10 (1988): 39–78.

31 Chalfin and McRary, "Effect of Police on Crime," discuss this issue in their review of the literature on policing and crime. Levitt, "Using Electoral Cycles," provides a discussion that is particularly useful here, because the method he developed to deal with the problem was our inspiration for the approach we used

to analyze the impact of nonprofits. Briefly, Levitt used year-to-year variation in city firefighters as an instrument for year-to-year variation in city police officers. The rationale is that support for firefighters is driven by general conditions around fiscal negotiations, budgets, and the strength of public sector unions in cities. Levitt utilized the variation in police department size that is driven by this variation in general conditions of support for public servants in order to estimate the impact of changes in police size on crime. In our analysis, we use year-to-year variation in the number of nonprofit organizations focusing on arts, the environment, and medical research as an instrument for year-to-year variation in the number of nonprofits focusing on crime, youth, and community problems like poverty and housing. Our justification for this approach mimics that of Levitt.

32   For details, see Patrick Sharkey, Gerard Torrats-Espinosa, and Delaram Takyar, "Community and the Crime Decline: The Causal Effect of Local Nonprofit Formation on Violent Crime," *American Sociological Review* (2018). The basic idea was to take advantage of the fact that nonprofits are formed partly in response to important social problems like crime, but they are also formed when funding becomes available from the state or from local philanthropists to support organizations for the arts, for the environment, for medical research, and for crime and violence. We isolated the changes in antiviolence nonprofits that were due to these shifts in funding conditions, rather than changes in crime, in order to get a better causal estimate of the impact on violence.

33   The story of Valley Interfaith is told in Robert D. Putnam, Lewis Feldstein, and Donald J. Cohen, *Better Together: Restoring the American Community* (New York: Simon and Schuster, 2004), chap. 1.

34   Ibid., p. 27.

35   A mid-1990s study of Washington Heights concluded that the entire community was overcome by fear of violence: "Adults fear youth. Immigrants fear authorities and community service institutions. People of different cultural origins misunderstand and fear one another." The problem of violence paralyzed the entire neighborhood. See Mindy Thompson Fullilove et al., "Injury and Anomie: Effects of Violence on an Inner-City Community," *American Journal of Public Health* 8, no. 6 (1998): 924–25. The report is quoted in Robert W. Snyder, *Crossing Broadway: Washington Heights and the Promise of New York City* (Ithaca, N.Y.: Cornell University Press, 2014).

36   Snyder, *Crossing Broadway.*

37   Von Hoffman, *House by House.* On the Dudley Triangle of Boston, see Putnam, Feldstein, and Cohen, *Better Together* and Peter Medoff and Holly Sklar, *Streets*

of Hope: The Fall and Rise of an Urban Neighborhood (Boston: South End Press, 1994). On the story of Little Village, see Robert Vargas, *Wounded City* (New York: Oxford University Press, 2016). On the change that has taken place in East Lake, Atlanta, see Chapter 9 of this book.

38   Steven Levitt and Stephen Dubner, *Freakonomics* (New York: William Morrow, 2005); and John Donohue and Steven D. Levitt, "The Impact of Legalized Abortion on Crime," *Quarterly Journal of Economics* 116, no. 2 (2001): 379–420.

39   Theodore J. Joyce, "Did Legalized Abortion Lower Crime?" *Journal of Human Resources* 39, no. 1 (2004): 1–28. See also Theodore J. Joyce, "A Simple Test of Abortion and Crime," *Review of Economics and Statistics* 91, no. 1 (2009): 112–23; Christopher L. Foote and Christopher F. Goetz, "The Impact of Legalized Abortion on Crime: Comment," *Quarterly Journal of Economics* 123, no. 1 (2008): 407–23; and Franklin E. Zimring, *The Great American Crime Decline* (New York: Oxford University Press, 2006). For a response to Joyce's 2004 article, see John J. Donohue and Steven D. Levitt, "Further Evidence That Legalized Abortion Lowered Crime: A Reply to Joyce," *Journal of Human Resources* 39, no. 1 (2004): 29–49.

40   Philip J. Cook and John H. Laub, "After the Epidemic: Recent Trends in Youth Violence in the United States," *Crime and Justice* 29 (2002): 1–37.

41   Zimring, *Great American Crime Decline*.

42   For instance, see the discussions in ibid.; in Alfred Blumstein and Joel Wallman, eds., *The Crime Drop in America* (Cambridge, U.K.: Cambridge University Press, 2006); and in Steven Pinker, *The Better Angels of Our Nature: Why Violence Has Declined* (New York: Viking, 2011).

43   The two primary sources of lead contamination are lead-based paint and leaded gasoline. Lead-based paint has become much less common over time, as it was banned for indoor use in 1950 and for all residential purposes in 1978. Similarly, the Clean Air Act of 1970 led to an almost complete removal of lead from gasoline between 1975 and 1985. As a result of these regulations, the average level of lead in the blood of Americans declined rapidly, and uniformly across all demographic groups, from the mid-1970s to the early 1990s. A new study with data from Rhose Island provides the most compelling evidence to date that exposure to lead has a causal effect on individual behavior leading to school suspensions and possibly incarceration. However, the study focuses on birth cohorts in a low-crime state who reached teenage years well after the drop in violence, and thus requires substantial extrapolation to be applicable for explaining the crime decline. See Anna Aizer and Janet Currie, "Lead and Juvenile Delinquency:

New Evidence from Linked Birth, School and Juvenile Detention Records," National Bureau of Economic Research, Working paper w23392 (2017). The most widely-cited previous study on lead and crime is Jessica Wolpaw Reyes, "Environmental Policy as Social Policy? The Impact of Childhood Lead Exposure on Crime," *BE Journal of Economic Analysis and Policy* 7, no. 1 (2007): 1–41. To identify the effect of changes in lead exposure on crime, Reyes exploited the fact that the amount of lead in gasoline was phased out at different rates across states, which were differentially affected by Clean Air Act regulations. Analyzing variations, within states, in the level of gasoline in lead while controlling for other characteristics that changed over time, Reyes found evidence that changes in the amount of lead in gasoline had large effects on rates of violent crime twenty-two years later. Although the strongest results from the Reyes study led the author to conclude that reduced lead in gasoline could account for more than half the national decline in violent crime, a closer look at the results suggests that this interpretation should be thought of as an upper bound estimate of how much lead may have contributed to the crime drop. Analyses that use different measures of lead exposure produce inconsistent results, with effect sizes that are much smaller and are not always statistically significant. Analyses that focus on the murder rate, instead of on the violent crime rate, show no significant effects in most of Reyes's preferred specifications. See also Janet L. Lauritsen, Maribeth L. Rezey, and Karen Heimer, "When Choice of Data Matters: Analyses of U.S. Crime Trends, 1973–2012," *Journal of Quantitative Criminology* 32, no. 3 (2016): 335–55.

44   Pinker, *Better Angels.*

45   Peter K. Enns, *Incarceration Nation: How the United States Became the Most Punitive Democracy in the World* (Cambridge, U.K.: Cambridge University Press, 2016).

46   Skeptics might argue that it is only natural that crime would fall the most in the places where it was most severe, that the crime decline can be explained by a simple "reversion to the mean." But this claim reflects a widespread misunderstanding of mean reversion. Reversion to the mean refers to a process where trends are driven by a combination of meaningful change and by random noise; data points that are far from the mean because of random noise are likely to return closer to the mean over time. This statistical metaphor is relevant for short-term fluctuations in violence, but it is entirely inappropriate for the analysis of long-term trends in violence. If cities had much higher levels of violence than the nation as a whole, for a long period of time, that violence cannot be said to reflect random noise. If violent crime declined in those cities over long periods

of time, the drop cannot be explained as simple "mean reversion," which is an empty explanation. If crime fell the most in the places that were most violent, we need to develop an understanding for why that happened.

47   Alfred Blumstein has done the most work on the relationship between crack cocaine and the crime decline. Much of this research is summarized in Blumstein and Wallman, *Crime Drop in America*.

48   Levitt, "Understanding Why Crime Fell," carried out a simple exercise to generate a rough estimate of how much the decline of the crack market contributed to the overall drop in homicides. He compared the drop in homicides for young black males, the group most directly enmeshed in the violence of the crack trade, with those of older black males and other groups who were less involved. He estimated that the end of the crack epidemic accounted for a minimum of 15 percent of the drop in homicide rates. See also Jeff Grogger and Michael Willis, "The Emergence of Crack Cocaine and the Rise in Urban Crime Rates," *Review of Economics and Statistics* 82 (2000): 519–29.

49   For example, consider the Lojack car security system, first introduced in the mid-1980s as a new approach to solving the enormous problem of car theft. Lojack installed a hidden radio transmission device inside vehicles, allowing the police to track the location of stolen ones. The Lojack system is extremely effective, as almost all stolen vehicles with it installed are recovered. But even more compelling is the way this new technology transformed the costs and benefits of car theft in cities, making every car more secure. In cities with Lojack, car thieves had to consider the possibility that any potential targeted car could be the one that led the police directly to the thief's home or chop shop. The economists Ian Ayres and Steven Levitt exploited the fact that Lojack was introduced to different cities at different times in order to assess the impact of the car security system on rates of motor vehicle theft. They found that every three Lojack installations resulted in about one fewer auto vehicle thefts in the city. Based on these estimates, the introduction of Lojack was probably more efficient than just about any publicly funded crime prevention program. See Ian Ayres and Steven D. Levitt, "Measuring Positive Externalities from Unobservable Victim Precaution: An Empirical Analysis of Lojack," *Quarterly Journal of Economics* 113, no. 1 (1998): 43–77. As for security cameras, although their use has generated pushback from civil rights organizations and is not the most effective approach to confronting crime, their presence has changed the nature of public space and has been shown to reduce crime. A review of 44 high-quality evaluations of CCTV surveillance systems found that they are effective in reducing certain types of crime, like auto theft and other property crime. Brandon C.

Welsh and David P. Farrington, "Public Area CCTV and Crime Prevention: An Updated Systematic Review and Meta-Analysis," *Justice Quarterly* 26, no. 4 (2009): 716–45.

4. THE PRESERVATION OF BLACK LIVES

1   Chicago Police Department, "2009 Annual Report," at http://home.chicago police.org/wp-content/uploads/2014/12/2009-Annual-Report.pdf.

2   Derrion Albert's murder, and its aftermath, are documented in Steve James's 2011 film *The Interrupters*. See also Azmat Khan, "Derrion Albert: The Death that Riled the Nation," *Frontline*, February 14, 2012; and Emma, G. Fitzsimmons, "4 Teenagers Charged in Youth's Beating Death," *New York Times*, September 28, 2009.

3   Alexia Cooper and Erica L. Smith, "Homicide Trends in the United States, 1980–2008," Bureau of Justice Statistics, U.S. Department of Justice (2011), at http://www.bjs.gov/content/pub/pdf/htus8008.pdf.

4   Michael is now an assistant professor of sociology at the University of Wisconsin, Whitewater. See Patrick Sharkey and Michael Friedson, "The Impact of the Homicide Decline on Life Expectancy of African American Males," *Demography* (2018).

5   The most comprehensive and careful analysis of changes in the racial gap in life expectancy is Glenn Firebaugh et al., "Why the Racial Gap in Life Expectancy Is Declining in the United States," *Demographic Research* 31, no. 32 (2014): 975–1006.

6   For details of the analysis, see Patrick Sharkey and Michael Friedson, "The Impact of the Decline in Homicide on Life Expectancy at Birth," NYU Working Paper (2017), at www.patricksharkey.net. To calculate life expectancy under the counterfactual assumption that homicide rates did not change from 1991 to 2012, we estimated life expectancy at birth for each of the four groups while holding mortality rates constant at 1991 levels. The central assumption we make is that average life expectancy of homicide victims is equivalent to life expectancy of individuals of the same race, age, and education level. The results are not sensitive to this assumption, however. If we relax this assumption and assume that homicide victims have lower life expectancy by several years, the effect of the homicide decline on life expectancy changes very little.

7   S. Jay Olshansky et al., "A Potential Decline in Life Expectancy in the United States in the 21st Century," *New England Journal of Medicine* 352, no. 11 (2005): 1138–45.

8   To provide another example, consider a separate study focused on one of the most important public health breakthroughs of the last thirty years, the

decline of smoking. Forecasting into the future, researchers at Harvard estimated how life expectancy for eighteen-year-olds would change if the prevalence of smoking continued to decline at the same pace at which it declined over the previous fifteen years. They estimated that if the enormous declines in smoking continued at the same pace for the next fifteen years, life expectancy of the American population would rise by .31 years. See Susan T. Stewart, David M. Cutler, and Allison B. Rosen, "Forecasting the Effects of Obesity and Smoking on U.S. Life Expectancy," *New England Journal of Medicine* 361, no. 23 (2009): 2252–60.

9   "Estimates of Funding for Various Research, Condition, and Disease Categories (RCDC)," National Institutes of Health, U.S. Department of Health and Human Services (February 10, 2016), at https://report.nih.gov/categorical_ spending.aspx.

10   Dawn Turner Trice, "Christmas Finally Returns to Derrion Albert's Family," *Chicago Tribune*, December 16, 2013.

11   Margaret Stroebe, Henk Schut, and Wolfgang Stroebe, "Health Outcomes of Bereavement," *Lancet* 370, no. 9603 (2007): 1960–73.

12   Michael Javen Fortner, *Black Silent Majority: The Rockefeller Drug Laws and the Politics of Punishment* (Cambridge, Mass.: Harvard University Press, 2015).

13   Karen Jordan, "Chicago Father of 3 Shot to Death in Kitchen Was Aspiring Cop," ABC7News, October 5, 2016.

14   Tyler Holmes, "After Prison, Raygene Jackson Was Working Toward a Better Future, But New Life Cut Short by Gun in a 'City in Ruins,'" *Homicide Watch Chicago*, September 27, 2016, at http://homicides.suntimes.com/2016/09/27/ after-prison-raygene-jackson-was-working-toward-a-better-future-but-new -life-cut-short-by-gun-in-a-city-in-ruins.

5. LEARNING IN FEAR

1   "DC Area Sniper Fast Facts," CNN, September 18, 2015.

2   Alex Mitchell, "Social Impacts of Fear: An Examination of the 2002 Washington, D.C. Sniper Shootings," University of Colorado, Boulder (2002), at https:// pdfs.semanticscholar.org/dbef/dd040bcc5540abd466fc11b0e4f5924ccf17.pdf.

3   As a sociologist by training, I faced a steep learning curve in attempting to understand how the brain responds to stress in the environment. I began by attending a nine-day, intensive "neuroscience boot camp" directed by the cognitive neuroscientist Martha Farah and administered by the University of Pennsylvania's Center for Neuroscience and Society. This remarkable course

provided a solid foundation of knowledge on the brain. Since then the research of scholars like Clancy Blair, Sonia Lupien, Bruce McEwen, Cybele Raver, and Robert Sapolsky has been enormously helpful in solidifying my understanding of how the brain responds to stress over short and long periods of time.

4   This summary reflects my own synthesis of many excellent research reviews on the topic. In addition to a set of overview and review articles from Bruce McEwen, the most influential texts for me have been two books by Robert M. Sapolsky. *Why Zebras Don't Get Ulcers* (New York: W. H. Freeman, 1994) is a more accessible version of the relationship between stress and the body. *Stress, the Aging Brain, and the Mechanisms of Neuron Death* (Cambridge, Mass.: MIT Press, 1992) is a more technical version that contains detailed reviews of the early empirical literature.

5   Benno Roozendaal, Bruce S. McEwen, and Sumantra Chattarji, "Stress, Memory and the Amygdala," *Nature Reviews Neuroscience* 10, no. 6 (2009): 423–33.

6   Sonia J. Lupien et al., "Stress Hormones and Human Memory Function Across the Lifespan," *Psychoneuroendocrinology* 30, no. 3 (2005): 225–42.

7   Roozendaal, McEwen, and Chattarji, "Stress, Memory and Amygdala."

8   Larry Cahill and James L. McGaugh, "Mechanisms of Emotional Arousal and Lasting Declarative Memory," *Trends in Neurosciences* 21, no. 7 (1998): 294–99.

9   Marian Joëls et al., "Learning Under Stress: How Does It Work?" *Trends in Cognitive Sciences*, 10, no. 4 (2006): 152–58.

10   Shaozheng Qin et al., "Understanding Low Reliability of Memories for Neutral Information Encoded Under Stress: Alterations in Memory-Related Activation in the Hippocampus and Midbrain," *Journal of Neuroscience*. 32, no. 12 (2012): 4032–41.

11   For a history of the project, see Robert J. Sampson, *Great American City: Chicago and the Enduring Neighborhood Effect* (Chicago: University of Chicago Press, 2012).

12   A fourth wave has also recently been collected with a subset of the original sample.

13   Julia Burdick-Will et al., "Converging Evidence for Neighborhood Effects on Children's Test Scores: An Experimental, Quasiexperimental, and Observational Comparison," in *Whither Opportunity? Rising Inequality, Schools, and Children's Life Chances*, ed. Greg Duncan and Richard Murnane (New York: Russell Sage Foundation, 2011); and Robert J. Sampson, Patrick Sharkey, and Stephen Raudenbush, "Durable Effects of Concentrated Disadvantage on Verbal Ability among African-American Children," *Proceedings of the National Academy of Sciences* 105 (2008): 845–52.

14   Patrick Sharkey, *Stuck in Place: Urban Neighborhoods and the End of Progress Toward Racial Equality* (Chicago: University of Chicago Press, 2013).

15   For details, see Patrick Sharkey and Felix Elwert, "The Legacy of Disadvantage: Multigenerational Neighborhood Effects on Cognitive Ability," *American Journal of Sociology* 116 (2011): 1934–81.

16   Dr. Champagne's publications and accomplishments are too numerous to list, but her lab's website "Champagne Lab: Psychobiology, Epigenetics, and Neuroscience," offers an introduction to her research: http://champagne lab.psych.columbia.edu/champagne.html.

17   Dr. David Diamond studies the effects of stress on brain, memory, and synaptic plasticity. He has conducted numerous experiments demonstrating that introducing a stressor to rats impairs memory and learning. His notable publications can be found at "Recent Publications of Dr. David Diamond," at http://psychology.usf.edu/publications/diamond.aspx. A review of the model of memory in the aftermath of severe stress can be found in David M. Diamond et al., "The Temporal Dynamics Model of Emotional Memory Processing: A Synthesis on the Neurobiological Basis of Stress-Induced Amnesia, Flashbulb and Traumatic Memories, and the Yerkes-Dodson Law," *Neural Plasticity* 2007 (2007): 60803–836; and Collin R. Park et al., "Acute Predator Stress Impairs the Consolidation and Retrieval of Hippocampus-Dependent Memory in Male and Female Rats," *Learning and Memory* 15, no. 4 (2008): 271–80.

18   The assumption made in this research is that the relative timing of children's assessments and local homicides is exogenous. Patrick Sharkey, "The Acute Effect of Local Homicides on Children's Cognitive Performance," *Proceedings of the National Academy of Sciences* 107 (2010): 11733–38, provides a series of tests to assess whether this assumption is valid. One test shows that children who were assessed just after a homicide occurred looked identical to other children assessed at a different time in terms of family characteristics, school engagement, grades, and other measures. Another test assessed whether there is an effect of being "exposed" to a homicide that occurs after a child is assessed. A homicide that occurs after the assessment should have no impact on the child's performance, and the analysis described in the appendix of that article confirms that all estimates of the impact of a homicide after the interview assessment hover around zero.

19   Johanna Lacoe and I analyzed data on reasonable suspicion stops in New York City and found that when a homicide occurs in a neighborhood, the number of police stops rises for every group, but it rises the most for African Americans. See Johanna Lacoe and Patrick Sharkey, "Life in a Crime Scene: Stop, Ques-

tion, and Frisk Activity in New York City Neighborhoods in the Aftermath of Homicides," *Sociological Science* 3 (2016): 116–34.

20   Patrick Sharkey et al., "High Stakes in the Classroom, High Stakes on the Street: The Effects of Community Violence on Students' Standardized Test Performance," *Sociological Science* 1 (2014): 199–220.

21   Seth Gershenson and Erdal Tekin, "The Effect of Community Traumatic Events on Student Achievement: Evidence from the Beltway Sniper Attacks," National Bureau of Economic Research, Working Paper no. 21055 (March 2015).

22   Paul Duggan, "Sniper's Imprint, Faded, Remains Indelible," *Washington Post,* November 11, 2009.

23   Steve Vogel, "Sandy Hook Elementary Shooting Leaves 28 Dead, Law Enforcement Sources Say," *Washington Post,* December 14, 2012.

24   James Alan Fox and Emma E. Fridel, "The Three R's of School Shootings: Risk, Readiness, and Response," in H. Shapiro, ed., *The Wiley Handbook on Violence in Education: Forms, Factors, and Preventions* (New York: Wiley/Blackwell Publishers, June 2018).

25   "Data Collection: National Crime Victimization Survey (NCVS)," Bureau of Justice Statistics, U.S. Department of Justice (2015), at http://www.bjs.gov/index.cfm?ty=dcdetail&iid=245#Publications_and_products.

26   "Youth Online: High School Youth Risk Surveillance System" (1991–2005), Centers for Disease Control and Prevention, at https://nccd.cdc.gov/youthonline/App/Default.aspx.

27   "Digest of Education Statistics: Table 230.70 Percentage of Students Ages 12–18 Who Reported Being Afraid of Attack or Harm, by Location and Selected Student and School Characteristics: Selected Years, 1995–2013," National Center for Education Statistics, U.S. Department of Justice and U.S. Department of Education (2015), at http://nces.ed.gov/programs/digest/d14/tables/dt14_230.70.asp?current=yes.

28   "National Assessment of Educational Progress (NAEP)," National Center for Education Statistics, at http://nces.ed.gov/nationsreportcard.

29   To carry out this analysis, I calculated average scores at the state level over two years of testing in the early 1990s and again in the late 2010s. Specific years varied depending on the age group. The main analysis focuses on fourth-grade reading scores and shows a strong bivariate relationship between state-level declines in homicide rates (and violent crime rates) and state-level changes in reading scores (with results weighted based on the number of test-takers). An additional analysis showed a similar bivariate relationship between changes

in homicide rates (and violent crime rates) and changes in black-white gaps in fourth-grade reading scores. Similar results are found for eighth graders and for math tests. Results are robust to controlling for changes in state-level demographics, but more elaborate analyses are not possible given the small sample size. I thank Sean Reardon for providing complete state-level data from the NAEP. See Andrew D. Ho and Sean F. Reardon, "Estimating Achievement Gaps from Test Scores Reported in Ordinal 'Proficiency' Categories," *Journal of Educational and Behavioral Statistics* 37, no.4 (2012): 489–517.

30   For details of the analysis, see Patrick Sharkey and Gerard Torrats-Espinosa, "The Effect of Violent Crime on Economic Mobility," *Journal of Urban Economics* (2017).

31   Anthony S. Bryk et al., *Organizing Schools for Improvement: Lessons from Chicago* (Chicago: University of Chicago Press, 2010); and James Garbarino et al., *Children in Danger: Coping with the Consequences of Community Violence* (San Francisco: Jossey-Bass, 1992).

32   Richard Arum, "Class and Racial Differences in U.S. School Disciplinary Environments," in *Improving Learning Environments: School Discipline and Student Achievement in Comparative Perspective,* ed. Richard Arum and Melissa Velez (Stanford, Calif.: Stanford University Press, 2012); Dewey G. Cornell and Matthew J. Mayer, "Why Do School Order and Safety Matter?" *Educational Researcher* 39, no. 1 (2010): 7–15; Johanna Lacoe, "Too Scared to Learn? The Academic Consequences of Feeling Unsafe at School," *Urban Education* (2016): 1–34.

33   Gershenson and Tekin, "Effect of Community Traumatic Events"; Sharkey, "Acute Effect of Local Homicides."

34   Burdick-Will et al., "Converging Evidence for Neighborhood Effects."

6. INEQUALITY AFTER THE CRIME DECLINE

1   For details of the attacks that night, see David E. Pitt, "Jogger's Attackers Terrorized at Least 9 in 2 Hours," *New York Times,* April 22, 1989. For a complete history of the incident, media coverage, and the legal aftermath see, Sarah Burns, *The Central Park Five: A Chronicle of a City Wilding* (New York: Alfred A. Knopf, 2011).

2   The reaction of Donald Trump, then a private citizen, provides an example of the most extreme public response to the crime. Trump took out a full-page ad in all four major newspapers with a headline in enormous capital letters: "BRING BACK THE DEATH PENALTY. BRING BACK OUR POLICE!" "They should

be forced to suffer," he wrote, "and when they kill, they should be executed for their crimes," He went further: "I no longer want to understand their anger. I want them to understand our anger. I want them to be afraid." See Oliver Laughland, "Donald Trump and the Central Park Five: The Racially Charged Rise of a Demagogue," *Guardian*, February 17, 2016.

3   Lisa W. Foderaro, "Dark Days Behind It, Central Park Pulses at Night," *New York Times,* December 28, 2011.

4   Ibid.

5   Emmanuel Saez and Gabriel Zucman, "Wealth Inequality in the United States Since 1913: Evidence from Capitalized Income Tax Data," *Quarterly Journal of Economics* 131, no. 2 (2016): 519–78; and Chad Stone et al., "A Guide to Statistics on Historical Trends in Income Inequality," Center on Budget and Policy Priorities (2016), at http://www.cbpp.org/research/poverty-and-inequality/a-guide-to-statistics-on-historical-trends-in-income-inequality.

6   Sean F. Reardon and Kendra Bischoff, "The Continuing Increase in Income Segregation, 2007–2012," Stanford Center for Education Policy Analysis (2016), at http://cepa.stanford.edu/content/continuing-increase-income-segregation-2007-2012.

7   Figures on the rise of gated community living are based on questions asked in the American Housing Survey that were first asked in 2001. On the rise in the percentage of Americans living in gated communities, see Rich Benjamin, "The Gated Community Mentality," *New York Times*, March 29, 2012. For the latest figures on the number of American families in high-poverty neighborhoods, see Paul A. Jargowsky, "Architecture of Segregation: Civil Unrest, the Concentration of Poverty, and Public Policy," Century Foundation (2015), at https://tcf.org/content/report/architecture-of-segregation/.

8   Lance Freeman, *There Goes the Hood: Views of Gentrification from the Ground Up* (Philadelphia: Temple University Press, 2011).

9   Monique Taylor, *Harlem Between Heaven and Hell* (Minneapolis: University of Minnesota Press, 2002). The best evidence available on crime and migration suggests that every crime that occurred in cities over the 1970s and 1980s led one additional city resident to depart, with most leaving for new suburban towns within the same metropolitan area. See Julie Berry Cullen and Steven D. Levitt, "Crime, Urban Flight, and the Consequences for Cities," *Review of Economics and Statistics* 81, no. 2 (1999): 159–69.

10   Freeman, *There Goes the Hood.*

11   Ibid. See also Alexander von Hoffman, *House by House, Block by Block: The*

Rebirth of America's Urban Neighborhoods (New York: Oxford University Press, 2003).

12   For details, see Gerard Torrats-Espinosa and Patrick Sharkey, "The Fall of Violence and the Reconfiguration of Urban Neighborhoods," NYU Working Paper (2018), at www.patricksharkey.net. To identify the effect of change in violent crime on economic segregation, we exploited variation in violence due to shocks such as (1) the timing of the crack epidemic that hit cities in the late 1980s and continued into the 1990s; and (2) the timing of cities' receipt of grants through the federal COPS program, which was unrelated to prior crime trends and has been shown to have affected crime.

13   Alan Ehrenhalt, *The Great Inversion and the Future of the American City* (New York: Knopf Doubleday, 2012); and Derek Hyra, *Race, Class, and Politics in the Cappuccino City* (Chicago: University of Chicago Press, 2017).

14   The threat of displacement has been studied extensively in the literature on gentrification, but the conclusions from this research are mixed. One of the most influential studies found minimal evidence that gentrifying neighborhoods lead to higher levels of displacement: Lance Freeman and Frank Braconi, "Gentrification and Displacement in New York City," *Journal of the American Planning Association* 70, no. 1 (2004): 39–52. However, this conclusion was driven by the finding that such neighborhoods already have high rates of turnover, as renters are constantly moving in and out. It does not mean that displacement is not an issue, but rather that there is no noticeable increase in the amount of movement out of the neighborhood as it undergoes change. This research was carried out in New York, which has more extensive protections for renters than many other cities. Other ethnographic research has found stronger evidence that the threat of displacement is amplified as neighborhoods gentrify and landlords seek to maximize the rent they can obtain in "hot" neighborhoods. Freeman reviews this literature in detail in *There Goes the Hood*. Derek Hyra also studies gentrification in Harlem, providing a less positive view that contrasts the experience of the black middle class and the black poor. See Derek Hyra, *The New Urban Renewal: The Economic Transformation of Harlem and Bronzeville* (Chicago: University of Chicago Press, 2008).

15   This claim is based on a national analysis focusing on the impact of neighborhood change in the most disadvantaged U.S. neighborhoods from 1970 to 2000. In each decade I examined, I found that when poverty becomes less concentrated, it typically does not mean that white newcomers are displacing black residents but rather that the neighborhood is becoming more ethnically diverse

as it becomes less racially segregated and experiences growth in the Hispanic population. See Patrick Sharkey, "An Alternative Approach to Addressing Selection Into and Out of Social Settings: Neighborhood Change and African American Children's Economic Outcomes," *Sociological Methods and Research* 41 (2012): 251–93. For a more general perspective on the misconceptions about gentrification, see John Buntin, "The Myth of Gentrification," *Slate* (January 14, 2015).

16   Jackelyn Hwang and Robert J. Sampson, "Divergent Pathways of Gentrification, Racial Inequality, and the Social Order of Renewal in Chicago Neighborhoods," *American Sociological Review* 79, no. 4 (2014): 726–51.

17   Raj Chetty et al., "Where Is the Land of Opportunity? The Geography of Intergenerational Mobility in the United States," *Quarterly Journal of Economics* 129, no. 4 (2014): 1553–623; Raj Chetty et al., "Is the United States Still a Land of Opportunity? Recent Trends in Intergenerational Mobility," *American Economic Review Papers and Proceedings* 104, no. 5 (2014): 141–47; Raj Chetty and Nathaniel Hendren, "The Impacts of Neighborhoods on Intergenerational Mobility: Childhood Exposure Effects and County Level Estimates," National Bureau of Economic Research, Working Papers no. 23001 and 23002 (2016).

18   We used two approaches to identify the causal effect of county-level changes in violent crime on upward economic mobility. First, we exploited variation in successive birth cohorts' exposure to violent crime from age fourteen to seventeen in a fixed-effects setup. This approach accounts for all time-invariant attributes of counties and controls for temporal trends that are common to all counties. Second, to address the possibility that the association between within-county changes in violent crime and changes in economic mobility may be driven by unobserved, time-varying characteristics of the county or its population, we used an instrumental variable strategy that exploits the timing of grants that local and state police departments received under the Community Oriented Policing Service (COPS) program. Prior research has shown that the addition of police officers through the COPS grants generated statistically significant reductions in violent and property crimes. The timing of receipt of the grants was uncorrelated with prior trends in crime, which makes this policy shock a candidate for an instrument for changes in within-county crime rates. See Patrick Sharkey and Gerard Torrats-Espinosa, "The Effect of Violent Crime on Economic Mobility," *Journal of Urban Economics* (2017).

19   Stone et al., "Guide to Statistics on Historical Trends."

20   Policy ideas to preserve affordable housing in communities with rising demand can be found in Patrick Sharkey, Robert D. Putnam, and Margery Turner, "Rebuilding Communities to Help Close the Opportunity Gap," in *Closing the*

Opportunity Gap: A Project of the Saguaro Seminar, ed. Thomas Sander and Toby Lester (Cambridge, Mass.: Harvard Kennedy School, 2016), at https://www.theopportunitygap.com/the-report.

21   For international comparisons of economic mobility, see Miles Corak, "Do Poor Children Become Poor Adults? Lessons from a Cross Country Comparison of Generational Earnings Mobility," IZA Discussion Paper no. 1993 (Bonn, Germany: Institute for the Study of Labor, 2006); Timothy M. Smeeding, Robert Erikson, and Markus Jantti, eds., *Persistence, Privilege, and Parenting: The Comparative Study of Intergenerational Mobility* (New York: Russell Sage Foundation, 2011); and Gary Solon, "Cross-Country Differences in Intergenerational Earnings Mobility," *Journal of Economic Perspectives* 16, no. 3 (2002): 59–66.

22   I borrow the label "age of extremes" from Douglas S. Massey, "The Age of Extremes: Concentrated Affluence and Poverty in the Twenty-First Century," *Demography* 33, no. 4 (1996): 395–412. Victimization rates are in "Data Collection: National Crime Victimization Survey (NCVS)," Bureau of Justice Statistics, U.S. Department of Justice, at http://www.bjs.gov/index.cfm?ty=dcdetail&iid=245#Publications_and_products.

23   In my own research I have found that African Americans making at least $100,000 in annual income live in more disadvantaged neighborhoods than whites making less than $30,000 per year. See Patrick Sharkey, "Spatial Segmentation and the Black Middle Class," *American Journal of Sociology* 119, no. 4 (2014): 903–54.

7. ABANDONMENT, PUNISHMENT, AND THE NEW COMPROMISE

1   Ross Tuttle and Erin Schneider, "Stopped-and-Frisked: 'For Being a F**king Mutt,'" *Nation*, October 8, 2012.

2   For details on racial discrepancies in the NYPD's use of "reasonable suspicion" stops, see Amanda Gelman, Jeffrey Fagan, and Alex Kiss, "An Analysis of the New York City Police Department's 'Stop and Frisk' Policy in the Context of Claims of Racial Bias," *Journal of the American Statistical Association* 102 (2007): 813–23; and Johanna Lacoe and Patrick Sharkey, "Life in a Crime Scene: Stop, Question, and Frisk Activity in New York City Neighborhoods in the Aftermath of Homicides," *Sociological Science* 3 (2016): 116–34. For an ethnographic account of the way young men of color are targeted by law enforcement see, Victor Rios, *Punished: Policing the Lives of Black and Latino Boys* (New York: New York University Press, 2011).

3   Jillian Jorgensen, "De Blasio Touts Lower Crime and Better Relationships,

Despite Criticism," *Observer,* December 2, 2014; and Benjamin Weiser, "Judges Decline to Reverse Stop-and-Frisk Ruling, All but Ending Mayor's Fight," *New York Times,* November 22, 2013. For trends in the use of "reasonable suspicion stops," see William J. Bratton, "Broken Windows and Quality-of-Life Policing in New York City," New York Police Department (2015), at http://www.nyc.gov/html/nypd/downloads/pdf/analysis_and_planning/qol.pdf.

4   Leah Libresco, "It Takes a Lot of Stop-and-Frisks to Find One Gun," FiveThirty Eight.com (June 3, 2015).

5   Matthew Bloch, Ford Fessenden, and Janet Roberts, "Stop, Question, and Frisk in New York City Neighborhoods," *New York Times,* July 11, 2010.

6   For documentation of the criminalization of black Americans throughout U.S. history, see Khalil Gibran Muhammad, *The Condemnation of Blackness* (Cambridge, Mass.: Harvard University Press, 2011). See also Jeffrey Fagan and Tracey Meares, "Punishment, Deterrence, and Social Control: The Paradox of Punishment in Minority Communities," *Ohio State Journal of Criminal Law* 6 (2008): 173–229.

7   In 2011, survey data indicated that 71 percent of individuals stopped on the street and 88 percent stopped in a car reported that the police officer "behaved properly." See Lynn Langton and Matthew Durose, "Police Behavior During Traffic and Street Stops, 2011," Bureau of Justice Statistics, U.S. Department of Justice (2013), at http://www.bjs.gov/content/pub/pdf/pbtss11.pdf.

8   Ta-Nehisi Coates, *Between the World and Me* (New York: Spiegel and Grau, 2015), p. 9.

9   Robert Sampson and Charles Loeffler, "Punishment's Place: The Local Concentration of Mass Incarceration," *Daedalus* 139, no. 3 (2010): 20–31; Jeffrey Fagan, Valerie West, and Jan Hollan, "Reciprocal Effects of Crime and Incarceration in New York City Neighborhoods," *Fordham Urban Law Journal* 30 (2003): 1555–602; Jeffrey Fagan et al., "Street Stops and Broken Windows Revisited: The Demography and Logic of Proactive Policing in a Safe and Changing City," in *Race, Ethnicity, and Policing: New and Essential Readings,* ed. Stephen Rice and Michael White (New York: New York University Press, 2010); and Becky Pettit and Bruce Western, "Mass Imprisonment and the Life Course: Race and Class Inequality in U.S. Incarceration," *American Sociological Review* 69, no. 2 (2016): 151–69.

10 Information on police violence has never been collected in a systematic way, so it is impossible to know exactly how often police resort to force, or even how often a police officer kills a civilian. The FBI relies on police departments to report every time an officer kills a felon in a "justifiable homicide," just as they

are asked to report every other homicide that has occurred over the course of each year. Efforts by journalists and activists to document every person who is killed by law enforcement have shown that the official figures, reported each year by the FBI, substantially underestimate the total number of individuals killed by law enforcement. Even if these figures are substantially biased, the numbers reported by the FBI are revealing. Data from the "Supplemental Homicide Reports" show that homicides occurring during robberies, drugs or gang disputes, arguments, or during the commission of other serious crimes all fell by somewhere between 40 percent and 80 percent since 1991. Almost every type of homicide has become less common over time, but there is one notable exception. From the early 1990s to the present, the number of "justifiable homicides" committed by police officers has been remarkably consistent. In the early 1990s, police officers usually killed about 475 people over the course of a year. Twenty years or so later, officers kill roughly 450 people each year. Pointing out the number of people killed by law enforcement tells us nothing about whether each incident was justified, whether police acted appropriately, or whether unnecessary force was used. What it does reveal, however, is a very consistent level of police force over time. As just about every other type of lethal violence has subsided over time, lethal violence from the police has remained constant. See "Uniform Crime Reporting Program Data: Supplementary Homicide Reports," FBI, U.S. Department of Justice (2014), at http://doi.org/10.3886/ICPSR36393.v1.

11   The most comprehensive treatment of the relationship between crime and public opinion is Peter K. Enns, *Incarceration Nation: How the United States Became the Most Punitive Democracy in the World* (Cambridge, U.K.: Cambridge University Press, 2016). It also documents the way perceptions of crime have fluctuated over the past several decades. Although Gallup's "most important problem" question is the simplest example of changes in public opinion toward crime, it is not the best measure. Events like terrorism, war, or changes in the national economy have shifted the public's attention away from crime and violence at different points in history. Enns uses an alternative measure of punitiveness to capture public sentiment about crime and criminals, and he finds a strong and robust relationship between trends in crime and violence and trends in punitiveness.

12   The riots in Detroit, Newark, Chicago, and Watts are described in detail in Michael Flamm, *Law and Order: Street Crime, Civil Unrest, and the Crisis of Liberalism in the 1960s* (New York: Columbia University Press, 2005); and Rick Perlstein, *Nixonland: The Rise of a President and the Fracturing of America* (New York: Simon and Schuster, 2010).

13   Lyndon B. Johnson, "Remarks Upon Signing Order Establishing the National Advisory Commission on Civil Disorders" July 29, 1967, at http://www.presidency.ucsb.edu/ws/?pid=28369.

14   National Advisory Commission on Civil Disorders and Otto Kerner, *Report of the National Advisory Commission on Civil Disorders* (Washington, D.C.: U.S. Government Printing Office, 1968).

15   Lyndon B. Johnson, "Special Message to the Congress on Law Enforcement and the Administration of Justice," March 8, 1965, at http://www.presidency.ucsb.edu/ws/?pid=26800.

16   My reading of the political and legislative history of this period relies heavily on the work of three scholars of the origins of mass incarceration: Enns, *Incarceration Nation*; Elizabeth Hinton, *From the War on Poverty to the War on Crime: The Making of Mass Incarceration in America* (Cambridge, Mass.: Harvard University Press, 2016); and Vesla M. Weaver, "Frontlash: Race and the Development of Punitive Crime Policy," *Studies in American Political Development* 21 (2007): 230–65.

17   J. Edgar Hoover, "An American's Challenge: Communism and Crime," October 9, 1962, *Vital Speeches of the Day* 29, no. 4 (1962): 98–101, p. 99. I became aware of this speech and Hoover's rhetoric in Weaver, "Frontlash."

18   Perlstein, *Nixonland*.

19   Ibid.

20   Hinton, *War on Poverty to War on Crime*.

21   Lyndon B. Johnson, "Statement by the President Following the Signing of Law Enforcement Assistance Bills," September 22, 1965, at http://www.presidency.ucsb.edu/ws/?pid=27270.

22   Ibid.

23   Richard M. Nixon, "Radio Address About the State of the Union Message on Community Development," March 4, 1973, at http://www.presidency.ucsb.edu/ws/?pid=4128.

24   Kerner, *Report of the National Advisory Commission on Civil Disorders*.

25   Moynihan used this term in a memo to President Nixon on the state of African Americans after the first year of his administration. Moynihan's argument suggested that economic progress for black Americans was continuing, yet anger was not subsiding. This led him to believe that it was time to focus less attention on the issue of race. See Dean J. Kotlowski. *Nixon's Civil Rights: Politics, Principle, and Policy* (Cambridge, Mass.: Harvard University Press, 2001).

26   Alexander von Hoffman, *House by House, Block by Block: The Rebirth of America's Urban Neighborhoods* (New York: Oxford University Press, 2003).

27   Margery Austin Turner et al., "Tackling Persistent Poverty in Distressed Urban Neighborhoods," Urban Institute (2014), at http://www.urban.org/research/ publication/tackling-persistent-poverty-distressed-urban-neighborhoods.

28   William Ahern, "Comparing the Kennedy, Reagan and Bush Tax Cuts," Tax Foundation (2004), at http://taxfoundation.org/article/comparing-kennedy-reagan-and -bush-tax-cuts.

29   Although it is impossible to know how cities would have fared in the absence of the Recovery Act, my own view is that the legislation was crucial to stabilizing poor communities until the economy regrouped and joblessness began to decline. See Patrick Sharkey, "The Urban Fire Next Time," *New York Times,* April 28, 2013.

30   German Lopez, "What Jeff Sessions Has Done So Far Is Toward One Goal: Unleashing the Police," *Vox.com* (May 4, 2017); Rebeca R. Ruiz, "Attorney General Orders Tougher Crime Sentences, Rolling Back Obama Policy," *New York Times*, May 12, 2017.

31   Michelle Alexander, *The New Jim Crow: Mass Incarceration in the Age of Colorblindness* (New York: New Press, 2012), pp. 235–36.

32   Alexander's argument shares features with the work of sociologist Loïc Wacquant, who has traced the systems of racial domination in the United States from slavery to Jim Crow, to the formation of the ghetto and finally to the prison. One central difference is that Wacquant focuses greater attention on class divisions and economic dislocation, noting that much of the black middle and upper class supported and benefited from the rise of mass incarceration that targeted the urban ghetto. See Loïc Wacquant, *Punishing the Poor: The Neoliberal Government of Social Insecurity* (Durham, N.C.: Duke University Press, 2009).

33   Ta-Nehisi Coates, "The Black Family in the Age of Mass Incarceration," *Atlantic,* October 2015.

34   Perkins is quoted in David Dagan and Steven M. Teles, "The Conservative War on Prisons," *Washington Monthly,* November–December 2012, an article describing the conservative movement for criminal justice reform.

35   Max Blumenthal, "Good Cop, Bad Cop," *Nation,* May 23, 2005.

36   This is part of the Family Research Council's mission statement, at http:// www.frc.org/mission-statement.

37   Tony Perkins, "Building Stronger Families and Safer Communities," Family Research Council (n.d.), at http://www.frc.org/op-eds/building-stronger-families -and-safer-communities.

38   Barbara Arnwine, on *Melissa Harris-Perry,* MSNBC, March 28, 2015, at http:// www.msnbc.com/transcripts/melissa-harris-perry/2015-03-28.

39   "Barbara Arnwine, Civil Rights Lawyer, Has Home Raided by Police," *Huffing-ton Post,* November 29, 2011.

40   All quotations are from the website of the Transformative Justice Coalition, at http://www.tjcoalition.org/about-tjc.

41   David Dagan and Steven M. Teles, *Prison Break: Why Conservatives Turned Against Mass Incarceration* (New York: Oxford University Press, 2016), p. xi.

42   Michael Grunwald, "Grover Norquist Isn't Finished," *Politico,* October 21, 2015.

43   Dagan and Teles, *Prison Break.*

44   Joan Walsh, "Rand Paul Just Wrecked His '16 Campaign: Watch His Awful Eric Garner Answer," *Salon,* December 5, 2015.

45   Hearings and working groups in both the House and the Senate formed to take on the issue of policing reform, with Republicans taking leadership positions in both cases. The hearings generated strong disagreement, but some of the most substantive actions proposed have come from politicians on the right. This pattern is reflected in statements and essays on criminal justice reform as well as policing reform. See M. Chettiar Inmai et al., "Solutions: American Leaders Speak Out on Criminal Justice," Brennan Center for Social Justice (2015), at https://www.brennancenter.org/publication/solutions-american-leaders-speak-out-criminal-justice. See also Rachel Bade, "House Hearing on Police Turns Ugly," *Politico,* May 19, 2015.

46   As an example, Grover Norquist shared the podium with Ben Jealous, former head of the NAACP, in an event publicizing the release of a new report on criminal justice reform. See Dagan and Teles, *Prison Break.*

47   Eric Cadora, "Justice Reinvestment in the U.S.," in *Justice Reinvestment: A New Approach to Crime,* ed. Robert Allen and Vivien Stern (London: International Centre for Prison Studies, 2007). See also Todd R. Clear and Natasha A. Frost, *The Punishment Imperative: The Rise and Failure of Mass Incarceration in America* (New York: New York University Press, 2015).

48   Lindsey Cramer et al., "The Justice Reinvestment Initiative: Experiences from the Local Sites," Urban Institute (2014), at http://www.urban.org/research/publication/justice-reinvestment-initiative-experiences-local-sites.

49   Eric Cadora, who conceived of the Justice Reinvestment approach and coined the term, has also written extensively about the limitations of the movement in practice. Cadora worked to create partners who would develop ways to reinvest savings from reductions in local prison populations into general investments to strengthen communities, but those initial plans did not materialize. Instead, savings from Justice Reinvestment initiatives have by and large been returned to criminal justice programs. For discussions of the "investment"

approach to Justice Reinvestment, see Susan Tucker and Eric Cadora, "Justice Reinvestment: To Invest in Public Safety by Reallocating Justice Dollars to Refinance Education, Housing, Healthcare, and Jobs," *Ideas for an Open Society* 3, no. 3 (2003): 1–5, at https://www.opensocietyfoundations.org/publications/ideas-open-society-justice-reinvestment; and Todd R. Clear, "A Private-Sector, Incentives-Based Model for Justice Reinvestment," *Criminology and Public Policy* 10, no. 3 (2011): 585–608. For a discussion of the implementation of Justice Reinvestment relative to these initial ideals, see Eric Cadora, "Civics Lessons: How Certain Schemes to End Mass Incarceration Can Fail," *Annals of the American Academy of Political and Social Science* 651, no. 1 (2014): 277–85.

50   Alexis de Tocqueville, *Democracy in America,* ed. and trans. Harvey C. Mansfield and Delba Winthrop (Chicago: University of Chicago Press, 2000). Tocqueville's observation seems remarkably prescient, as does his suggestion that an armed force would be necessary to deal with the problem of urban marginality. Yet this passage does not seem to have been noticed by many social scientists studying urban poverty. Discussions can be found in Edward Banfield, *The Unheavenly City* (Boston: Little, Brown, 1970); and Thomas Bender, *The Unfinished City: New York and the Metropolitan Idea* (New York: New York University Press, 2007).

51   Quoted in Banfield, *Unheavenly City.*

52   Nicholas Lemann, "The Myth of Community Development," *New York Times,* January 9, 1994.

8. THE END OF WARRIOR POLICING

1   On the origins of CompStat and the myriad attempts to utilize the principles laid out by Jack Maple on that napkin at Elaine's, see Robert D. Behn, *The PerformanceStat Potential: A Leadership Strategy for Producing Results* (Washington, D.C.: Brookings Institution Press, 2014).

2   David Weisburd et al., "Reforming to Preserve: CompStat and Strategic Problem Solving in American Policing," *Criminology and Public Policy* 2, no. 3 (2003): 421–56.

3   For a description and update of the Mayor's Action Plan, see http://www1.nyc.gov/assets/operations/downloads/pdf/pmmr2016/mayors_action_plan_for_neighborhood_safety.pdf.

4   George L. Kelling and James Q. Wilson, "Broken Windows: The Police and Neighborhood Safety," *Atlantic Monthly,* March 1982.

5   William J. Bratton, "Broken Windows and Quality-of-Life Policing in New York

City," New York Police Department (2015), at http://www.nyc.gov/html/nypd/downloads/pdf/analysis_and_planning/qol.pdf.

6   George Kelling, "How New York Became Safe: The Full Story," *City Journal*, July 2009, at http://fsjna.org/wp-content/uploads/2012/07/Time_To_Restore_Order.pdf.

7   Issa Kohler-Hausmann, "Managerial Justice and Mass Misdemeanors," *Stanford Law Review* 66, no. 3 (2014): 611–94.

8   Bratton, "Broken Windows and Quality-of-Life Policing."

9   Bernard E. Harcourt, *Illusion of Order: The False Promise of Broken Windows Policing* (Cambridge, Mass.: Harvard University Press, 2009).

10   Howard N. Snyder, "Arrest in the United States, 1990–2010," Bureau of Justice Statistics, U.S. Department of Justice (2012), at http://www.bjs.gov/content/pub/pdf/aus9010.pdf.

11   "Crime in the United States 2015—Arrests," FBI, U.S. Department of Justice (2015).

12   Data on stop, question, and frisk published by the NYPD can be found at "Stop-and-Frisk Data," New York Civil Liberties Union (n.d.), at http://www.nyclu.org/content/stop-and-frisk-data.

13   Bratton, "Broken Windows and Quality-of-Life Policing."

14   "Final Report of the President's Task Force on 21st Century Policing," Office of Community Oriented Policing Services (2015), at http://www.cops.usdoj.gov/pdf/taskforce/taskforce_finalreport.pdf.

15   Anthony Braga, David Hureau, and Andrew Papachristos, "The Relevance of Micro Places in Citywide Robbery Trends: A Longitudinal Analysis of Robbery Incidents at Street Corners and Block Faces in Boston," *Journal of Research in Crime and Delinquency* 48, no. 1 (2011): 7–32; Anthony Braga, Andrew Papachristos, and David Hureau, "The Concentration and Stability of Gun Violence at Micro Places in Boston, 1980–2008," *Journal of Quantitative Criminology* 26 , no. 1 (2010): 33–53; and David Weisburd et al., "Trajectories of Crime at Places: A Longitudinal Study of Street Segments in the City of Seattle," *Criminology* 42, no. 2 (2004): 283–322.

16   Several field experiments test the temporary effect of supplementary police deployment to crime "hot spots" and find that extra police patrols reduce crime and disorder. For a meta-analysis and reviews of the literature, see Anthony A. Braga, "Hot Spots Policing and Crime Prevention: A Systematic Review of Randomized Controlled Trials," *Journal of Experimental Criminology* 1 (2005): 317–42; Anthony A. Braga, Andrew V. Papachristos, and David M. Hureau, "The Effects of Hot Spots Policing on Crime: An Updated Systematic Review

and Meta-Analysis," *Justice Quarterly* 31, no. 4 (2012): 633–63; and Lawrence W. Sherman, "Hot Spots of Crime and Criminal Careers of Places," in *Crime and Place*, ed. John E. Eck and David Weisburd (Washington, D.C.: Police Executive Research Forum, 1995).

17   Andrew V. Papachristos, Christopher Wildeman, and Elizabeth Roberto, "Tragic, but Not Random: The Social Contagion of Nonfatal Gunshot Injuries," *Social Science and Medicine* 125 (2015): 139–50.

18   Andrew V. Papachristos and Christopher Wildeman, "Network Exposure and Homicide Victimization in an African American Community," *American Journal of Public Health* 104, no. 1 (2014): 143–50.

19   Daniel W. Webster et al., "Effects of Baltimore's Safe Streets Program on Gun Violence: A Replication of Chicago's CeaseFire Program," *Journal of Urban Health* 90, no. 1 (2013): 27–40.

20   David M. Kennedy, *Don't Shoot: One Man, a Street Fellowship, and the End of Violence in Inner-City America* (New York: Bloomsbury, 2011).

21   Andrew Papachristos, Tracey Meares, and Jeffrey Fagan, "Attention Felons: Evaluating Project Safe Neighborhoods in Chicago," *Journal of Empirical Legal Studies* 4, no. 2 (2007): 223–72.

22   "Final Report of the President's Task Force on 21st Century Policing."

23   Sue Rahr and Stephen K. Rice, "From Warriors to Guardians: Recommitting American Police Culture to Democratic Ideals," National Institute of Justice, U.S. Department of Justice (2015), at https://www.ncjrs.gov/pdffiles1/nij/248654.pdf.

24   Ibid.

25   Kate Mather, "LAPD Urges Officers to Be Community Guardians, Not Warriors on Crime," *Los Angeles Times*, April 20, 2015.

26   For a history of how policing has transformed and the roots of the "warrior cop" mentality, see Radley Balko, *Rise of the Warrior Cop: The Militarization of America's Police Forces* (New York: PublicAffairs, 2013).

9. THE NEXT URBAN GUARDIANS

1   The section on the East Lake Community is based on my own conversations with staff from Purpose Built Communities; an analysis of census data from Atlanta; and several histories of the community: "East Lake Story," East Lake Foundation, at http://www.eastlakefoundation.org/the-east-lake-story; "Transforming East Lake: Systematic Intentionality in Atlanta," Center for Promise, at https://www.americaspromise.org/sites/default/files/EastLake%20FINAL.pdf; "Who

We Are," Purpose Built Communities, at http://purposebuiltcommunities.org/
who-we-are/; Tom G. Cousins, "The Atlanta Model for Reviving Poor Neighborhoods," *Wall Street Journal*, September 14, 2013; and Alexander von Hoffman,
House by House, Block by Block: The Rebirth of America's Urban Neighborhoods
(New York: Oxford University Press, 2003). Special thanks to David Edwards
for discussions of the organization and the East Lake community with me.

2   Cousins is quoted in "Who We Are," Purpose Built Communities, at http://
purposebuiltcommunities.org/who-we-are/history.

3   Jeff Humphreys et al., "A Chance to Succeed: Economic Revitalization of Atlanta's East Lake Community," Selig Center for Economic Growth, University of
Georgia (2008), at http://www.terry.uga.edu/media/documents/selig/east_lake_
study.pdf.

4   Stuart M. Butler, Michael B. Horn, and Julia Freeland, "Schools as Community
Hubs: Integrating Support Services to Drive Educational Outcomes," Brookings
Institution (2015), at https://www.brookings.edu/research/schools-as-community
-hubs-integrating-support-services-to-drive-educational-outcomes.

5   Details about Community Renewal International can be found on its website,
http://communityrenewal.us.

6   The story of community planning and the long-term work of the Dudley Street
Neighborhood Initiative is told in Robert D. Putnam, Lewis Feldstein, and
Donald J. Cohen, *Better Together: Restoring the American Community* (New
York: Simon and Schuster, 2004). An earlier book on Dudley Street recounts the
beginning of the neighborhood's transformation:, Peter Medoff and Holly Sklar,
Streets of Hope: The Fall and Rise of an Urban Neighborhood (Boston: South
End Press, 1994).

7   Jane Jacobs, *The Death and Life of Great American Cities* (New York: Random
House, 1961).

8   Robert J. Sampson, Stephen W. Raudenbush, and Felton Earls, "Neighborhoods
and Violent Crime: A Multilevel Study of Collective Efficacy," *Science* 277 (1997):
918–24; Robert J. Sampson, and Stephen W. Raudenbush, "Systematic Social
Observation of Public Spaces: A New Look at Disorder in Urban Neighborhoods," *American Journal of Sociology* 105, no. 3 (1999): 603–51.

9   Robert J. Sampson and Per-Olof Wikström, "The Social Order of Violence in
Chicago and Stockholm Neighborhoods: A Comparative Inquiry," in *Order, Con-
flict, and Violence*, ed. Stathis Kalyvas, Ian Shapiro, and Tarek Masoud (New
York: Cambridge University Press, 2008). See also Robert J. Sampson, *Great
American City: Chicago and the Enduring Neighborhood Effect* (Chicago: Uni-
versity of Chicago Press, 2012).

10   Jens Ludwig and Phillip J. Cook, "The Benefits of Reducing Gun Violence: Evidence from Contingent-Valuation Survey Data," *Journal of Risk and Uncertainty* 22, no. 3 (2001): 207–26.

11   Mark Cohen and colleagues have used a similar approach to estimate the social costs of specific types of crime to the public. Based on responses to a question about willingness to pay for programs that reduce crime by 10 percent, they estimated in 2004 that every armed robbery and sexual assault cost over $200,000 and every murder cost almost $10 million. See Mark A. Cohen et al., "Willingness-to-Pay for Crime Control Programs," *Criminology* 42 (2004): 89–110. Other approaches focusing on jury awards to victims or direct costs to public agencies and to victims have also been used, but the willingness-to-pay approach is most persuasive when considering the benefits to the public of any effort to reduce crime.

12   John R. Logan and Harvey Molotch, *Urban Fortunes: The Political Economy of Place* (Berkeley: University of California Press, 1988).

13   Devin Pope and Jaren Pope, "Crime and Property Values: Evidence from the 1990s Crime Drop," *Regional Science and Urban Economics* 42, no. 1 (2012): 177–88; Ingrid Gould Ellen and Katherine O'Regan, "Reversal of Fortunes: Lower-Income Neighborhoods in the Urban U.S. in the 1990s," *Urban Studies* 45, no. 4 (2008): 845–69; and Keith Ihlanfeldt and Tom Mayock, "Panel Data Estimates of the Effects of Different Types of Crime on Housing Prices," *Regional Science and Urban Economics* 40, nos. 2–3 (2010): 161–72.

14   Robert J. Shapiro and Kevin A. Hassett, "The Economic Benefits of Reducing Violent Crime: A Case Study of 8 American Cities," Center for American Progress (2012), at https://www.americanprogress.org/wp-content/uploads/issues/2012/06/pdf/violent_crime.pdf.

15   This figure is a rough approximation of the "direct" costs to the criminal justice system of aggravated assault. The direct costs of each robbery or sexual assault are higher than $10,000, and the costs of each murder are at least $400,000 or more. Note also that these estimates do not include the direct costs to victims from lost property, injury, and loss of productivity. Estimates are approximated from Kathryn E. McCollister, Michael T. French, and Hai Fang, "The Cost of Crime to Society: New Crime-Specific Estimates for Policy and Program Evaluation," *Drug and Alcohol Dependence* 108, no. 1 (2010): 98–109.

16   Lawrence W. Sherman et al., "Preventing Crime: What Works, What Doesn't, What's Promising," National Institute of Justice, Office of Justice Programs, U.S. Department of Justice (1998), at http://www.soc.umn.edu/~uggen/whatworks.pdf; and Arthur L. Kellerman et al., "Preventing Youth Violence: What Works," *Annual Review of Public Health* 19 (1998): 271–91.

17   Closing the Gap Clearinghouse, "The Role of Community Patrols in Improving
     Safety in Indigenous Communities," Australian Government (July 2013), at http://
     www.aihw.gov.au/uploadedFiles/ClosingTheGap/Content/Publications/2013/
     ctg-rs20.pdf; and Sharon Gray, "Community Safety Workers: An Exploratory
     Study of Some Emerging Crime Prevention Occupations," International Centre
     for the Prevention of Crime (2006), at http://www.crime-prevention-intl.org/en/
     publications/report/report/article/community-safety-workers.html.

18   "The Royal Commission into Aboriginal Deaths in Custody: Timeline of Events
     and Aftermath," *NITV News* (April 15, 2016). The full report can be found at
     "The Royal Commission Into Aboriginal Deaths in Custody," Indigenous Law
     Resources (1998), http://www.austlii.edu.au/au/other/IndigLRes/rciadic. On
     the royal commission, see "Fact Sheet 112," National Archives of Australia, at
     http://www.naa.gov.au/collection/fact-sheets/fs112.aspx.

19   Harry Blagg, "Models of Best Practice: Aboriginal Community Patrols in West-
     ern Australia," Crime Research Centre, University of Western Australia (2006).

20   In New York City, for instance, several groups of civilian patrols are trained
     to oversee public spaces and work with the police. Perhaps the best example
     of a local group that was established to look out for the community while also
     controlling crime is the Shomrim of Brooklyn. These organized groups of Ortho-
     dox Jews act as intermediaries between community members and the police
     in neighborhoods like Crown Heights and Flatbush. Equipped with vans that
     bear a close resemblance to those operated by the NYPD, the Shomrim patrol
     communities, respond to calls for assistance, and act as the NYPD's "eyes and
     ears." When a child goes missing or a member of the community is victimized,
     calls often go to the Shomrim first and the police department later.

10. A WAR ON VIOLENCE

1   Edward Glaeser, *Triumph of the City* (New York: Pan MacMillan, 2012), pro-
     vides the best example of the optimistic view of cities. Richard Florida, *The
     New Urban Crisis* (New York: Basic Books, 2017), provides a complementary
     argument about the need to expand the benefits of cities to a larger share of the
     population.

2   Over the course of U.S. history, major social unrest frequently emerges at times
     of sharply rising crime and violence, an observation that is troubling given the
     degree of unrest in the summers of 2015 and 2016. See Eric H. Monkkonen,
     Murder in New York City (Berkeley: University of California Press, 2001).

3   See Patrick Sharkey, *Stuck in Place: Urban Neighborhoods and the End of*

Progress Toward Racial Equality (Chicago: University of Chicago Press, 2013), chap. 7.

4   On connecting people to cities with greater opportunity, see Florida, *New Urban Crisis*. On responding to the crisis of affordable housing, see Barbara Sard and Will Fischer, "Key Features of a Federal Renters' Tax Credit," Center on Budget and Policy Priorities (2015), at http://www.cbpp.org/research/housing/ key-features-of-a-federal-renters-tax-credit; "2016 Public Policy Agenda," National Low Income Housing Coalition (2016), at http://nlihc.org/sites/default/ files/2016AG_Chapter_1-2.pdf. On confronting concentrated poverty and providing mobility programs that lead to sustained, transformative moves, see Margery Austin Turner et al., "Tackling Persistent Poverty in Distressed Urban Neighborhoods," Urban Institute (2014), at http://www.urban.org/sites/default/ files/alfresco/publication-pdfs/413179-Tackling-Persistent-Poverty-in-Distressed -Urban-Neighborhoods.pdf. On improving work opportunities and supporting families, see "Opportunity, Responsibility, and Security: A Consensus Plan for Reducing Poverty and Restoring the American Dream," AEI-Brookings Working Group on Poverty and Opportunity, Brookings Institution (2015), at https:// www.brookings.edu/wp-content/uploads/2015/12/full-report.pdf. On ideas to support children, families, and civil society, see Robert D. Putnam, *Our Kids: The American Dream in Crisis* (New York: Simon & Schuster, 2016).

INDEX

Note: Page numbers in *italics* indicate figures.